A Sociopolitical Agenda for TESOL Teacher Education

Critical Approaches and Innovations in Language Teacher Education

SERIES EDITOR: Bedrettin Yazan (University of Texas at San Antonio, USA)

The series is dedicated to advancing critical language teacher education research that can transform the dominant practices of language teaching in educational contexts around the world. Language education has become more important than ever, to facilitate the crossing of physical and ideological borders of nation-states, and to meet the needs of increasingly ethnically and linguistically diverse student populations. This series helps inform the preparation of resilient and agentive language teachers with critical social justice orientations. It presents state-of-the-art research to support the formation of teachers who identify as democratic, social agents of formal schooling, and devoted to improving learning experiences of marginalized students. The titles in this series appeal to language teachers, teacher educators, and researchers and can be used as educational materials in graduate and undergraduate studies.

ADVISORY BOARD

Darío Banegas (University of Edinburgh, UK)
Osman Barnawi (Royal Commission Colleges & Institutes, Saudi Arabia)
Yasemin Bayyurt (Bogaziçi University, Turkey)
Ester de Jong (University of Florida, USA)
Andy Xuesong Gao (University of New South Wales, Australia)
Icy Lee (Chinese University of Hong Kong, Hong Kong)
Gloria Park (Indiana University of Pennsylvania, USA)
Ingrid Piller (Macquarie University, New South Wales, Australia)
Richard Smith (University of Warwick, UK)
Zia Tajeddin (Tarbiat Modares University, Iran)

Forthcoming in the series:

Critical Autoethnography in Language Teacher Education, Bedrettin Yazan
Critical Dialogic TESOL Teacher Education: Preparing Future Advocates and Supporters of Multilingual Learners, edited by Fares J. Karam and Amanda Kibler
International Perspectives on Critical English Language Teacher Education: Theory and Practice, edited by Ali Fuad Selvi and Ceren Kocaman
Language Teacher Education Beyond Borders: Multilingualism, Transculturalism, and Critical Approaches, edited by Fernando Zolin-Vesz, Dario Luis Banegas, Luciana C. de Oliveira
Teacher Education for Global Englishes Language Teaching, Denchai Prabjandee

A Sociopolitical Agenda for TESOL Teacher Education

Edited by
Peter I. De Costa and Özgehan Uştuk

BLOOMSBURY ACADEMIC
LONDON • NEW YORK • OXFORD • NEW DELHI • SYDNEY

BLOOMSBURY ACADEMIC

Bloomsbury Publishing Plc, 50 Bedford Square, London, WC1B 3DP, UK
Bloomsbury Publishing Inc, 1385 Broadway, New York, NY 10018, USA
Bloomsbury Publishing Ireland, 29 Earlsfort Terrace, Dublin 2, D02 AY28, Ireland

BLOOMSBURY, BLOOMSBURY ACADEMIC and the Diana logo are
trademarks of Bloomsbury Publishing Plc

First published in Great Britain 2024
This paperback edition published in 2025

Copyright © Peter I. De Costa, Özgehan Ustuk and Contributors, 2024

Peter I. De Costa, Özgehan Ustuk and Contributors have asserted their right under the
Copyright, Designs and Patents Act, 1988, to be identified as Editors of this work.

For legal purposes the Acknowledgments on p. xvii and p. 138 constitute an extension of
this copyright page.

Cover design: Grace Ridge
Cover image © rudchenko and Anastasia Shemetova via iStock

All rights reserved. No part of this publication may be: i) reproduced
or transmitted in any form, electronic or mechanical, including photocopying,
recording or by means of any information storage or retrieval system without
prior permission in writing from the publishers; or ii) used or reproduced in any
way for the training, development or operation of artificial intelligence (AI)
technologies, including generative AI technologies. The rights holders expressly
reserve this publication from the text and data mining exception as per
Article 4(3) of the Digital Single Market Directive (EU) 2019/790.

Bloomsbury Publishing Plc does not have any control over, or responsibility for,
any third-party websites referred to or in this book. All internet addresses given
in this book were correct at the time of going to press. The author and publisher
regret any inconvenience caused if addresses have changed or sites have ceased
to exist, but can accept no responsibility for any such changes.

A catalogue record for this book is available from the British Library.

A catalog record for this book is available from the Library of Congress.

ISBN: HB: 978-1-3502-6284-3
PB: 978-1-3502-6288-1
ePDF: 978-1-3502-6285-0
eBook: 978-1-3502-6286-7

Series: Critical Approaches and Innovations in Language Teacher Education

Typeset by RefineCatch Limited, Bungay, Suffolk

For product safety related questions contact productsafety@bloomsbury.com.

To find out more about our authors and books visit www.bloomsbury.com
and sign up for our newsletters.

Contents

List of Figures	vii
List of Tables	viii
Series Editor Foreword	ix
Foreword: On Developing Fluency in Humaning *Maggie Kubanyiova*	xiv

1 Introduction: A Sociopolitical Agenda for TESOL Teacher Education and Why It Matters *Peter I. De Costa and Özgehan Uştuk* — 1

Part One Theoretical Underpinnings of the Sociopolitical Agenda

2 The Imperative of Language Teacher Leadership in an Unjust World *Dudley Reynolds* — 13

3 Pedagogical and Conceptual Principles of Teacher Professional Learning in TESOL: Teacher Stories from Turkey *Kenan Dikilitaş and Irem Çomoğlu* — 27

4 (Non)Native Speakerism in English Language Teaching: Changing Perspectives, Resilient Discourses, and Missing Links *Ali Fuad Selvi* — 45

5 Critical Engagement with Achievement Gap Discourses and Data: Narrowing or Not? *Jamie L. Schissel and Nancy H. Hornberger* — 65

Part Two Setting the Sociopolitical Agenda

6 "Figuring Out My End Game": Supporting Novice ESOL Teachers' Emerging Identities as Humanizing Practitioners and Advocates through Peer Interaction *Megan Madigan Peercy, Danielle Gervais Sodani, and Wyatt Hall* — 87

7 Implementing an Intersectional Pedagogy in a TESOL Methods Course: A Narrative Approach *Hayriye Kayi-Aydar* — 107

8 Teacher Identity in Critical Autoethnographic Narrative: Making Sense of the Political in the Personal *Bedrettin Yazan* 123

9 Developing Decolonizing Language Teachers in Colonial Sociopolitical Contexts *Mario E. López-Gopar, Vilma Huerta Cordova, William M. Sughrua, Juan Ignacio Martínez Martínez, and Denisse Zárate Ríos* 145

Afterword: Interrogating and Destabilizing the Canon of TESOL Teacher Education *Peter Sayer* 169

List of Contributors 181

Index 187

Figures

0.1	Ideologies in language teacher education	xi
2.1	Static perspectives on teacher leadership	16
4.1	Three pillars of the *NNEST* movement	51
5.1	Occurrence of the term "achievement gap," 1940–2019	66
5.2	Number of unaccompanied children per fiscal year as reported by ORR	71
5.3	The number of Spanish-English test versions taken by subject and year	78
5.4	The number of Spanish-speaking students classified as ELs in Pennsylvania by year	79
8.1	Visual map of Kateryna's CAN	131
9.1	Ms. Ana selling bread	159
9.2	Jacobo coloring	161

Tables

6.1 Study participants   91
8.1 Implementation of CAN in Spring 2018   129

Series Editor Foreword

When I was preparing the initial proposal for this book series with Bloomsbury Academic, I was asked to justify why there should be a separate book series on critical and innovative language teacher education (LTE). The scholarly conversation on LTE has taken place in venues that have a broader scope and occurs in fields of applied linguistics, TESOL (Teaching English to Speakers of Other Languages), modern language education, or general teacher education. While this interdisciplinarity gives the field of LTE both scope and depth, at times it feels scattered across these various venues of scholarship. Thus, the first aim of this series was to curate and compile volumes centered around the common topic of LTE. The second aim in the series is to highlight the need in our field to focus on critical approaches to innovating LTE due to the ways that language (and, therefore, language teaching) is intertwined with cycles of privilege and marginalization and power dynamics among speakers. I feel that this need to bring together scholarship that is critical and simultaneously innovative in nature has been clear to us as members of the research communities who are interested in studying policies, pedagogies, and practices of teacher education. Therefore, the inception of this series was timely.

With the support of the contributing authors, editors, and editorial board members, what I seek to accomplish with this series is to bring together colleagues from around the world to share their efforts in pedagogy-oriented research in LTE and extend the existing scholarly work further toward the direction of continued criticality and innovation in the interest of social justice. At the same time, practitioners and researchers of LTE can use the publications in this series, partly or fully, as resources in advancing their work.

The two significant constructs undergirding this book series are *criticality* and *innovation*, and their relationship therein. Ideally, *innovation*, or the process of engaging in continuous efforts to create new ways of supporting teachers and teacher educators at all phases of their careers in response to changing dynamics at their institutions and society in general, in LTE should contribute to teachers', teacher educators', researchers', and administrators' increasingly critical approaches to language teaching and learning. What I mean by *criticality* here are the combined efforts to address oppressive language ideologies that inform institutions' and people's stances, decisions, and actions, thus shaping their professional practices as educators writ large. Those language ideologies are never about "language" *per se*; they are always intertwined with ideologies of culture, nationality, race, ethnicity, gender, sexuality, and ableism, among others (see Kubota 2020; Motha 2014; Park 2017).

Very much contextually bound and situated, language ideologies operate invisibly and impact the activities within the scope of LTE at three interlocking layers: language learners, language teachers, and language teacher education. To parse them out, at one layer, language ideologies shape how we understand the nature, acquisition, and use of language, which subsequently impacts our understanding of the identity positions hierarchically available for language users and learners (Pavlenko and Blackledge 2004). At another layer, we have ideologies that pertain to teaching languages and being language teachers, the most salient of such ideologies being the monolingual fallacy, the "native" speaker fallacy, and the subtractive fallacy as discussed by Phillipson (2013). As examples, these three fallacies provide dichotomous identity positions for language teachers, reducing the nuance and complexity of teacher identity and essentializing what "good" teachers and teaching practices should be. At a third layer, we encounter ideologies about the formal preparation of language teachers, as well as what it means to become and grow as a language teacher within local educational contexts where economic and cultural globalization are variably accepted or opposed as national educational goals (Hawkins 2011). Those ideologies include the hierarchical positioning of certain academic content as superior to or more important than others based on or aligned with the standards or directives coming from governing bodies that manage the activities of teacher education (e.g., Higher Education Council in Turkey, State legislative mandates on K-12 curriculum content in the US). Such hierarchies are typically perpetuated through external high-stakes assessments which operate as gatekeeping mechanisms. Additionally, to reiterate their interconnected nature, ideologies of LTE also encompass the ideologies in circulation around language teaching which therefore also involve the ideologies around language learning and language use. Ideologically-laden hierarchies, variably based on the sociopolitical context, define and confine what a language teacher educator is allowed and supposed to be, do, and feel when preparing teachers to work with language learners.

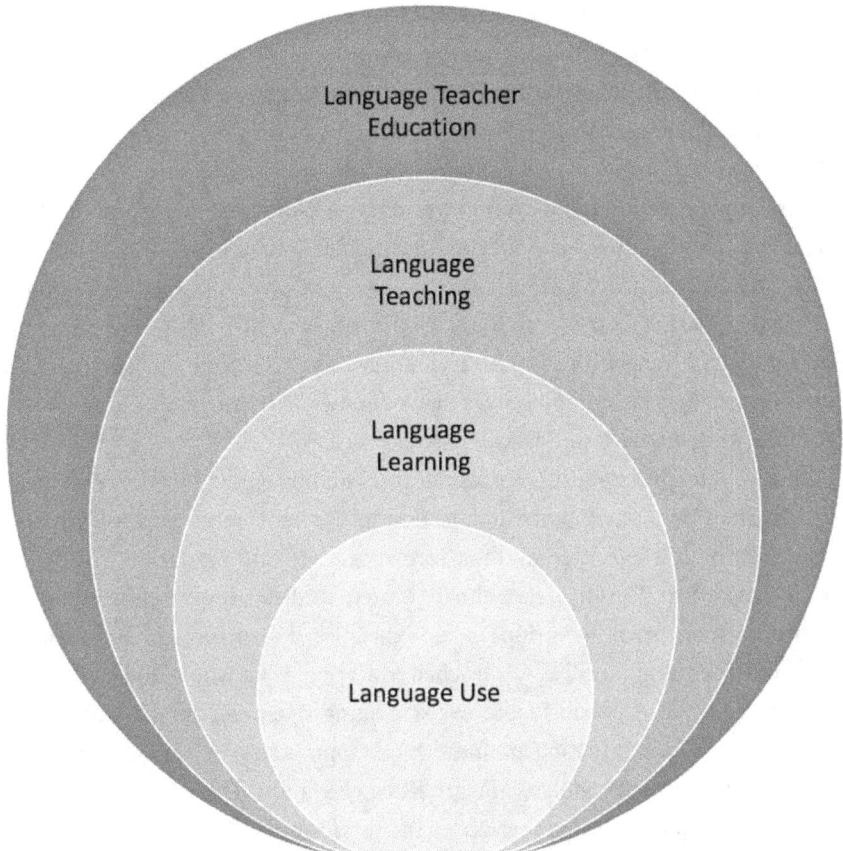

Figure 0.1 Ideologies in language teacher education.

In the last three decades, critical scholarship in our field (e.g., Canagarajah 2020; Norton and Toohey 2004; Varghese et al. 2016) has called for persistent push-back against dominant language ideologies and the corresponding ways in which institutions and the people ultimately maintain the asymmetrical power relations in society. As the "mission" of LTE is to prepare language teachers (who experience varying degrees of privilege and marginalization) who are going to work with language learners (who also experience varying degrees of privilege and marginalization), LTE practices have strong potential to effect change in society. It is my hope that the scholarly work published in this series will contribute to that change in various educational contexts around the world. I suggest that we, as practitioners and researchers of LTE, keep in mind these two aspects of being critical: first, there are many ways of being critical and acting critically in our contexts and our practices, and identities that inform our criticality are situated at the intersection of personal, professional, and political dimensions of language learning, teaching, and teacher education (Rudolph 2022). Second, being critical requires us to keep critiquing our own criticality by self-reflexively questioning, reconsidering, and innovating our practices to address oppressive forces, uneven power relations, and systemic inequities that impact our efforts as teacher educators. Such reflexivity in which we engage and model for our students could also involve endeavors toward developing "ideological clarity" (Bartolomé 2004). This includes identifying, problematizing, examining, and reflecting on our orientation *vis-à-vis* dominant ideologies to better understand the complex ways they operate and our identities as language users, learners, teachers, and teacher educators.

Reviewed by peers at different stages, this volume, edited by Peter De Costa and Özgehan Uştuk, is the first publication in the book series and will make a great contribution to critical and innovative research and practice in LTE, with specific regard to TESOL. The editors curated studies from a select group of contributors situated in various socio-educational contexts to put forth a sociopolitical agenda for TESOL teacher education. As a whole, this collection offers a renewed response to the ever-changing dynamics in the world that require continuous updating of the critical approaches we adopt as teacher educators. Prominent scholars Maggie Kubanyiova and Peter Sayer wrote the foreword and afterword, respectively. In her foreword, Maggie situates the volume within the "rapidly shifting discourses" in the world to which the chapter contributors are responding through their research. In the afterword, Peter discusses how the book is contributing to "interrogating and destabilizing the canon of TESOL teacher education." I believe that this book will open new conversations around critical scholarship in TESOL and that researchers and practitioners of LTE will enjoy reading it from cover to cover.

References

Bartolomé, L. I. (2004), "Critical Pedagogy and Teacher Education: Racializing Prospective Teachers," *Teacher Education Quarterly*, 31 (1): 97–122.

Canagarajah, A. S. (2020), *Transnational Literacy Autobiographies as Translingual Writing*, New York: Routledge.

Hawkins, M. R., ed. (2011), *Social Justice Language Teacher Education*, Vol. 84, Bristol: Multilingual Matters.

Kubota, R. (2020), "Confronting Epistemological Racism, Decolonizing Scholarly Knowledge: Race and Gender in Applied Linguistics," *Applied Linguistics*, 41 (5): 712–732.

Motha, S. (2014), *Race, Empire, and English Language Teaching: Creating Responsible and Ethical Anti-Racist Practice*, New York: Teachers College Press.

Norton, B., and Toohey, K., eds. (2004), *Critical Pedagogies and Language Learning*, Cambridge: Cambridge University Press.

Park, G. (2017), *Narratives of East Asian Women Teachers of English: Where Privilege Meets Marginalization*, Bristol: Multilingual Matters.

Pavlenko, A., and Blackledge, A., eds. (2004), *Negotiation of Identities in Multilingual Contexts*. Bristol: Multilingual Matters.

Phillipson, R. (2013), "TESOL Expertise in the Empire of English," *TESOL in Context*, 22 (2): 5–16.

Rudolph, N. (2022), "Narratives and Negotiations of Identity in Japan and Criticality in (English) Language Education: (Dis)Connections and Implications, *TESOL Quarterly*. https://doi.org/10.1002/tesq.3150.

Varghese, M., S. Motha, J. Trent, G. Park, and J. Reeves, eds. (2016), "Language Teacher Identity in Multilingual Settings," *TESOL Quarterly*, 50 (3): 545–571.

Foreword: On Developing Fluency in Humaning

Maggie Kubanyiova

A discipline that deals with questions of *education, language,* and *"other"* should probably have something useful to say about how we (teach or learn to) live our lives in the world of diverse others. If this aspiration is anything close to being shared within the TESOL community, it is hard to imagine TESOL teacher education that does not explicitly engage with its sociopolitical agenda. Such an agenda has, of course, for better or worse, always shaped TESOL (teacher education) debates and pedagogies, not to mention spaces in which these have occurred. The politics, in other words, have always been there. Present and powerful. The silences that have often surrounded such questions have had less to do with their relevance and infinitely more to do with the politics of platform.

Judging from the debates that have increasingly claimed that platform, a discourse has been shifting rapidly over the past few years. There's no doubt that the change has been accelerated by recent momentous sociopolitical events that have shaken the world. Especially those parts of it that have, despite consistent bids for interruptions, tended to exude unshakeable confidence in a mandate to guard that platform and mold an exportable variety of TESOL; one that can and must strive to resist inconveniences of context. There is now an acute awareness in some of those corners that TESOL, just like any other area of education, cannot be divorced from the world in which it is practiced and in which it is meant to intervene. Its central concern with a specific language heightens this imperative: the language of opportunity and oppression, erudition and erasure, conviviality and colonization, development and depletion; in short, the language of stark contrasts and paradoxes compels the world of TESOL to expose its societal assumptions and face its political consequences.

This volume enters the picture in such a moment of reckoning and joins the ever-intensifying chorus of voices to ask what this growing sociopolitical consciousness might mean for TESOL teacher education and for public bodies established to support it and advocate for it. I see the chapters assembled here as revolving around two fundamental understandings shared by the broader domain of applied linguistics: that reducing people to labels is a damaging way of living in the world of diverse others and that doing the same to people's language can often have the same effect. How these insights might translate into TESOL teacher education curricula and pedagogies is what this book helps those charged with designing and implementing them ponder.

The chapters lay out ways in which essentializing difference in TESOL research, practice, or policy veils the uniqueness of circumstances and the heterogeneity of needs. This is true of students, their teachers, and their teacher educators. Native speakerism, for instance, and the discriminatory practices associated with it have not gone away despite a longstanding movement within the academy, professional organizations, and public bodies. But we are also reminded of a similarly reductive effect of its counter-ideology, nonnative speakerism. Both forms build hierarchies, neither serves the cause.

Just what that cause is or should be is in fact central to the discipline's reflection on its sociopolitical agenda. Efforts to reduce the "achievement gap" of students in US mainstream education for whom English is an additional language sound like a worthwhile cause for TESOL and therefore for TESOL teacher education in those specific settings. Until its fallacy is exposed through a meticulous examination of linguistic and value assumptions behind measures designed to push an agenda which misses its elephants. Such as an "opportunity gap." Or the fact that failing to meet arbitrary proficiency criteria marks one as a non-achiever for life, a non-citizen, a security threat, and, unspeakably, a non-person (Flores and Rosa 2019; Khan 2019). Striving nevertheless to conform to such benchmarks in tests and relationships is often done out of hope for acceptance or safety from the violence of dehumanization. It is often encouraged "out of (a sometimes misguided) love. A love that tells people that who they are isn't enough, but that they can at least perform in a way that will make others believe they are enough until an ecosystem fully embraces them" (Abdurraqib 2021: 91). Helping TESOL professionals to get closer to these soul-piercing truths as part of their education, the truths that govern their students' lives and probably their own too, will not dismantle such an ecosystem. But it might get closer to disturbing it (Sharma, Allen, and Ibrahim 2022; Si'ilata 2019).

Along with the broader debates in applied linguistics (Bagga-Gupta 2018; Canagarajah 2013; Creese and Blackledge 2019; Krause 2022; Kubota 2013; Moriarty and Kusters 2021; Valente 2020), this volume helps us appreciate how labeling language varieties, speakerhoods, or proficiencies is an ideological process that has its place but misses what matters most: how people actually use language to relate to one another and the world around them. That it is not in judging what language should be, but in paying attention to what it is already doing that new vistas for sociopolitically engaged TESOL teacher education can open up. The many examples of teacher education initiatives discussed here, be it through the critically conscious narrative reflections or the rich descriptive accounts of teachers' and teacher educators' community-building efforts, are instructive and necessary. They also present additional opportunities: to become the very spaces in which historically, spatially, and biographically situated, fluid, and embodied communication practices that cross all sorts of boundaries in order to make contact with others become a firm focus of attention and TESOL teacher education praxis.

Doing so will enable the discipline to remain in close conversation with what I suggested in the introduction might be its bigger purpose. It is one which is pointing away from an imposition of a fixed notion of what language is, what it sounds like, or whose language counts, and towards a fuller participation in ongoing "humaning", which is how Erasmus (2018: xxii) writes about "life-in-the-making with others." Paying attention to language as lived life and fully participating in it is the kind of language (teacher) education that helps to grow a sense of when to speak, what to say, and, mostly, how to listen in order to encounter the other. I would venture to suggest that this might well be the most radical part of the sociopolitical agenda for TESOL and, by extension, for TESOL teacher education: to enable those participating in it to develop their fluency in humaning. It is one that is neither acquired nor learned and it is therefore impossible to *equip* anyone *for* it. But TESOL teacher education can become the space that allows teachers, and then their students, to *open* themselves *to* it.

Because it is this fluency in being neighbors to one another when it's impossible to breathe and our home is burning that, to my mind, should occupy our minds. It is not a concern that somehow stands apart from TESOL. Acknowledging that TESOL, on the contrary, is very much part of it is what books such as these enable the larger community to do, even if it might not come easily (Motha 2020). The chapters in this volume exemplify how TESOL teacher education can help locate the act of doing TESOL, for which the teachers are practicing, in its larger ecology of educational systems, societal structures, and, I would add, the natural environment. But a reminder that it is precisely this kind of fluency that teachers will ultimately be asked to teach their students must be central to this discussion. Who the teachers are and the biographies, stigmas, visions, and activism that they uniquely bring to their educational relationships matter greatly. They can only educate as themselves, not as someone else. But sociopolitically-conscious TESOL teacher education is one that also teaches educators to leave the scene to let their students engage in "life-in-the-making with others." As themselves, not as someone else.

The chapters in this volume testify that pursuing TESOL teacher education with sociopolitical sensibilities in mind but without the larger society's support can and does easily lead to frustration, burnout, and resignation. It is not easy to lead a major international organization, an institution, a teacher education program, or a teacher development initiative, when it's part of a society or a system that seems patently uninterested in what cannot be counted and is even less invested in what it deems not to count. When society is not ready to listen and do its bit, the act of language (teacher) education is easily stifled before it's had a chance to take root. But the chapters offered in this book also show that openings for resisting and acting responsively (Kubanyiova 2020), however constrained and seemingly inconsequential, do exist (cf. Kuchah 2020). The resignation that comes with deliberately turning away from them is the more dangerous variety and one to which the history of TESOL teacher education will not be kind. That is the point and strength of volumes such as this: to compel the TESOL community as a whole not to look the other way.

Acknowledgment

The development of this chapter has been supported by the Arts and Humanities Research Council grant: "Ethics and Aesthetics of Encountering the Other: New Frameworks for Engaging with Difference" (AH/T005637/1)

References

Abdurraqib, H. (2021), *A Little Devil in America: In Praise of Black Performance*, London: Allen Lane.

Bagga-Gupta, S. (2018), "Going Beyond 'Single Grand Stories' in the Language and Educational Sciences: A Turn Towards Alternatives," *Aligarh Journal of Linguistics*, 8: 127–147.

Canagarajah, A. S. (2013), *Translingual Practice: Global Englishes and Cosmopolitan Relations*, London: Routledge.

Creese, A., and A. Blackledge (2019), "Translanguaging and Public Service Encounters: Language Learning in the Library," *Modern Language Journal*, 103 (4): 800–814.

Erasmus, Z. (2018), *Race Otherwise: Forging a New Humanism for South Africa*, Johannesburg: Wits University Press.

Flores, N., and J. Rosa (2019), "Bringing Race into Second Language Acquisition," *Modern Language Journal*, 103 (suppl.): 145–151.

Khan, K. (2019), *Becoming a Citizen: Linguistic Trials and Negotiations*, London: Bloomsbury.

Krause, L.-S. (2022), *Relanguaging Language from a South African Township School*, Bristol: Multilingual Matters.

Kubanyiova, M. (2020), "Language Teacher Education in the Age of Ambiguity: Educating Responsive Meaning Makers in the World," *Language Teaching Research*, 24 (1): 49–59.

Kubota, R. (2013), "'Language is Only a Tool': Japanese Expatriates Working in China and Implications for Language Teaching," *Multilingual Education*, 3: 4. https://multilingual-education.springeropen.com/articles/10.1186/2191-5059-3-4

Kuchah, K. H. (2020), "Staying Resilient, Responding to a Global Crisis'" *ELT Journal*, 74 (3): 366–367.

Moriarty, E., and A. Kusters (2021), "Deaf Cosmopolitanism: Calibrating as a Moral Process," *International Journal of Multilingualism*, 18 (2): 285–302.

Motha, S. (2020), "Is an Antiracist and Decolonizing Applied Linguistics Possible," *Annual Review of Applied Linguistics*, 40: 128–133.

Sharma, M., A. Allen, and A. Ibrahim, eds. (2022), *Disruptive Learning Narrative Framework: Analyzing Race, Power, and Privilege in Post-Secondary International Service Learning*, London: Bloomsbury.

Si'ilata, R. K. (2019), "Teachers' Professional Learning and Practice with Multilingual Pacific/Pasifika Learners in Aotearoa/New Zealand," in S. Hammer, K. Mitchell Viesca, and N. L. Commins (eds.), *Teaching Content and Language in the Multilingual Classroom: International Research on Policy, Perspectives, Preparation and Practice*, 168–191, London: Routledge.

Valente, J. M. (2020), "In between Spiderman and the Incredible Hulk," in I. W. Leigh and C. A. O'Brien (eds.), *Deaf Identities*, 349–369, Oxford: Oxford University Press.

1

Introduction: A Sociopolitical Agenda for TESOL Teacher Education and Why It Matters

Peter I. De Costa and Özgehan Uştuk

In his recent article, "Critical applied linguistics in the 2020s," invoking an article he wrote three decades earlier, "Towards a critical applied linguistics for the 1990s" (Pennycook 1990), Alastair Pennycook asserted that "critical work has to be responsive to a changing world, and a great deal has happened in the last twenty or thirty years from a more urgent need to deal with climate change to the rise of neoliberal political and economic forms of governance" (2022: 1). He noted how critical work needs to move in rhythm with changes to the world. Such changes to applied linguistics in general and TESOL in particular, as elaborated further in this introductory chapter, have been characterized by a host of factors that range from the neoliberal turn in education to climate change. Indeed, as a field, we have made valuable inroads into unpacking and problematizing the sociopolitics of language education, spanning from Hall and Eggington's edited volume, *The Sociopolitics of English Language Teaching* (2000), to Mirhosseini and De Costa's more recent *The Sociopolitics of English Language Testing* (2020). These investigations into the sociopolitics of English language education need to be seen in conjunction with recent calls to explore social justice issues in language education (e.g., Avineri et al. 2019; Ortaçtepe Hart and Martel 2020). Importantly, and taking a step back, one might ask what is it about English language instruction that draws such an enduring interest in the sociopolitical milieu in which it is embedded? And more specifically, what is our justification for putting out an edited volume that centers on a sociopolitical agenda for TESOL teacher education?

To address the above questions, we would like to establish from the outset that we cannot—and nor should we—divorce sociopolitically-inflected TESOL teacher education concerns from broader teacher education developments that address inequities in education. Put differently, the problems confronting

TESOL teacher education (see Yuan et al. 2022 for a comprehensive recent review of research involving TESOL teacher educators) are also endemic in general teacher education. And to large extent, the sentiments raised by Pennycook (1990, 2022) echo the calls by educational scholar, Marilyn Cochran-Smith, who in her 2005 presidential address to the American Educational Research Association, aptly observed that:

> [T]he new teacher education is complex, especially when understood in terms of the larger educational, economic, social, and political conditions in which it is emerging: market-based reforms in education and a whole range of other human services, increasing global competition, ... high-stakes accountability, and persistent social and educational inequities.... [T]he new teacher education should embrace the political aspects of educational policy as the inevitable stuff of social institutions in human societies.
>
> Cochran-Smith 2005: 13–14

In coupling education with society, Cochran-Smith and critical language teacher educators (e.g., De Costa 2018; Kubanyiova 2020; Pennycook 2022) remind us that because classrooms constitute a microcosm of society, we need to be aware that what goes on in classrooms is impacted by developments in society as well as geopolitical shifts in the world. In fact, like Cochran-Smith and Pennycook, we argue that TESOL teacher educators need to look beyond classrooms, and think about how national and global concerns have begun to intrude upon our classrooms.

Macro Concerns: Why They Matter

What macro concerns exactly should we be concerned with? In essence, we need to come to terms with the fact that we live in an age of precarity. As noted earlier, a strong neoliberal streak has been coursing through education for a while now. In TESOL, these neoliberal demands are manifested in high stakes accountability standards imposed upon TESOL professionals (Sayer 2019) and the "publish or perish" pressure experienced by TESOL teacher educators (Li and De Costa 2021). Not surprisingly, these overwhelming expectations often lead to teacher burnout and vulnerability (Benesch 2020; De Costa, Li, and Rawal 2020).

Relatedly, and given that English is inextricably tied to political economy (O'Regan 2021; Ricento 2015), TESOL educators have had to grapple with the fallout from a slew of economically-related phenomena such as Covid-19, which in particular severely impacted the lives and livelihoods of English learners and teachers, and more recently a huge influx of refugees who have had to flee their home countries because of adverse climate change (Goulah and Katunich 2020) and collapsing economies. The latter phenomenon has become rampant in recent months following the attack of Ukraine by Russia. Together these disasters, both natural and man-made, along with runaway inflation in almost every country, have led to financial turmoil. As we write this introduction, stock markets across the globe are in free fall, and we are increasingly confronted by the specter of a global recession. Perturbingly, it is not just Global South nations such as Argentina, Pakistan, and Sri Lanka which have debts issued in the U.S. currency that are in peril; even Global North nations like Canada and the UK have fallen prey to this economic downturn. Again, what does all this have to do with TESOL? The large numbers of risk-taking refugee learners of English who cross borders in search of better lives will translate into a ballooning ESL population across all levels of education. But more importantly, are TESOL professionals adequately equipped to deal with linguistically and culturally diverse students who will increasingly populate our classrooms? And how will they cope with tensions within wider society that are increasingly characterized by resurgent nationalism (McIntosh and McPherron 2023) and led by factions that are often hostile to such diversity?

Identity Politics and Ideological Wars in the Classroom: Designing Effective Solutions

The contact zone of the ESL classroom thus becomes contested terrain as students and teachers alike find themselves embroiled in an identity politics of recognition as they negotiate ideological battlefields. Ultimately at stake is whose communicative repertoires are validated, and whose are not. That identity and ideology are inextricably linked is underscored by Jenks (2017), who reminds us that racial discrimination and White normativity are deeply entrenched in the practices and ideologies of English language teaching. Thus, teacher identity—as is illustrated in several chapters in this volume—comes under scrutiny because one way of addressing this burgeoning problem is to facilitate the development of reflexive teacher identities so that TESOL educators are able to critically question and remedy injustices that might emerge in and from their ESL classroom. To that end, we have seen a growing research interest in examining teacher agency (e.g., Kayi-Aydar 2019; Peña-Pincheira and De Costa 2021; Uştuk and De Costa, 2021; Venegas-Weber 2019; Vitanova 2018), teacher reflexivity (e.g., Edge 2011; Kennedy and De Costa 2022; Uştuk 2022a; Uştuk and Çomoğlu 2021), and teacher mentoring (e.g., De Costa, Ojha, and Zang 2022b; Helgevold, Næsheim-Bjørkvik, and Østrem 2015; Uştuk 2022b; Uştuk and Çomoğlu 2019) opportunities to support the professional development of teachers. This expanding second language teacher education agenda is further solidified by exhortations to foster critical translingual awareness (Cinaglia and De Costa 2022; see also Deroo, Ponzio, and De Costa 2020). Crucially, many of these critically-oriented TESOL pedagogical efforts seek to disrupt and unsettle a hegemonic and often monolingual "standard" English ideology that has prevailed in school, especially in contexts where English is the dominant language in society. And as the chapters in this volume will reveal, a concerted and multi-pronged effort—one that combines a destabilization of the TESOL education canon that has long favored a monolingual native-speaker episteme—is needed.

In this Volume ...

As part of our aforementioned plan to develop a sociopolitical agenda for TESOL teacher education, we would like to emphasize that we conceive of TESOL teacher education as including all *teacher learning* activities across different phases of a TESOL professional's teaching career, namely, initial teacher education, early career teacher orientation/induction programs, and in-service professional learning. In that respect, this volume seeks to provide a blueprint for TESOL teacher educators to refine their instructional practices in ways that will help ESL teachers navigate our volatile profession by, specifically, showcasing an activist sociopolitical agenda that can be put into practice.

Following the introductory chapter, we introduce the two sections that comprise this volume. The chapters in the first section unfold the theoretical underpinnings of our proposed sociopolitical agenda. Building upon these theoretical underpinnings, the chapters in the second section exemplify how to actualize our agenda in real TESOL teacher education contexts, primarily through engaging in acts of professional reflexivity and developing sociopolitically responsive pedagogical practices.

Part I opens with a chapter by Dudley Reynolds on TESOL teacher leadership. In Chapter 2, Reynolds (a former TESOL president) provides a vivid example of how sociopolitics has impacted even the content of his presidential keynote: on one hand, there was the opportunity to foster professionalism as a TESOL leader by delivering a speech that focused merely on academic issues in a decontextualized manner; on the other hand, the keynote afforded him the opportunity to demonstrate his leadership by engaging with the issues associated with "the unjust world." Reynolds explains how he elected to pursue the second type of leadership, underscoring why it is vitally important for teachers today to make sense of the world, connect it to their classrooms, and identify ways to exercise moral agency.

In Chapter 3, long-time collaborators, Kenan Dikilitaş and Irem Çomoğlu, introduce several principles that underpin sociopolitically-oriented L2 teacher professional learning, and share three teacher stories from the Turkish context. Positioning themselves as teacher educators who challenge the understanding of L2 teachers as passive recipients of knowledge, Dikilitaş and Çomoğlu challenge current understandings of TESOL teacher *training* and propose a new TESOL teacher education initiative that enables teachers to create an agentic space. Such a space, they argue, allows teachers to be critical decision-makers of their professional *learning* even when the wider meso-level (e.g., institutional) and macro-level (e.g., national and global) systems that surround their classrooms do not necessarily facilitate teacher agency.

In the fourth chapter, Ali Fuad Selvi elaborates on how (non)native speakerism has long plagued the English language teaching (ELT) profession. Following a problematization of discussions around native speakerism and an exploration of inequities and injustices within ELT, Selvi calls for a reconceptualization of critical concepts such as the *(non)native speaker*. Specifically, he notes that TESOL teacher educators should interrogate Western, White, Male, and Global North hegemony. Importantly, Selvi's chapter reminds us of the need for TESOL practitioners to understand the discourses, practices, policies, and the politics of critical issues such as (non)native speakerism.

In Chapter 5, the last chapter in the first section of this book, Jamie Schissel and Nancy Hornberger analyze achievement gap discourses and existing data that have been mobilized to fuel the circulation of these discourses. Focusing on the *grand narrative* of the achievement gap, they highlight how such discourses compromise the educational opportunities available to English learners in the US. TESOL practitioners, Schissel and Hornberger argue, need to be aware of the linguistic biases that impact their classrooms and assessment practices. They add that practitioners also need to interpret test score data with a critical lens, and not passively accept interpretations of scores by so-called "specialists" who have little or no access to their classrooms.

The chapters in Part II of the book not only push forward the conceptualizations introduced in Part I but also show us how to become sociopolitically-aware TESOL practitioners and reflexive teacher educators. In particular, the chapters in the second part of the book highlight the significance of local praxis in TESOL teacher education. Megan Madigan Peercy, Danielle Gervais Sodani, and Wyatt Hall (Chapter 6) report how TESOL practitioners, who work with multilingual learners, can emerge as equity-minded and *humanizing* language teaching professionals. Pointing out that multilingual learners are systematically marginalized, Peercy and colleagues argue that novice teachers require more than prescriptive and vertically hierarchal induction programs—where novice teachers are only monitored and advised by senior colleagues—to become change agents in such a system.

In Chapter 7, Hayriye Kayi-Aydar provides a narrative account of how she implemented an intersectional pedagogical approach in her TESOL methodology course in order to help future TESOL practitioners understand the diversity and inequalities of an uneven world. Incorporating diverse voices in the Global South and problematizing labels such as multilingualism and multilingual learners that define critical concepts of TESOL into her curriculum, she illustrates how a TESOL methodology module can shape the identity and agency of language educators.

Bedrettin Yazan (Chapter 8) recommends the use of critical autoethnographic narratives as a way to deal with the complexities of TESOL teacher identity. Arguing that existing TESOL teacher education practices are often in alignment with the neoliberal ideologies, he posits that teacher educators need to challenge a standardized way of preparing teachers by priming them with "best," one-size-fits-all practices; instead, Yazan calls for an integration of identity into teacher education and the promotion of reflexivity so that teachers can customize their teaching according to the needs of their learners.

In Chapter 9, Mario López-Gopar, Vilma Huerta Cordova, William Sughrua, Juan Ignacio Martínez Martínez, and Denisse Zárate Ríos transport readers to Mexico, and demonstrate how TESOL teacher education can be decolonized by addressing the challenges encountered by Indigenous and linguistic minorities who are culturally and historically marginalized. Their decolonial efforts are realized through the creation of a *praxicum* (Pennycook 2004) that enables TESOL practitioners to act and reflect together.

The volume ends with an afterword by Peter Sayer, who underscores the need to always stay focused on the local concerns and struggles of ESL students and their teachers as the latter enact what he describes as "social justice as pedagogical practice." In closing, we recognize that we may have started on a relatively somber and pessimistic note. But as you page through the chapters of this book, you will find that the sociopolitical agenda put forward by our contributing authors does indeed offer much hope for our field. We are indeed fortunate in that our enterprise to advocate for English learners and teachers is buoyed by parallel efforts within the broader field to uplift TESOL education through efforts to (1) queer pedagogical practices (e.g., Cahnmann-Taylor, Coda, and Jiang 2022), (2) engage in anti-racist work (e.g., De Costa 2021a; Gordon et al. 2021), (3) promote epistemic access to multilingual learners (e.g., Kerfoot and Bello-Nonjengele 2022), (4) revitalize the languages of Indigenous people who are at risk of losing their land rights and, correspondingly, their cultures (De Costa 2021b), and (5) bridge the research-practitioner gap in TESOL that needs to be narrowed (De Costa et al. 2022a; Rose 2019). Such efforts are also richly deserving of our support and attention, especially if we are to realize Kumaravadivelu's vision of "helping language teaching professionals become strategic thinkers, exploratory researchers, and transformative intellectuals" (2012: x) as we address contemporary sociopolitical issues that surround us in ways that will enhance learning and teaching outcomes. At the same time, however, we cannot afford to turn a blind eye to the valuable contributions and insights that our colleagues from the Global South have to offer (Heugh et al. 2021), especially if we are to mount a successful decolonial dismantle of a historically hegemonic field like TESOL (Motha 2014). If anything, we need to manage this significant enterprise in a deeply humanizing and ethical manner in order to benefit all who are committed to our endeavor. We are indeed poised to experience some turbulent but exciting moments ahead of us. Let's wait and see how the next three decades of TESOL teacher education research unfold.

References

Avineri, N., L. R. Graham, E. J. Johnson, R. Conley Riner, and J. Rosa, eds. (2019), *Language and Social Justice in Practice*, New York: Routledge.

Benesch, S. (2020), "Emotions and Activism: English Language Teachers' Emotion Labor as Responses to Institutional Power," *Critical Inquiry in Language Studies*, 17 (1): 26–41.

Cahnmann-Taylor, M., J. Coda, and L. Jiang (2022), "Queer Is as Queer Does: Queer L2 Pedagogy in Teacher Education," *TESOL Quarterly*, 56 (1): 130–153.

Cinaglia, C., and P. I. De Costa (2022), "Cultivating Critical Translingual Awareness: Challenges and Possibilities for Teachers and Teacher Educators," *RELC Journal*, 53 (2): 452–459.

Cochran-Smith, M. (2005), "The New Teacher Education: For Better or for Worse?," *Educational Researcher*, 34 (7): 3–17.

De Costa, P. I. (2018), "Toward Greater Diversity and Social Equality in Language Education Research," *Critical Inquiry in Language Studies*, 15 (4): 302–307.

De Costa, P. I. (2021a), "Anti-Asian Racism: How It Affects TESOL Professionals Like You and Me," *TESOL Journal*, 12: e620. https://doi.org/10.1002/tesj.620.

De Costa, P. I. (2021b), "Indigenous Language Revitalization: How Education Can Help Reclaim 'Sleeping' Languages," *Journal of Language, Identity, and Education*, 20 (5): 355–361.

De Costa, P. I., W. Li, and H. Rawal (2020), "Should I Stay or Leave? Exploring L2 Teachers' Profession an Emotionally-Inflected Framework," in C. Gkonou, J. M. Dewaele, and J. King (eds.), *Language Teaching: An Emotional Rollercoaster*, 211–227, Bristol: Multilingual Matters.

De Costa, P. I., K. Gajasinghe, L. Ojha, and A. Ahmed (2022a), "Bridging the Researcher-Practitioner Divide Through Community Engaged Action Research: A Collaborative Autoethnographic Exploration," *The Modern Language Journal*, 106 (3): 547–563.

De Costa, P. I., L. P. Ojha, and L. Zang (2022b), "Mentoring Through Modeling and Socialization: Insights from China and Nepal," in M. Wyatt and K. Dikilitaş (eds.), *International Perspectives on Mentoring in English Language Education*, 53–69, Cham: Springer.

Deroo, M. R., C. M. Ponzio, and P. I. De Costa (2020), "Reenvisioning Second Language Teacher Education Through Translanguaging Praxis," in Z. Tian, L. Aghai, P. Sayer, and J. L. Schissel (eds.), *Envisioning TESOL through a Translanguaging Lens*, 111–134, Cham: Springer.

Edge, J. (2011), *The Reflexive Teacher Educator in TESOL: Roots and Wings*, New York: Routledge.

Gordon, R. R., H. L. Reichmuth, L. Her, and P. I. De Costa (2021), "Thinking Beyond 'Languaging' in Translanguaging Pedagogies: Exploring Ways to Combat White Fragility in an Undergraduate Language Methodology Course," in U. Lanvers, A. S. Thomson, and M. East (eds.), *Language Learning in Anglophone Countries*, 445–462, Cham: Springer.

Goulah, J., and J. Katunich, eds. (2020), *TESOL and Sustainability: English Language Teaching in the Anthropocene Era*, London: Bloomsbury.

Hall, J. K., and W. G. Eggington, eds. (2000), *The Sociopolitics of English Language Teaching*, Bristol: Multilingual Matters.

Helgevold, N., G. Næsheim-Bjørkvik, and S. Østrem (2015), "Key Focus Areas and Use of Tools in Mentoring Conversations during Internship in Initial Teacher Education," *Teaching and Teacher Education*, 49: 128–137.

Heugh, K., C. Stroud, K. Taylor-Leech, and P. I. De Costa, eds. (2021), *A Sociolinguistics of the South*, New York: Routledge.

Jenks, C. (2017), *Race and Ethnicity in English Language Teaching: Korea in Focus*, Bristol: Multilingual Matters.

Kayi-Aydar, H. (2019), "Language Teacher Agency: Major Theoretical Considerations, Conceptualizations and Methodological Choices," in Hayriye Kayi-Aydar, X. Gao, R. E. Miller, M. Varghese, and G. Vitanova (eds.), *Theorizing and Analyzing Language Teacher Agency*, 10–21, Bristol: Multilingual Matters.

Kennedy, L. M., and P. I. De Costa (2022), "Reflexivity, Emerging Expertise, and Mi[S-STEP]s: A Collaborative Self-Study of Two TESOL Teacher Educators," in S. Consoli and S. Ganassin (eds.), *Reflexivity in Applied Linguistics: Opportunities, Challenges, and Suggestions*, 153–170, New York: Routledge.

Kerfoot, C., and B. O. Bello-Nonjengele (2022), "Towards Epistemic Justice: Constructing Knowers in Multilingual Classrooms," *Applied Linguistics*. https://doi.org/10.1093/applin/amac049.

Kubanyiova, M. (2020), "Language Teacher Education in the Age of Ambiguity: Educating Responsive Meaning Makers in the World," *Language Teaching Research*, 24 (1): 49–59.

Kumaravadivelu, B. (2012), *Language Teacher Education for a Global Society: A Modular Model for Knowing, Analyzing, Recognizing, Doing, and Seeing*, New York: Routledge.

Li, W., and P. I. De Costa (2021), "Problematizing Enterprise Culture in Global Academic Publishing: Linguistic Entrepreneurship through the Lens of Two Chinese Visiting Scholars in a U.S. University," *Multilingua*, 40 (2): 225–250.

McIntosh, K., and P. McPherron, eds. (2023), "Teaching English in a Time of Resurgent Nationalism," *TESOL Quarterly* (Special Issue).

Mirhosseini, S.-A., and P. I. De Costa, eds. (2020), *The Sociopolitics of English Language Testing*, London: Bloomsbury.

Motha, S. (2014), *Race, Empire, and English Language Teaching: Creating Responsible and Ethical Anti-Racist Practice*, New York: Teachers College Press.

O'Regan, J. P. (2021), *Global English and Political Economy*, New York: Routledge.

Ortaçtepe Hart, D., and J. Martel (2020), "Exploring the Transformative Potential of English Language Teaching for Social Justice: Introducing the Special Issue," *TESOL Journal*, 11: e568. https://doi.org/10.1002/tesj.568.

Peña-Pincheira, R. S., and P. I. De Costa (2021), "Language Teacher Agency for Educational Justice-Oriented Work: An Ecological Model," *TESOL Journal*, 12: e561. https://doi.org/10.1002/tesj.561.

Pennycook, A. (1990), "Towards a Critical Applied Linguistics for the 1990s," *Issues in Applied Linguistics*, 1 (1): 8–28.

Pennycook, A. (2004), "Critical Moments in a TESOL Praxicum," in B. Norton and K. Toohey (eds.), *Critical Pedagogies and Language Learning*, 327–346, Cambridge: Cambridge University Press.

Pennycook, A. (2022), "Critical Applied Linguistics in the 2020s," *Critical Inquiry in Language Studies*, 19 (1): 1–21.

Ricento, T., ed. (2015), *Language Policy and Political Economy: English in a Global Context*, Oxford: Oxford University Press.

Rose, H. (2019), "Dismantling the Ivory Tower in TESOL: A Renewed Call for Teaching-Informed Research," *TESOL Quarterly*, 53 (3): 895–905.

Sayer, P. (2019), "The Hidden Curriculum of Work in English Language Education," *AILA Review*, 32 (1): 36–63.

Uştuk, Ö. (2022a), "Drama-in-Teacher-Education: A 'Metaxical' Approach for Juxtaposing EFL Teacher Identity and Tensions," *Language Teaching Research*. https://doi.org/10.1177/13621688221118644.

Uştuk, Ö. (2022b), "How Massive Open Online Courses Constitute Digital Learning Spaces for EFL Teachers: A Netnographic Case Study," *Teaching English with Technology*, 22 (3–4): 43–62.

Uştuk, Ö., and İ. Çomoğlu (2019), "Reframing as a Mentor-Coaching Technique in Initial EFL Teacher Education," in K. Dikilitaş, M. Wyatt, A. Burns, and G. Barkhuizen (eds.), *Energizing Teacher Research*, 19–26, Faversham: IATEFL.

Uştuk, Ö., and İ. Çomoğlu (2021), "Reflexive Professional Development in Reflective Practice: What Lesson Study Can Offer," *International Journal for Lesson & Learning Studies*, 10 (3): 260–273.

Uştuk, Ö., and P. I. De Costa (2021), "Reflection as Meta-action: Lesson Study and EFL Teacher Professional Development," *TESOL Journal*, 12: e531. https://doi.org/10.1002/tesj.531.

Venegas-Weber, P. (2019), "Bi/Multilingual Teachers' Professional Holistic Lives: Agency to Enact Inquiry-Based and Equity-Oriented Identities across School Contexts," in H. Kayi-Aydar, X. Gao, E. R. Miller, M. Varghese, and G. Vitanova (eds.), *Theorizing and Analyzing Language Teacher Agency*, 121–138, Bristol: Multilingual Matters.

Vitanova, G. (2018), "'Just Treat Me as a Teacher!' Mapping Language Teacher Agency through Gender, Race, and Professional Discourses," *System*, 79: 28–37.

Yuan, R., I. Lee, P. I. De Costa, M. Yang, and S. Liu (2022), "TESOL Teacher Educators in Higher Education: A Review of Studies from 2010 to 2020," *Language Teaching*, 55 (4): 434–469.

Part One

Theoretical Underpinnings of the Sociopolitical Agenda

The Imperative of Language Teacher Leadership in an Unjust World

Dudley Reynolds

Introduction

From March 2016 until March 2017, I had the honor of serving as the elected leader of TESOL International Association. One of the most momentous events of my presidential year was planned to be the association's annual conference held at the end of my term, where I would deliver the Presidential Keynote address. I was asked for a title and abstract shortly after I assumed office in the summer of 2016. One of my goals for the year was to encourage members of our professional association to envision themselves as professionals and promote a greater understanding of professionalism within the association. I chose the title "PROFESSIONAL English Language Teachers in a 2.0 World" and submitted a brief abstract:

> Educational systems everywhere want to educate more students to higher standards while cutting resources for teacher education and development. Why do they think they can? Why do we know they cannot? The 2.0 world prizes non-traditional learning, interdisciplinarity, and technology. What do "professional" English language teachers offer this world?

In November 2016, however, the US Presidential election results began to create a series of issues that undermined my understanding of what made the world "2.0," and shortly after the Presidential inauguration ceremony in January 2017, the Executive Director and I felt compelled to write to all members around the world outlining how the association was responding to unfolding events, which we described this way:

> Last week, the President of the United States issued a series of executive orders that directly impact TESOL professionals, their students and communities. One

set of executive orders authorizes the construction of a U.S.-Mexico border wall; the stripping of federal grant money to sanctuary cities; hiring 5,000 more Border Patrol agents; and ending "catch-and-release" policies for undocumented immigrants. Another executive order imposes a 120-day suspension of the refugee program and a 90-day ban on travel to the U.S. from citizens of seven predominantly Muslim countries: Iraq, Iran, Syria, Libya, Yemen, Somalia and Sudan.

I had wanted my Presidential Keynote to be about the value of a sense of professionalism for teachers, but suddenly, I found myself in what felt like an unprecedented time that compelled me to think more about my own role as a leader—and how I might encourage our members to engage with this new world—than about my academic understanding of professionalism. Most language teachers will not become the elected leader of a professional association, and unless their career aspirations include some form of administrative role, they may not see "leadership" as a central topic for their professional development. My experience, however, leads me to think differently. In an unjust world, where so much of the injustice has an intercultural dimension, leadership is an imperative focus for language teacher education and development.

Teachers play a pivotal role at the nexus of inherited and emergent societies. They are entrusted with passing on what the world has already figured out—as well as where it has failed—to those who will have the power to enact change. Language teachers at that nexus are particularly crucial for helping societies to address challenges created by cultures in contact: the social and economic inequalities produced by colonialism, racialized identities, the use of language to empower and disempower. It is important therefore to understand the leadership role that language teachers play at this nexus and to think how we may support and scaffold them.

Numerous studies have argued that the concept of "teacher leadership" is murky at best (Berg and Zoellick 2018; Whitehead and Greenier 2019). The confusion stems in part from whether teacher leadership is seen as referring to a role that teachers can play within educational systems (e.g., Allen 2018; Al-Taneiji and Ibrahim 2017; Cheung et al. 2018; Cosenza 2015; Nerlino 2020) or as a set of traits exhibited by some teachers (e.g., Greenier and Whitehead 2016; McGee, Haworth, and MacIntyre 2015; Russell and von Esch 2018; Warren 2021; Whitehead and Greenier 2019). Both of these perspectives adopt the view that teacher leadership only applies to a subset of teachers: some people will be leaders and the rest will be followers. Moreover, whether the emphasis is on the influence of the role on the system or the impact of teaching like a leader, the tendency is to treat teacher leadership as a static quality, be it a title or a style of teaching.

This chapter argues for a more contextualized understanding of language teacher leadership, seeing it as a dynamic role that is part and parcel of being a teacher. It is a role that responds to and is shaped by temporal events (cf., Kubanyiova 2008; Kubanyiova and Crookes 2016; Kubanyiova and Feryok 2015) and affordances for teacher agency (Vitanova 2018; Kayi-Aydar et al. 2019; Peña-Pincheira and De Costa 2021; Tao and Gao 2021). As such, teacher educators (Gao 2019; Kubanyiova and Crookes 2016), school administrators (Barakat and Brooks 2016), and teachers themselves (Dove and Honigsfeld 2010; Lai and Cheung 2015) must prepare for the eventuality that every teacher will encounter opportunities to lead.

Static Perspectives on Teacher Leadership

Calls to promote greater "teacher leadership" are central in many recent discussions around improving learning outcomes (e.g., Berg and Zoellick 2018; Warren 2021) and general educational reform (e.g., National Education Association 2020). A focus on the improvement of educational outcomes for language learners has also been central in studies related specifically to language teacher leadership (e.g., Greenier and Whitehead 2016; McGee, Haworth, and MacIntyre 2015; Whitehead and Greenier 2019). Across this literature, however, one of the frequent observations is the lack of consensus about the concept's meaning. Berg and Zoellick (2018), for example, identify three strands of research: how a system enables teacher leaders, the characteristics of teacher leaders, and the relation between teacher leadership and student learning. Whitehead and Greenier similarly contrast definitions that focus on roles teachers may hold within an educational system with definitions that seek to identify traits and practices belonging to individuals identified as teacher leaders: "something teachers do in the broader school context that contributes to shaping the learning culture" (2019: 962) versus "a dynamic set of qualities, characteristics, and behaviors exhibited inside and outside the classroom that positively influence learners not only in their learning, but also in their lives" (963). For their study, Whitehead and Greenier interviewed 20 Korean undergraduate English learners about the ways in which language teachers are leaders and the "features and characteristics [that] contribute to good language teacher leadership" (965). They then grouped the characteristics identified by the learners

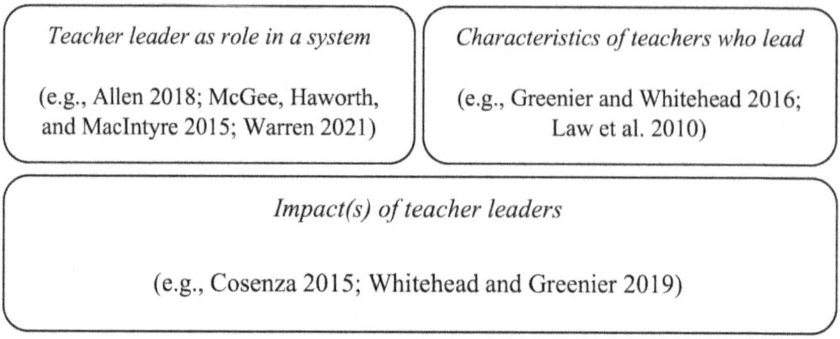

```
┌─────────────────────────────────────┐  ┌─────────────────────────────────────┐
│ Teacher leader as role in a system  │  │ Characteristics of teachers who lead│
│                                     │  │                                     │
│ (e.g., Allen 2018; McGee, Haworth,  │  │ (e.g., Greenier and Whitehead 2016; │
│ and MacIntyre 2015; Warren 2021)    │  │           Law et al. 2010)          │
└─────────────────────────────────────┘  └─────────────────────────────────────┘
┌───────────────────────────────────────────────────────────────────────────────┐
│                         Impact(s) of teacher leaders                          │
│                                                                               │
│            (e.g., Cosenza 2015; Whitehead and Greenier 2019)                  │
└───────────────────────────────────────────────────────────────────────────────┘
```

Figure 2.1 Static perspectives on teacher leadership.

according to four themes: "passion, rapport, purpose, and balance and flexibility" (971).

The common thread that has connected examinations of the roles teacher leaders can play in a system with studies attempting to identify the characteristics of teacher leaders is the influence that individuals identified as teacher leaders ultimately have not just on student learning but on the broader educational context. Drawing on interviews with 22 elementary and middle school teachers in California, Cosenza concludes:

> The participants in this study portray teacher leadership primarily as a collaborative activity that draws them into the decision making process. This is a powerful affirmation that teachers are beginning to see themselves as professionals who have a voice in their own profession. Overall, this outcome supports the definition of teacher leadership put forward by the Institute for Educational Leadership (2001), which suggests that teachers are leaders when they seek additional challenges outside the confines of their classrooms.
>
> 2015: 96

Whitehead and Greenier similarly found that students identified characteristics of good classroom teaching but also characteristics that "transcended the immediate connection to learning and learning objectives at the classroom level and involved stimulating learners in the overall process of language learning inside and outside the classroom" (2019: 979). Seeing (language) teacher leaders as classroom and system "influencers" acknowledges their social power and explains why the push to promote teacher leadership has been taken up by legislatures in the United States (Allen 2018), professional associations like TESOL International Association ("ELT Leadership

Management Certificate Program," n.d.), and local school districts in the United States (Cheung et al. 2018) and Hong Kong (Law et al. 2010).

One effect of this push to institutionalize teacher leadership, however, is a tendency to emphasize the goal as a seemingly static trait, whether of systems or individuals. For example, based on a review of literature on teacher leadership and its impact on student learning, Warren describes an ideal system in which "stakeholders in education . . . place significant emphasis on promoting classroom teacher leadership. They . . . design effective strategies to ensure that the current crop of teachers understands the importance and role of teacher leaders. They . . . ensure that more non-leader teachers transform into leaders" (2021: 14). Greenier and Whitehead draw similar conclusions about the ideal English teacher in a study surveying English teachers about characteristics of good teaching and how they show leadership in their classrooms:

> To positively affect their community of learning and be authentic classroom leaders, teachers *must continuously reflect*, be open and honest but conscious of how they communicate their feelings, wholeheartedly consider students' needs, and act in a manner that is both principled and respectful. Such leadership skills require *an ongoing effort* that utilizes both teaching knowledge and the capacity to engage and motivate learners by understanding their needs, their culture, and their individual characteristics.
>
> 2016: 90, emphasis added

For Greenier and Whitehead, being a language teacher leader is a constant aspiration, much as learner motivation is often viewed as a general state informed by a sense of future-self. For learner motivation research, however, Dörnyei argues that such aspiration-based conceptualizations overlook the need for "a situation-specific constituent" (2019: 21). He notes: "For some language learners the initial motivation to learn a language does not come from internally or externally generated self-images but rather from successful engagement with the actual language learning process (e.g., because they discover that they are good at it)" (2009 as quoted in Dörnyei 2019: 22). This chapter argues that more attention is needed to language teacher leadership as a dynamic construct describing teacher engagement with actual situations and issues.

Teacher Leadership as a Dynamic Construct

The concerns that prompted my email to TESOL members in January 2016 were real and significant. The external contexts motivating English learners worldwide and in which English learners in the United States specifically were learning, not to mention the ways in which specific cultural groups were being characterized, were changing rapidly; TESOL's Executive Director and I felt a need for immediate collective action. Static conceptualizations of teacher leadership that focus on standing positions within an organization and characteristics such as passion, rapport, and purpose are useful for identifying individuals pre-positioned to act and the general tenor of their discourse; they are less useful in understanding the potential within the field to take meaningful, collective action in real time.

Larsen-Freeman notes that: "In our daily lives complexity and constant change can be difficult to live with. We cope by reducing the complexity—by adopting routines and telling stories about our life experiences, and by reifying constant change, for instance, nominalizing dynamic processes, which then connotes stasis" (2012: 206). This is what we do to the action of leading when we reify it as leadership roles and qualities. In her work, Larsen-Freeman rejects the adoption of static characterizations of human action, and in particular language, proposing instead a Complexity Theory/Dynamic Systems Theory for language, which "aims to account for how the interacting parts of a complex system give rise to the system's collective behavior and how such a system simultaneously interacts with its environment" (206). In order to model the potential for language teachers' collective response to a complex and changing set of concerning issues, we need a dynamic understanding of what teachers know to do.

Teacher cognition as emergent sense-making

Kubanyiova and Feryok approach this question by examining teacher cognition, which they see as key to understanding "How do language teachers create meaningful learning environments for their students? How can teacher education, continuing professional development, and the wider educational and sociocultural context facilitate such learning in language teachers?" (2015: 435). They reject cognitivist approaches as too static, however, and argue instead that teacher cognition should be seen as "emergent sense making in action" (2015: 436). If we view teachers' cognition of leadership as "emergent," then we emphasize both the contingent nature of the need to lead and the inherent negotiation of what constitutes leadership in a given situation.

In my Presidential Keynote, I contrasted two senses of what was making the world "2.0." When I had written the abstract, I had seen globalization as the force that was changing the world and posing existential threats to the teaching profession. Driven by the neoliberal imperative to do more with less, it was blurring distinctions between expert and lay teachers, arguing that technology could achieve the same ends as a classroom teacher, and questioning the need for language classrooms when sink-or-swim immersion seemed to work perfectly well. By the time I was ready to deliver the Keynote, however, I had come to see nationalistic ideologies as an even bigger threat to Kubanyiova and Feryok's "meaningful learning environment" (2015: 435). A refugee crisis meant that displaced young people were too often out of school because they had no status in a foreign country (UNESCO 2018). Political leaders in the United States and Europe were stereotyping ethnic and religious groups in ways that not only made international students studying in their countries feel excluded but in some cases even made it difficult for them to return from a vacation in order to continue their studies. The segmentation of the world according to ethnicities, religions, and passports was not just downgrading the quality of what happened in the classroom, it was denying students the right to even enter it.

Since the time of my Presidential Keynote, the challenges for language classrooms presented by both globalization and nationalism have continued. They cannot be ignored, nor can the new challenges that have presented themselves since 2017 such as the social and emotional impact on students and teachers of the global Covid-19 pandemic and the potential for extreme weather events induced by global warming to disrupt education. Any conceptualization of teacher leadership must recognize the contingent need for teachers to make sense of these challenges as they emerge, to see the impact that they have on their own ability to support students' learning, and to counter the ways in which these challenges demotivate and exclude students. In an article sharing lessons about leadership taken from interviews with former leaders of professional associations for language teachers, Stephenson shares this quote from Peter Grundy, a former President of IATEFL:

> I think leadership skills are developed on the job and come about by thinking hard about people and the situation and remembering that in a sense the leader is only there, and certainly only leading effectively, because others agree to it. The few things I know are all particularized to contexts and people and so are unlikely to result from formal training.
>
> 2018: 194

Teacher leadership emerges through making sense of world events, specific contexts, and the people involved.

Moral teacher agency

Teacher leadership is more than sense-making, however; it is also an expression of agency. Ecological perspectives on teacher agency (e.g., Peña-Pincheira and De Costa 2021; Priestley et al. 2012) see the act of doing, like the act of sense-making, as emergent. Tao and Gao write: "an individual's past experience, present conditions, and future goals form an iterative relationship in performing agentic choices and actions. When agency is individual and contextually resourced, it becomes something emergent in a particular context rather than an individual capacity" (2021: 8). It is also contingent as Vitanova notes: "agency is more of a relational phenomenon and is both positioned within an environment that is occupied by other individuals and is marked by temporality. Thus, agency, similar to identity, is not a constant or immutable entity one possesses; an individual may enact more or less agency depending on the contexts and different temporal frames" (2018: 28). Seeing one's agency as something other than a possessed, immutable entity wards off the deterministic fatalism embedded in the question: "how could I make a difference?" It emphasizes that whether the context that presents on a given day is a student struggling to stay awake in class because of problems at home or a new Ministry policy that denies multilingual learners additional time on a standardized assessment, agency is something that is found and acted upon in the moment. The possibility for action, the decisions made when acting, and the lessons learned from action are emergent and contingent.

When the Executive Director and I sent our email to more than 12,000 TESOL members and when I delivered my Presidential Keynote to an audience of over 2,000 conference attendees, I euphorically sensed that I was enacting more agency than ever before in my career. As noted earlier, however, most language teachers will not find themselves president of an international professional association. Does this mean that their sense of agency must be more limited, more "realistic?" My sense of agency in those moments was constructed relative to my previous experiences and the affordances of the position I was in at the moment; I felt that I was taking advantage of the role I was in. Kubanyiova and Crookes argue that

> the contribution of the "additional language" teacher across language learning contexts (e.g., foreign, second, bilingual, heritage, complementary, immersion, etc.) is to promote, maintain, and strengthen the multicultural nature of his or her society, enable students to navigate the complex language learning demands in their multilingual lifeworlds, and in some cases act as an advocate for minority cultures within a dominant culture and country.
>
> 2016: 119

In this role, they see the language teacher as a "moral agent" (119).

Dynamic perspectives of language teacher leadership do not call for more leadership roles in schools or workshops on influencing and motivating students; rather, they advocate for equipping language teachers to be moral agents who sense the connections between the affordances of their classrooms and a more just and equitable society. I concluded my Keynote: "As professional English language teachers in a 2.0 world, we must engage the issues and problems of our day, not just the issues and problems of our classrooms." Preparing language teachers for this role offers them the potential to feel as agentive as I felt watching the audience leave my Keynote.

Preparing for Every Language Teacher to Lead: Acting on the Vision

When I delivered my Keynote, I moved away from the content promised in my abstract because I felt that the time I was living in required me to do so. More importantly, I felt it was my professional responsibility to encourage other educators to make sense of how their classrooms connected with the social and political changes happening around them and envision their own moral agency with respect to an unjust world. Preparing language teachers to lead, however, is not a task that should be delegated—or relegated—to a TESOL President; it is a shared responsibility for teacher educators (Gao 2019; Kubanyiova and Crookes 2016), school administrators (Barakat and Brooks 2016), professional associations (Stephenson 2018, 2020), and teachers themselves (Dove and Honigsfeld 2010; Lai and Cheung 2015). If the language teacher leadership needed in an unjust world is emergent and contingent, then it cannot be developed in one lesson or by one voice; it must be a collective exercise in building capacity for action "based on the notion that leadership learning is complex, multidimensional, socially constructed and grounded in shared experiences that allow new knowledge to emerge" (Stephenson 2020: 204).

Connecting the world to the classroom

This capacity-building must begin by encouraging every teacher to make sense of who is in their classroom, who is not, and why the students who are feel more, or less, empowered. This means considering the impact of historical forces such as colonialism and climate change, global economic models such as neoliberalism, and political rhetoric that often divides communities in an attempt to "carve out" supporters. It also means considering ways in which language resources can both exacerbate and counter such social and political forces. Peña-Pincheira and De Costa argue that

> although English can serve as an equalizer, it can also create large fractures in society by dividing the "haves" and the "have nots." That, unfortunately, is the trade-off of embracing neoliberalism in any educational system.... Because of this reality, English teachers need to step up and determine how they can become effective agents of change in school and society.
>
> 2021: 10

Language teachers are uniquely positioned to observe the human faces of social and economic inequality, historic prejudices, misguided nationalism, and other forces that attempt to proscribe individual opportunity. They can see that while educational institutions worldwide promote their impact on how societies develop with taglines such as "we prepare the leaders of tomorrow today" and "where the future is born," social forces such as neoliberal globalization and nationalism actually shape participation in these institutions and opportunities to learn. Teachers in language classrooms are also positioned to understand and recognize individual and collaborative ability. They see what students can do when social and economic constraints are at least lessened. They observe group work that engages individuals who news media might stereotype as "marginalized populations" or even sometimes "warring parties." When language teachers engage in "sense-making," they can come to understand both the impact and the potential of the world outside the classroom. It is important therefore to consider how this ability to sense-make can be cultivated and scaffolded.

Sense-making as described here is an act of interpretation, of going beyond surface realities and observations to consider who is present in the classroom, who is not, and why. The same type of questions can be asked about students' engagement, learning histories, future goals, and myriad other factors that standard language education curricula teach as important to language learning. To prepare teachers for such interpretation, they need to engage readings with critical perspectives on human and social capital, discuss alternative perspectives on opportunity with peers, observe classroom ecologies, and follow-up with reflective analysis of key interactions. Just as literature majors learn to interpret and critique creative works, language teachers can learn to interpret and critique educational environments and systems.

Identifying opportunities for moral agency

If teacher leadership involves going beyond sense-making to the exercise of moral agency, then a second key question is how to enhance teachers' ability to act. Kubanyiova and Crookes argue that:

> it seems crucial to begin to think of the core task of language teacher education in terms of facilitating the development of the kinds of moral visions that will enable language teachers to adapt, innovate, and survive in the face of political, economic, and other realities they must face in order to enhance language learning experiences for diverse language learners, users, and persons in their classrooms.
>
> 2016: 126

Two common approaches for developing the ability to act are scenarios and practicum experiences. Scenarios may be introduced through role-play activities or as reflection prompts. Kubanyiova and Crookes' reference to adapting, innovating, and surviving could provide a useful taxonomy for ensuring scenarios cover a range of actions. Practicum experiences, on the other hand, provide opportunities for supervised "learning on the job" as Grundy phrases it; they also offer opportunities to observe the messiness of actual interactions and reflect on "how to enhance language learning experiences," as Kubanyiova and Crookes describe the goal. A third, less common approach to teaching the ability to act is to study actors. Stephenson's (2018) interviews with Peter Grundy and other professional association leaders offer a useful example. Whether working through scenarios, debriefing class observations, or reading leader profiles, it will be important to focus on the potential influence teachers have in and outside the classroom and the kinds of techniques and characteristics identified in the literature on teacher leadership (e.g., Whitehead and Greenier 2019) that enhance that influence.

Finally, in considering ways to support teachers' exercise of moral agency, it is important to remember that agency is not only emergent but also contingent on opportunity. Gao argues that "language teacher educators not only need to provide knowledge and experience to enable transformation among language teachers; they should also explore ways to create and sustain the contextual conditions that are conducive to changes in their learning and professional practice" (2019: 165). It is not enough to encourage action; teacher educators and researchers must strive to influence elements of the educational system like curriculum guides and standards, teacher licensing requirements, and even conceptualizations of learning and language that limit what teachers see as possible.

Leadership is Part of Every Teacher's Role

This chapter has argued that language teachers are uniquely positioned to lead responses to many of the social and political injustices that characterize our world. If we are to build that capacity to respond, we must adopt a dynamic understanding of teacher leadership that goes beyond static perspectives focusing simply on creating leadership roles within an educational system or promoting generic leadership traits. Dynamic perspectives of teacher leadership view it as a capacity that emerges as teachers make sense of their times and contexts and which is contingent on their moral agency in the moment. The very dynamic nature of the capacity moreover means that it is the responsibility of the educational ecosystem as a whole—teacher educators, system administrators, teachers themselves—to nurture the capacity, to seek out opportunities to promote reflection and practice.

The imperative of teacher leadership, however, does not lie in the urgency of the social crises and conflicts to which this chapter has argued teachers should be equipped to respond. Rather, it lies in the value of what teacher leaders can offer, their micro-level experiences with the problems and the solutions of the classroom that help them analyze and advocate at the meso and macro levels of school and community. As discussions of agency often note, the potential for action does not ensure that actions when taken will be helpful or hurtful. Teacher leadership is an emergent phenomenon that will manifest in relation to context and time. When it does, teachers need to be as prepared as possible to see how the meaning-making happening in the classroom is shaped by—and can shape—the schools and communities of which the classroom is part. This is not a matter that anyone in the educational ecosystem can afford to leave to chance.

References

Allen, L. Q. (2018), "Teacher Leadership and the Advancement of Teacher Agency," *Foreign Language Annals*, 51 (1): 240–250.

Al-Taneiji, S., and A. Ibrahim (2017), "Practices of and Roadblocks to Teacher Leadership in the United Arab Emirates' Schools," *International Education Studies*, 10 (6): 87–99.

Barakat, M., and J. S. Brooks (2016), "When Globalization Causes Cultural Conflict: Leadership in the Context of an Egyptian/American School," *Journal of Cases in Educational Leadership*, 19 (4): 3–15.

Berg, J. H., and B. Zoellick (2018), "Teacher Leadership: Toward a New Conceptual Framework," *Journal of Professional Capital and Community*, 4 (1): 2–14.

Cheung, R., T. Reinhardt, E. Stone, and J. W. Little (2018), "Defining Teacher Leadership: A Framework," *Phi Delta Kappan*, 100 (3): 38–44.

Cosenza, M. N. (2015), "Defining Teacher Leadership: Affirming the Teacher Leader Model Standards," *Issues in Teacher Education*, 24 (2): 79–99.

Dörnyei, Z. (2009), "The L2 Motivational Self System," in Z. Dörnyei and E. Ushioda (eds.), *Motivation, Language Identity and the L2 Self*, 9–42, Bristol: Multilingual Matters.

Dörnyei, Z. (2019), "Towards a Better Understanding of the L2 Learning Experience, the Cinderella of the L2 Motivational Self System," *Studies in Second Language Learning and Teaching*, 9 (1): 19–31.

Dove, M., and A. Honigsfeld (2010), "ESL Coteaching and Collaboration: Opportunities to Develop Teacher Leadership and Enhance Student Learning," *TESOL Journal*, 1 (1): 3–22.

Gao, X. (Andy) (2019), "The Douglas Fir Group Framework as a Resource Map for Language Teacher Education," *The Modern Language Journal*, 103 (S1): 161–166.

Greenier, V. T., and G. E. K. Whitehead (2016), "Towards a Model of Teacher Leadership in ELT: Authentic Leadership in Classroom Practice," *RELC Journal*, 47 (1): 79–95.

Kayi-Aydar, H., X. (Andy) Gao, E. R. Miller, M. Varghese, and G. Vitanova, eds. (2019), *Theorizing and Analyzing Language Teacher Agency*, Bristol: Multilingual Matters.

Kubanyiova, M. (2008), "Rethinking Research Ethics in Contemporary Applied Linguistics: The Tension between Macroethical and Microethical Perspectives in Situated Research," *The Modern Language Journal*, 92 (4): 503–518.

Kubanyiova, M., and G. Crookes (2016), "Re-Envisioning the Roles, Tasks, and Contributions of Language Teachers in the Multilingual Era of Language Education Research and Practice," *The Modern Language Journal*, 100 (S1): 117–132.

Kubanyiova, M., and A. Feryok (2015), "Language Teacher Cognition in Applied Linguistics Research: Revisiting the Territory, Redrawing the Boundaries, Reclaiming the Relevance," *The Modern Language Journal*, 99 (3): 435–449.

Lai, E., and D. Cheung (2015), "Enacting Teacher Leadership: The Role of Teachers in Bringing about Change," *Educational Management Administration & Leadership*, 43 (5): 673–692.

Larsen-Freeman, D. (2012), "Complex, Dynamic Systems: A New Transdisciplinary Theme for Applied Linguistics?," *Language Teaching*, 45 (2): 202–214.

Law, E., M. Galton, and S. Wan (2010), "Distributed Curriculum Leadership in Action: A Hong Kong Case Study," *Educational Management Administration & Leadership*, 38 (3): 286–303.

McGee, A., P. Haworth, and L. MacIntyre (2015), "Leadership Practices to Support Teaching and Learning for English Language Learners," *TESOL Quarterly*, 49 (1): 92–114.

National Education Association (NEA) (2020), "The Teacher Leader Model Standards," Washington, DC: National Education Association. https://www.nea.org/resource-library/teacher-leader-model-standards (accessed July 22, 2022).

Nerlino, E. (2020), "A Theoretical Grounding of Teacher Leadership," *Journal of Professional Capital and Community*, 5 (2): 117–128.

Peña-Pincheira, R. S., and P. I. De Costa (2021), "Language Teacher Agency for Educational Justice-Oriented Work: An Ecological Model', *TESOL Journal*, 12 (2): e561. https://doi.org/10.1002/tesj.561.

Priestley, M., R. Edwards, A. Priestley, and K. Miller (2012), "Teacher Agency in Curriculum Making: Agents of Change and Spaces for Manoeuvre," *Curriculum Inquiry*, 42 (2): 191–214.

Russell, F. A., and K. S. von Esch (2018), "Teacher Leadership to Support English Language Learners," *Phi Delta Kappan*, 99 (7): 52–56.

Stephenson, L. (2018), "Developing Leadership Capacity through Leadership Learning Opportunities," in A. Elsheikh, C. Coombe, and O. Effiong (eds.), *The Role of Language Teacher Associations in Professional Development*, Second Language Learning and Teaching, 187–200, Cham: Springer.

Stephenson, L. (2020), "Developing Leadership Capacity in English Language Teaching," in C. Coombe, N. J. Anderson, and L. Stephenson (eds.), *Professionalizing Your English Language Teaching*, Second Language Learning and Teaching, 197–206, Cham: Springer.

Tao, J., and X. Gao (2021), *Language Teacher Agency*, Cambridge Elements in Language Teaching, Cambridge: Cambridge University Press.

TESOL International Association (n.d.), "ELT Leadership Management Certificate Program." https://www.tesol.org/attend-and-learn/certificate-leadership-programs/elt-leadership-management-certificate-program (accessed February 13, 2023).

UNESCO (2018), "Migration, Displacement & Education: Building Bridges, Not Walls," Global Education Monitoring Report, Paris: UNESCO. https://en.unesco.org/gem-report/report/2019/migration.

Vitanova, G. (2018), "'Just Treat Me as a Teacher!' Mapping Language Teacher Agency through Gender, Race, and Professional Discourses," *System*, 79: 28–37.

Warren, L. L. (2021), "The Importance of Teacher Leadership Skills in the Classroom," *Education Journal*, 10 (1): 8–15.

Whitehead, G. E. K., and V. T. Greenier (2019), "Beyond Good Teaching Practices: Language Teacher Leadership from the Learners' Perspective," *TESOL Quarterly*, 53 (4): 960–985.

3

Pedagogical and Conceptual Principles of Teacher Professional Learning in TESOL: Teacher Stories from Turkey

Kenan Dikilitaş and Irem Çomoğlu

Introduction

Traditional pedagogies in teacher education position teachers as "passive subjects" who have little or no say in their development and teaching, and who are expected to comply rather than take action for change (Kohli et al. 2015). Yet, the dialectic between practice and theory, according to Freire (2005: 143), needs to be fully embodied in the training of educators. Thus, recent approaches to teacher development have started to position teachers in an agentive role in their professional journeys and consider professional development as "dialogic action" and "praxis" to be better educators (Freire 1970; Kemmis 2010). This relationship between theory and practice resulting in informed action (Kincheloe 2008; Monchinski 2008) forms the basis of critical pedagogies in teacher education which aim to provoke cooperative dialogue, build unity, provide shared leadership, and meet the critical needs of teachers (Kohli et al. 2015).

In defining critical pedagogies, López-Gopar (2019) emphasizes transformation as a process of developing agency, being responsive, and displaying resistance to social injustice and discrimination, including the imposition of fixed expert knowledge, lack of time to plan, an overwhelming schedule of work, and lack of constructive feedback and non-judgmental pedagogical support. Thus, teachers "become architects of their own transformation" (Vetter 2012: 44) and create their own space and opportunities to engage in professional learning. Considering teacher change as identity work, "professional development becomes something that teachers do for themselves rather than what is done to teachers" (Vetter 2012: 44).

Consequently, teacher professional development as a continuum from initial teacher education through in-service professional development has recently become personally driven (Attard 2017), idiosyncratically self-regulated (Harris, Graham, and Adkins 2015), multimodally-engaged (Yi and Angay-Crowder 2016), research-based (Dikilitaş 2015; Dikilitaş and Çomoğlu 2022; Wyatt and Dikilitaş 2016), and more reflective and reflexive (Beauchamp 2015; Shaw 2013). A shift is occurring from expert-based, transmission-oriented professional development to contextually-situated, transformative teacher development (Burns 2017), which includes identity construction (Edwards and Burns 2016; Yuan and Burns 2017), critical inquiry, and collaboration (Richards 2008). Teachers have become more and more at the epicenter of their own learning (Borg 2013) by making their own choices of mode (online, face-to-face, (a)synchronous), and exercising agency (Miller and Gkonou 2018) for professional development. Rather than teachers waiting to be provided with knowledge and opportunities by others, they have started to self-initiate their learning and self-create their own professional path. More widespread recognition of the ineffectiveness of top-down teacher professional development policies, coupled with the sociopolitical turn in teacher professional development (Gandara, Maxwell-Jolly, and Driscoll 2005; Uştuk and Çomoğlu 2019, 2021), has led both scholarship and practice to encourage teachers' ownership of their own learning.

Although in global contexts one can find fine examples of these principles of critical pedagogies as embedded into teacher education, there are countries where teacher professional development practices are still top-down and transmission-oriented. For instance, in an educational context, Turkey is not seen as a successful provider of professional development programs for its teachers (Balta, Arslan, and Duru 2015; Koç 2016; Korkmazgil and Seferoğlu 2013). Due to sparsely provided support, Turkey's professional development activities for teachers are short-lived, non-systematic, and unsustainable. In the country's education system, both at pre-service and in-service levels, teacher education is often designed to provide decontextualized knowledge which includes standardized techniques and approaches regardless of local contexts. In the Turkish context, teachers are provided with externally-driven support that commodifies and imposes knowledge without any consideration of their own voice and critical interpretation. Although more recent teacher development programs in the world have started to recognize teachers' agency and autonomy by creating space and time to research, reflect, and contextualize knowledge through meaningful experiences (see Borg 2013; Burns 2017; Mills and Goos 2017; Munthe and Rogne 2015; Saglam and Dikilitas 2020), it is not clear how these are understood and enacted in countries like Turkey, where the mere transmission of knowledge by external trainers is still prevalent and teachers are positioned as receivers of knowledge. Therefore, in this chapter, we aim to discuss how teachers at both pre-service and in-service levels need to create their own professional development stories in such a system through the presentation of four cases. We believe the stories showcasing critical developmental trajectories provide examples of how teachers in such contexts with no or little identified institutional support can navigate their professional selves and gain new insights about self, others, and the sociopolitical realities of teaching.

Issues in teacher education in Turkey

Although approaches to professional development have come to encompass more critical theories that prioritize concepts such as autonomy, reflectivity, empowerment, identity, and social justice, we still see "scripted PD" and "one-size-fit-all workshops" as "passive and dehumanizing" processes for teachers (Kohli et al. 2015; Patton, Parker, and Tannehill 2015) in countries such as Turkey. The country has recently seen several reforms in its English language teacher education policies at both pre-service and in-service levels (HEC 2018; MoNE 2021); however, additional reforms are needed in the quest to develop meaningful teacher professional development in a country where top-down policies are still pervasive at all levels (Başar, Çeliktürk, and Çomoğlu 2020). In 2017, for instance, the Ministry of National Education (MoNE) introduced generic and field-specific teacher competencies to set standards at the national level (http://oygm.meb.gov.tr/dosyalar/StPrg/). The generic teacher competencies include six main competencies, 31 sub-competencies, and 233 performance signs. Yet, this rather well-prepared and comprehensive document seems to be a dream far from reality, considering the current problems in the education system in Turkey, such as insufficient initial teacher education programs, regional socioeconomic differences, and teachers' heavy workloads (Atmaca 2018). In Turkey, English language teachers are trained in four-year programs at faculties of education and graduates can teach at all levels of education, from pre-school to tertiary, both in public and private schools. Since there are more education faculty graduates than jobs available, they are required to take the Selection Examination for Professional Posts in Public Organizations (KPSS), a large-scale standardized test for recruitment to public schools. Teachers with low scores on the KPSS are appointed to the eastern and southeastern parts of the country where the standard of living is lower and social services are limited or inaccessible.

According to the University Monitoring and Evaluation Report (HEC 2020), the universities in the country are monitored and evaluated according to several criteria including their KPSS success rate.

As of 2021, there were 97 education faculties in Turkey with a total student population of 235,753 (https://istatistik.yok.gov.tr/). In 2018, the HEC updated teacher education programs in all subject fields, placing increased emphasis on courses related to content knowledge and pedagogical knowledge as well as restructuring and extending teaching practice periods. The education faculties are now partially allowed to self-design some courses if they follow the ratios determined by the HEC. For the English language teacher education (ELTE) programs, the course categories and their ratios determined by the HEC are as follows: 18% (General Culture), 34% (Pedagogical Knowledge), and 48% (Content Knowledge) (https://www.yok.gov.tr/). Students are admitted to ELTE programs based on their scores in the university entrance exam prepared and administered by the Student Selection and Placement Centre (OSYM). The English section of the university entrance exam tests only grammar and vocabulary knowledge, and reading skills; therefore, students wishing to become English teachers strive to master test-taking and do not feel obligated to improve their ability to communicate in English (Hatipoğlu 2016; Öztürk and Aydın 2019).

This over-centralized, exam-oriented, and theory-based nature of the higher education system in the country has some negative consequences for teacher education, as supported by Eret-Orhan, Ok, and Capa-Aydin (2018), who investigated the perceptions of 1,856 pre-service teachers from various subject fields, including English language teaching, about the adequacy of pre-service teacher education programs. They found that pre-service teachers consider the teaching practicum aspect of the program ineffective and that they need more experience-based practical exposures and more interactive and authentic teaching methods and techniques for improving their teaching skills. Similarly, Öztürk and Aydın (2019) highlight the top-down implementation of the updated ELTE program and express doubts about the eventual impact of this program on ensuring standardization in ELTE programs throughout the country.

The case of in-service teacher education is not much different in terms of its limitations and challenges. In Turkey, the Teacher Training and Development General Directorate authorized by the MoNE centrally provides in-service training, including induction programs for teachers in public schools (http://oygmen.meb.gov.tr/). Private schools can determine their own professional development policy priorities according to their contextual needs. Studies conducted with public school teachers reveal that the MoNE's professional development policies and practices organized as one-shot workshops by outside experts do not satisfy them professionally (Ayvaz-Tuncel and Çobanoğlu 2018; Balta, Arslan, and Duru 2015; Koç 2016; Öztürk and Aydın 2019). Irrelevant content, valuing theory over practice, a lack of interactivity, collaboration and reflectivity, and the low quality of trainers and learning materials have been highlighted as some of the challenges Turkish teachers face.

It is also a serious deficit in these pre-service and in-service programs that teacher research is not considered a component that can support teacher learning as well as student learning. Extant literature proposes several functions of research conducted by teachers. The most cited is teacher research for *improving teachers' own in-class practices* (Burns 2019; Wyatt 2011), which is often at the heart of practitioner research. The second is *school development*, where teachers engage in collective or individual research to investigate curriculum issues (Oolbekkink-Marchand, van der Steen, and Nijveldt 2014). The third includes *emancipation and empowerment* as argued in the literature regarding action research (Burns 2019; Stern 2019). Teachers conducting research, both at pre-service and in-service levels, open the way for co-reflection and co-development, thereby increasing transparency and accountability in education. Teachers developing with their students by engaging in inquiry and research initiatives could function as an interaction point for mutual evaluation of the lessons and create a more fluid space where there is a safe environment for both themselves and their students to co-criticize and co-learn, which is seriously needed in teacher professional development in Turkey.

It is sadly the case that the highly centralized and institutionally structured system of teacher education both at pre-service and in-service levels in the country does not permit the space for teachers to pursue their own professional development path in accordance with their own and their students' needs and interests. Neither ELTE programs nor in-service teacher development programs provide flexibility for teachers' individual development. There are very few exemplary teacher development stories on emerging understandings about self, others, and the sociopolitical realities of teaching in the Turkish context, as we show and discuss in the rest of this chapter.

Language Teacher Stories from Turkey

Below, we present four cases from Turkey—one pre-service teacher, one in-service teacher, one MA teacher group, and one PhD graduate teacher—to showcase their unique developmental trajectories within the domain of professional development. The four cases are based on collaborative endeavors with practitioners in our capacity as teacher educators for over 20 years and as their course lecturers and supervisors. We wrote the narrative cases drawing on extensive field notes and hour-long informal conversations we had with the teachers, which we inductively thematized in order to reveal the process of the self-regulation of their professional development. We used pseudonyms throughout. Each case we selected showcases one teacher's professional development trajectory despite a myriad of micro and macro factors that do not support teacher professional learning. Yet, we believe that the stories provide successful examples of professional development in TESOL in multiple ways, modes, and contexts with little or no identified institutional support.

Case 1: Ayşen

Ayşen, a pre-service teacher, was a participant in Mumford and Dikilitaş' (2020) study of pre-service language teachers' reflection development involving online interaction in a hybrid learning course at a private university in Turkey. The developmental trajectory of Ayşen showed marked changes as she became involved in reflective practice in the final year of her education. The online course aimed to help pre-service teachers to develop reflective skills by drawing on observation during the practicum. The course also included face-to-face components which supported the development of a relationship between the students and the instructor, and created space for expanding on written (chatbox) interaction in the online component. This course, which was her first online course at the university, was a totally new phenomenon for Ayşen as a pre-service teacher. The course instructor believed that various courses that would provide pre-service teachers with space to reflect were needed to support their autonomous learning process and critical reflective development.

Early in the course, in an online conversation with her instructor, Ayşen complained about a teaching challenge she faced during the practicum and expressed sadness that it was impossible to find an activity that would please every student. However, when the instructor asked her to reflect more critically on the experience by asking questions such as, "Why did some students not like songs?," "Why did others like it?," "How can you turn your comments into evidence, synthesizing to help understand the case?," Ayşen came to realize the importance of contextual factors in her teaching and wrote in the chatbox: "I want to be more effective in different contexts of learning." In the same lesson,

Ayşen also wrote: "The public school students do not understand the lesson if done in English. I once tried to speak in English. They panicked."

It was apparent that writing and reflecting in the chatbox enabled Ayşen as a pre-service teacher to critically evaluate the contextual factors in her teaching. Describing the chatbox, Ayşen said:

> It's very useful. Words fly but the writing stays, it's very useful, the [written] words. The most important thing, sometimes we speak but if we write, it really helps us to process information better. You read it and think about it in a different way, e.g., thinking out loud helps, but ... you read and think about it more effectively. It helps you, online!

The online component of the course enabled Ayşen to critically reflect on the sociocultural and socioeconomic differences between public and private schools in Turkey. As Ayşen gained more teaching experience in various schools and reflected more on her teaching in online lessons through chatbox conversations with her instructor, she came to describe the socioeconomic status of students, physical conditions of the school, neighborhood, and teacher as the four most important contextual components. For instance, Ayşen once compared her use of songs in private and public school contexts and reflected in the chatbox; "The use of songs in public school was very effective and motivating. I expected the same in a private school in lower ages, however, some of them gave me some negative comments and I was surprised." This shows Ayşen's growing awareness of the difference between private and public schools and of the influence of socioeconomic context on teaching practices.

Case 2: Nilgün

Nilgün became a language teacher in 2006 after graduating in German and English (as a minor degree) and started to teach both languages at K-12 schools in Izmir, Turkey. After working as an English as a Foreign Language (EFL) and German as a Foreign Language (GFL) teacher for 10 years, she began work at another private school which intended to initiate a Turkish-English bilingual kindergarten education system in 2017. Although she accepted the job offer, she was not fully aware of what bilingual education would be like at that time. The other teachers who were involved in this program had no experience in bilingual pedagogies either. However, this was an important initiative for the school to attract financially advantaged parents. In Turkey, parents who are financially well off tend to choose private education for their children to ensure that they get a good start in life by learning English in a private school. Compared to public schools, private schools in the country are known for their better quality English teaching (Kırkgöz 2007).

In such a competitive and neoliberal context in the private education sector, Nilgün's new school—situated in one of the most prestigious and socioeconomically privileged neighborhoods in the city—initiated this bilingual kindergarten program. The program supported children's use of both Turkish and English for communicative purposes. It was designed to ensure that children's use of English was not limited to a particular area but rather was integrated into daily activities and topics. The bilingual program aimed for both Turkish and English to become a normal part of the children's everyday experience. This kindergarten bilingual program stood out as an attractive option for parents who might consider sending their children to a college/university abroad.

Despite feeling weak and powerless at the very beginning of her new job assignment due to her lack of experience of bilingual issues, Nilgün grew in stature with the appointment of an experienced teacher educator as the mentor for the bilingual program. From then on, Nilgün, whose understanding of how bilingual education worked began to grow, did not consider her situation in a negative light. On the contrary, she became very enthusiastic about the new program and the opportunities afforded her professionally through her mentor's support and guidance. Within the emerging bilingual community of practice in her school, Nilgün positioned herself in an agentive role, pushing herself and her peers to co-decide what knowledge to use and what new pedagogies might be appropriate in the school context. In Nilgün's case, this particular professional collaboration created an opportunity to reconstruct and develop her teacher identity, as she explained:

> Having the opportunity to learn from my mentor has made a substantial change both in my career and identity. Switching from being an EFL teacher to a bilingual teacher has been a great journey for me. The more I learned about bilingualism the more I felt inspired by it. Developing the syllabus together with the homeroom teachers and the use of two languages in the lessons have been a good start for me to dive into being a bilingual education teacher. That valuable experience made me feel more connected with children both linguistically and socially as I feel the same with my colleagues.

During the training provided by her mentor, Nilgün was committed to collaboration, active in all tasks, and motivated to help others. She developed a close relationship with her mentor and was very ambitious to develop. Her qualities and abilities to work as part of a team and to lead the team emerged during her training, which enabled her to reconstruct and develop her teacher identity despite the powerlessness she felt at the very beginning of her journey.

Case 3: MA teacher group

It is still the case in Turkey that teachers are perceived as the sole providers of knowledge and students as the receivers of this knowledge (Tekel and Öztekin-Bayır 2021; Tüzel-İşeri and Akin 2019). Within this traditional education system where knowledge is acquired from teachers, a group of public and private school teachers, who were taking the MA ELT course delivered in 2019 at a private university in Istanbul, were asked to develop an action research plan that positions their students as co-researchers and includes them in pedagogical decisions.

The teachers in the group had to pay the tuition fees for the MA program themselves as there was no financial support from the school and/or governmental systems, something that most teachers in Turkey cannot afford. Teachers need to hold a master's degree in order to work in higher education contexts, a practice introduced in 2018. Therefore, the motive for enrolling in these programs is a requirement for induction rather than solely for professional development. However, the program offers a number of opportunities for practical professional development as we describe below.

In this Participatory Action Research assignment, the teacher educator aimed to help the teachers to share their agentic teacher power with their students and to investigate the process of this shift by observing their students and self-reflecting on their new role as co-researchers with their students. In other words, the assignment strove to promote and honor students' voices in the classroom and acknowledge their needs in the course design as well as enable teachers to share their agentic power with them. Such a teacher-student collaboration was not a practice they were used to, which created challenges and opportunities, as one of the participants explained:

> I observed the importance and value of getting reflection from students to assess the classroom activities. As the main purpose is to make more competent learners, I will get my students' ideas about the activities, tasks, and practices we do in class, and consider their ideas for planning lessons. Students' reflections and expectations are extremely important for also my professional development as students are the most important assessors of what teachers do.

Apparently, this was a new and empowering experience for the teachers and their students, who were not used to students' involvement in the knowledge generation process. The Participatory Action Research project assignment within this MA course enabled the teacher group to "co-produce knowledge that is action oriented" and led to "changing and improving practices, finding practical solutions to problems, or changing power relations," as supported by Hammad, Alunni, and Alkhas (2019: 166).

Case 4: Samuel

Samuel's developmental trajectory as a native EFL instructor at a private English medium instruction (EMI) university in Turkey and a PhD student in an ELT program highlights the potency of multidimensional experiences as the sources of deeper identity change cultivated by practical experiences in multiple arenas. At the beginning of Samuel's PhD journey, his supervisor's understanding was that if he had focused on his context as the research setting, on his teaching subject as the overall topic, and his experiences as the overall purpose of delineation and analysis, this would have provided him with agency over the process thanks to a familiarity with the context, topic, and people, and overcome potential challenges that might occur. As a result of repeated online meetings of varying length with his supervisor, Samuel selected as his topic "narrating academic writing teachers' identity" based on Cultural Historical Activity Theory in a collective case study. The identified topic fitted with the context, experiences, and his main roles.

The participants in Samuel's PhD study were four EAP teachers, three of whom were native speakers of English. One of these native speakers of English had an education/teaching background, yet the other two did not, i.e., they came to teaching from careers in other sectors. In Turkey, native speakers from a non-education background are allowed to teach in areas they themselves have not studied. This was the case with Samuel's two participants who had no relevant academic writing experience. As Samuel explored their academic writing identity, he began to develop a sociopolitical stance toward the employment of native speakers as EAP teachers solely dependent on their native speaker background, having no specific pedagogical training for teaching academic language. Samuel reflected on this issue as follows:

> I think when I started teaching academic writing, I didn't really understand what it was, but through writing, and writing about writing, I began to understand it better. This is the paradox, if you don't write academically yourself, you don't have the means to understand writing, regardless of your native language. So, if you are a native speaker who doesn't write, you see academic writing as advanced

English which focuses on accuracy and text structure, rather than being a means of self-expression and a tool for developing thinking.

The research process held a mirror for Samuel's own reflection as he was also a native speaker who invested in learning to teach academic language not only by writing up and publishing academic papers, but also by investigating the teaching of academic language through a series of interviews and observations. On the whole, Samuel's PhD process, which enabled the constitutive relationship of teaching and research, helped him nurture his identities through research activities enriched by peer support and new research practices. This research and supervision process, which provided the opportunity for him to combine his practice of teaching with his PhD research activities, also provided Samuel with a sociopolitical understanding of the employment of native speakers as EAP teachers solely dependent on their native speaker background.

Discussion and Implications

Let us now discuss each of these in turn, four pre-service/in-service teachers who needed to create their own professional development stories in a context with little or no identified institutional support but with relevance to self, their students, and the sociopolitical realities of language education.

In Ayşen's case, we observe the sociopolitical awareness being shaped by noticing and reflecting on the differences between the students' profiles and language learning processes in private and public schools. Ayşen's course instructor supported her reflective engagement, which led her to discover contextual differences in learning and to reflect upon these as part of her learning during and beyond the course. As Mumford and Dikilitaş (2020) explained in their study, Ayşen's increasing reflective capacity and development of a sociopolitical stance on language education were facilitated by the online component of the course facilitated by her instructor. In undergraduate programs, it might be helpful to have pre-service teachers analyze multiple contexts of teaching where they can develop their own sociopolitical stance and adapt their teaching according to the context they are to teach, including student profiles. Experiencing multiple contexts of teaching and reflecting on each critically will lead to emerging understandings about self and others as well as the sociopolitical realities of teaching. These opportunities are especially important in countries like Turkey where initial language teacher education programs lack a reflective component (Turhan and Kırkgöz 2021).

Similarly, Nilgün transformed herself into promoting bilingual education in the school where she was exposed to teaching experiences for which she received no training in her bachelor's degree. The competitive nature of the private sector, which forces teachers to deal with the unknown themselves, was turned into an opportunity by Nilgün. She revisited her teacher roles since she was supposed to teach with a homeroom teacher to facilitate exposure to two languages using a jointly constructed bilingual syllabus. She also had to develop new skills such as critical collaboration before (planning a bilingual course), during (co-teaching harmoniously), and after the bilingual lessons (reflecting on and assessing the experiences). The new skills that she needed to develop also included adapting to a new program by co-implementing instructional translanguaging practices designed in the syllabus and facilitating translanguaging by allowing children to use their choice of language when interacting with the teachers in the classroom. These were new practices that she needed to reflect upon, understand, and sustain as part of her professional position in the school.

Although Nilgün had not been supported and guided in her bilingual context at the very beginning, the school administration later sought help from a mentor, an expert in teacher education. Nilgün's mentor created the space and opportunity for her to recognize her competence in the bilingual program and co-design context-driven bilingual practices with her peers. Because of the "recognition of competence" and "legitimacy of access to practice" (Tsui 2007: 675) afforded her, the experience was an empowering one for Nilgün. In other words, in Nilgün's case, the earlier contradiction between how she positioned herself as an EFL teacher and how she was positioned by the school and sociopolitical realities had "transformative potential" through the collaborative efforts of her peers and mentors (Johnson and Golombek 2020: 120).

In the case of the MA students, their sociopolitical stance was reshaped by their realization of the role of the student voice in learning. The teachers reported taking a critical look into their own practices when they stepped back and observed their students taking control of learning activities when designing and implementing them in the classroom. The participating teachers' awareness of the students' engagement when granted choice and agency in self-regulating their own learning helped them to redefine their position and role in the classroom in relation to those of their students.

It is clear that the teachers began to conceptualize their learners "as research partners with valuable voices" (Lind 2007: 371) and recognized their capacity "to be participative in research projects that become a platform for the learning of academics, field-based practitioners, and the community at large" (Groundwater-

Smith and Mockler 2016: 173). This assignment changed the nature and practice of teacher-learner power relations, which is an important element and dimension of the research conducted by teachers. Such a small project raised their awareness of using students' criticality and learning-related genuineness as a basis for their future pedagogy. Repositioning themselves as observers and space-openers by displacing their traditional roles, the teachers started to engage their students in their decision-making on planning, course delivery, and course evaluation.

Similarly, Samuel's PhD story under the supervision of a teacher educator in Turkey displayed how he grew into new identities and how this learning-in-practice experience shaped his identities as a learner, teacher, and researcher. For Samuel, the supervision process gave him the reflective space to link theory with classroom practice throughout his PhD journey, resulting in meaningful learning and discoveries about his own assumptions associated with the native/non-native teacher divide (Lee and Canagarajah 2019; Portelli and McMahon 2004). This locally appropriate development opportunity, which was responsive to Samuel and his peers' needs (Johnson and Golombek 2020), enabled him to develop an improved understanding of the sociopolitical dimensions of the employment of native speakers as EAP teachers in Turkey. In other words, Samuel's identity development process was nurtured not by a single source of experiences, but by interlinked sources of experiences interacting in complex ways simultaneously over a period long enough to influence the emerging identities. Empowerment and agency (Dikilitaş and Yayli 2018; Goodnough 2010) were the two important elements that facilitated his identity reconstruction and development process.

The four cases presented in this chapter suggest that once provided with space, guidance, and the appropriate tools to navigate their own professional development, teachers can function as "knowledge generators" (Yazan 2018) and "transformative intellectuals" (Gray 2019) rather than inactive actors in their professional learning. Therefore, language teacher education pedagogy, including in-service professional development providers, needs to involve critical teacher education practices and collaborative dialogue to construct and mediate meanings and understandings (Hawkins and Norton 2009). Teachers provided with professional development opportunities designed on the basis of critical pedagogy could develop emerging understandings about self, students, and the sociopolitical realities of teaching. We agree with López-Gopar (2019) that critical pedagogies "co-creating agency and transformation" need to lie at the heart of all practices in teacher professional learning in TESOL. Therefore, we believe it is important to create opportunities for teachers to develop a critical stance toward their own professional learning even if such an approach is not supported by the current macro-social and macro-political dynamics.

References

Atmaca, Ç. (2018), "Are Generic and English Teacher Competencies Sufficient and Realistic Enough?," *European Journal of Foreign Language Teaching*, 3 (2): 44–67.

Attard, K. (2017), "Personally Driven Professional Development: Reflective Self-Study as a Way for Teachers to Take Control of Their Own Professional Development," *Teacher Development*, 21 (1): 40–56.

Ayvaz-Tuncel, Z., and F. Çobanoğlu (2018), "In-Service Teacher Training: Problems of the Teachers as Learners," *International Journal of Instruction*, 11 (4): 159–174.

Balta, N., M. Arslan, and H. Duru (2015), "The Effect of In-Service Training Courses on Teacher Achievement: A Meta-Analysis Study," *Journal of Education and Training Studies*, 3 (5): 254–263.

Başar, S., H. Çeliktürk, and I. Çomoğlu (2020), "English Language Teachers' Insights into Continuous Professional Development: A Cross-Case Exploration," *The Literacy Trek*, 6 (2): 55–80.

Beauchamp, C. (2015), "Reflection in Teacher Education: Issues Emerging from a Review of Current Literature," *Reflective Practice*, 16 (1): 123–141.

Borg, S. (2013), *Teacher Research in Language Teaching: A Critical Analysis*, Cambridge: Cambridge University Press.

Burns, A. (2017), "Innovating Teacher Development: Transformative Teacher Education through Classroom Inquiry," in T. Gregerson and P. MacIntyre (eds.), *Innovations in Teacher Education*, 187–203, New York: Springer.

Burns, A. (2019), "Action Research in English Language Teaching: Contributions and Recent Developments," in X. Gao (ed.), *Second Handbook of English Language Teaching*, 991–1005, Cham: Springer.

Dikilitaş, K. (2015), "Professional Development through Teacher-Research," in K. Dikilitaş, R. Smith, and W. Trotman (eds.), *Teacher-Researchers in Action*, 47–58, Faversham: IATEFL.

Dikilitaş, K., and I. Çomoğlu (2022), "Pre-Service English Teachers' Reflective Engagement with Stories of Exploratory Action Research," *European Journal of Teacher Education*, 45 (1): 26–42.

Dikilitaş, K., and D. Yayli (2018), "Teachers' Professional Identity Development through Action Research," *ELT Journal*, 72 (4): 415–424.

Edwards, E., and A. Burns (2016), "Language Teacher-Researcher Identity Negotiation: An Ecological Perspective," *TESOL Quarterly*, 50 (3): 735–745.

Eret-Orhan, E., A. Ok, and Y. Capa-Aydin (2018), "We Train, But What Do They Think? Preservice Teachers' Perceptions of the Adequacy of Their Teacher Education in Turkey," *Asia-Pacific Journal of Teacher Education*, 46 (2): 183–198.

Freire, P. (1970), *Pedagogy of the Oppressed*, New York: Seabury Press.
Freire, P. (2005), *Teachers as Cultural Workers: Letters to Those Who Dare Teach*, Boulder, CO: Westview Press.
Gandara, P., J. Maxwell-Jolly, and A. Driscoll (2005), *Listening to Teachers of English Language Learners: A Survey of California Teachers' Challenges, Experiences, and Professional Development Needs*, Santa Cruz, CA: Center for the Future of Teaching and Learning.
Goodnough, K. (2010), "The Role of Action Research in Transforming Teacher Identity: Modes of Belonging and Ecological Perspectives," *Educational Action Research*, 18 (2): 167–182.
Gray, J. (2019), "Critical Language Teacher Education?," in S. Walsh and S. Mann (eds.), *The Routledge Handbook of English Language Teacher Education*, 68–81, Abingdon: Routledge.
Groundwater-Smith, S., and N. Mockler (2016), "From Data Source to Co-Researchers? Tracing the Shift From 'Student Voice' to Student–Teacher Partnerships in Educational Action Research," *Educational Action Research*, 24 (2): 159–176.
Hammad, S., A. Alunni, and T. Alkhas (2019), "Reflections on the Potential (and Limits) of Action Research as Ethos, Methodology and Practice: A Case Study of a Women's Empowerment Programme in the Middle East," *Action Research*, 17 (2): 162–185.
Harris, K. R., S. Graham, and M. Adkins (2015), "Practice-Based Professional Development and Self-Regulated Strategy Development for Tier 2, At-Risk Writers in Second Grade," *Contemporary Educational Psychology*, 40: 5–16.
Hatipoğlu, Ç. (2016), "The Impact of the University Entrance Exam on EFL Education in Turkey: Pre-Service English Language Teachers' Perspective," *Procedia-Social and Behavioral Sciences*, 232: 136–144.
Hawkins, M., and B. Norton (2009), "Critical Language Teacher Education," in A. Burns and J. Richards (eds.), *Cambridge Guide to Second Language Teacher Education*, 30–39, Cambridge: Cambridge University Press.
Higher Education Council (HEC) (2018), "New Teacher Training Undergraduate Programs," Ankara: HEC. https://www.yok.gov.tr/kurumsal/idari-birimler/egitim-ogretim-dairesi/yeni-ogretmen-yetistirme-lisans-programlari (accessed November 1, 2021).
Higher Education Council (HEC) (2020), "University Monitoring and Evaluation Report," Ankara: HEC. https://www.yok.gov.tr/Documents/Yayinlar/Yayinlarimiz/2021/universite-izleme-ve-degerlendirme-genel-raporu-2020.pdf (accessed November 1, 2021).
Johnson, K. E., and P. R. Golombek (2020), "Informing and Transforming Language Teacher Education Pedagogy," *Language Teaching Research*, 24 (1): 116–127.
Kemmis, S. (2010), "Research for Praxis: Knowing Doing," *Pedagogy, Culture & Society*, 18 (1): 9–27.
Kincheloe, J. L. (2008), *Critical Pedagogy Primer*, New York: Peter Lang.

Kırkgöz, Y. (2007), "English Language Teaching in Turkey: Policy Changes and Their Implementations," *RELC Journal*, 38 (2): 216–228.

Koç, E. M. (2016), "A General Investigation of the In-Service Training of English Language Teachers at Elementary Schools in Turkey," *International Electronic Journal of Elementary Education*, 8 (3): 455–466.

Kohli, R., B. Picower, A. N. Martinez, and N. Ortiz (2015), "Critical Professional Development: Centering the Social Justice Needs of Teachers," *International Journal of Critical Pedagogy*, 6 (2): 7–24.

Korkmazgil, S., and G. Seferoğlu (2013), "Exploring Non-Native English Teachers' Professional Development Practices," *Boğaziçi University Journal of Education*, 30 (1): 1–10.

Lee, E., and S. Canagarajah (2019), "Beyond Native and Nonnative: Translingual Dispositions for More Inclusive Teacher Identity in Language and Literacy Education," *Journal of Language, Identity & Education*, 18 (6): 352–363.

Lind, C. (2007), "The Power of Adolescent Voices: Co-Researchers in Mental Health Promotion," *Educational Action Research*, 15 (3): 371–383.

López-Gopar, M. E. (2019), "Introducing International Critical Pedagogies in ELT," in M. E. López-Gopar (ed.), *International Perspectives on Critical Pedagogies in ELT*, 1–15, Cham: Palgrave Macmillan.

Miller, E. R., and C. Gkonou (2018), "Language Teacher Agency, Emotion Labor and Emotional Rewards in Tertiary-Level English Language Programs," *System*, 79: 49–59.

Mills, M., and M. Goos (2017), "The Place of Research in Teacher Education? An Analysis of the Australian Teacher Education Ministerial Advisory Report Action Now: Classroom Ready Teachers," in M. A. Peters, B. Cowie, & I. Menter (eds.), *A Companion to Research in Teacher Education*, 637–650, Singapore: Springer.

Ministry of National Education (MoNE) (2021), "Improved and Updated In-Service Teacher Education Programs," Ankara: MoNE. http://oygm.meb.gov.tr/dosyalar/StPrg/ (accessed November 2, 2021).

Monchinski, T. (2008), *Critical Pedagogy and the Everyday Classroom*, Dordrecht: Springer.

Mumford, S., and K. Dikilitaş (2020), "Pre-Service Language Teachers Reflection Development through Online Interaction in a Hybrid Learning Course," *Computers & Education*, 144: 103706. https://doi.org/10.1016/j.compedu.2019.103706.

Munthe, E., and M. Rogne (2015), "Research Based Teacher Education," *Teaching and Teacher Education*, 46: 17–24.

Oolbekkink-Marchand, H. W., J. van der Steen, and M. Nijveldt (2014), :A Study of the Quality of Practitioner Research in Secondary Education: Impact on Teacher and School Development," *Educational Action Research*, 22 (1): 122–139.

Öztürk, G., and B. Aydin (2019), "English Language Teacher Education in Turkey: Why Do We Fail and What Policy Reforms Are Needed?," *Anadolu Journal of Educational Sciences International*, 9 (1): 181–213.

Patton, K., M. Parker, and D. Tannehill (2015), "Helping Teachers Help Themselves: Professional Development that Makes a Difference," *NASSP Bulletin*, 99 (1): 26–42.

Portelli, J., and B. McMahon (2004), "Why Critical Democratic Engagement?," *Journal of Maltese Education Research*, 2 (2): 39–45.

Richards, J. C. (2008), "Second Language Teacher Education Today," *RELC Journal*, 39 (2): 158–177.

Saglam, A. L. G., and K. Dikilitas (2020), "Evaluating an Online Professional Learning Community as a Context for Professional Development in Classroom-Based Research," *Electronic Journal for English as a Second Language*, 24 (3): 1–17.

Shaw, R. (2013), "A Model of the Transformative Journey into Reflexivity: An Exploration into Students' Experiences of Critical Reflection," *Reflective Practice*, 14 (3): 319–335.

Stern, T. (2019), "Participatory Action Research and the Challenges of Knowledge Democracy," *Educational Action Research*, 27 (3): 435–451.

Tekel, E., and Ö. Öztekin-Bayır (2021), "Turkish Education System from the Eyes of Future Teachers: Metaphorical Perceptions," *Educational Policy Analysis and Strategic Research*, 16 (2): 179–207.

Tsui, A. (2007), "Complexities of Identity Formation: A Narrative Inquiry of an EFL Teacher," *TESOL Quarterly*, 41 (4): 657–680.

Turhan, B., and Y. Kırkgöz (2021), "A Critical and Collaborative Stance Towards Retrospective Reflection in Language Teacher Education," *European Journal of Teacher Education*. https://doi.org/10.1080/02619768.2021.1917545.

Tüzel-İşeri, E., and U. Akin (2019), "Perceptions of Primary School Teacher Candidates Towards the Turkish Education System, School, Teacher, and Student: A Metaphor Analysis," *International Journal of Higher Education*, 8 (4): 239–253.

Uştuk, Ö., and İ. Çomoğlu (2019), "Lesson Study for Professional Development of English Language Teachers: Key Takeaways from International Practices," *Journal of Efficiency and Responsibility in Education and Science*, 12 (2): 41–50.

Uştuk, Ö., and İ. Çomoğlu (2021), "Reflexive Professional Development in Reflective Practice: What Lesson Study Can Offer," *International Journal for Lesson & Learning Studies*, 10 (3): 260–273.

Vetter, A. (2012), "Teachers as Architects of Transformation: The Change Process of an Elementary School Teacher in a Practitioner Researcher Group," *Teacher Education Quarterly*, 39 (1): 27–49.

Wyatt, M. (2011), "Teachers Researching Their Own Practice," *ELT Journal*, 65 (4): 417–425.

Wyatt, M., and K. Dikilitaş (2016), "English Language Teachers Becoming More Efficacious through Research Engagement at Their Turkish University," *Educational Action Research*, 24 (4): 550–570.

Yazan, B. (2018), "Toward Identity-Oriented Teacher Education: Critical Autoethnographic Narrative," *TESOL Journal*, 10: e388. https://doi.org/10.1002/tesj.388.

Yi, Y., and T. Angay-Crowder (2016), "Multimodal Pedagogies for Teacher Education in TESOL," *TESOL Quarterly*, 50 (4): 988–998.

Yuan, R., and A. Burns (2017), "Teacher Identity Development through Action Research: A Chinese Experience," *Teachers and Teaching*, 23 (6): 729–749.

4

(Non)Native Speakerism in English Language Teaching: Changing Perspectives, Resilient Discourses, and Missing Links

Ali Fuad Selvi

Introduction

Scientific disciplines and fields of inquiry rely on a comprehensive repertoire of concepts (e.g., *neoliberalism* in economics, *artificial intelligence* in computer science, or *culturally responsive pedagogy* in educational sciences, just to name a few), broadly referred to as scientific terminology. These lexical constructions serve as systematic mental representations allowing scholars to (re-)define, (re-/de-)construct, understand, explore, and interpret the world around us and various phenomena, entities, beings, processes, and structures therein. From an inquiry standpoint, they serve as the foundation of scientific inquiry and their connections to discourses and implications in the form of policies and practices. From a professional standpoint, they remain essential ingredients of scientific discourse and academic socialization, and their meaning must be mutually agreed upon by those who engage in these discourses either as consumers (e.g., students) or contributors (e.g., researchers). This notion of shared construct representativeness brings about conversational practicality and thereby eliminates the need to define, operationalize, and contextualize concepts every time we employ or talk about these concepts. Nevertheless, nuances, ambiguities, inconsistencies, and variations in interpretations around the meaning of concepts will continue to exist within and beyond the scientific community. Therefore, deliberate scrutiny, critical analysis, and dynamic reconceptualization of the concepts widely employed in a field of inquiry must be both the ethical and professional commitment and responsibility of those who engage in the construction, dissemination, and communication of scientific knowledge. This mission is aligned with Pennycook's stance on critical applied linguistics, which entails:

...a constant skepticism, a constant questioning of the normative assumptions of applied linguistics. It demands a restive problematization of the givens of applied linguistics and presents a way of doing applied linguistics that seeks to connect it to questions of gender, class, sexuality, race, ethnicity, culture, identity, politics, ideology, and discourse.

2001: 10

The fields of applied linguistics and English Language Teaching (henceforth, ELT) are no different in this regard. Over the years, scholars working within and beyond disciplinary borders of these fields coined and defined various concepts (e.g., *Communicative Language Teaching* in methodology, *achievement tests* in assessment, *fossilization* in Second Language Acquisition, or *English as a Lingua Franca* (or ELF) in applied linguistics) to pursue various questions around them in multiple settings, populations, conceptual lenses, and methodological tools. Among those, perhaps no other concept employed in the relatively short yet rich history of applied linguistics has ever generated so much tension, conjecture, or controversy than the *native speaker*[1] *(NS)* and its accompanying extensions— *nonnative speaker (NNS), native English-speaking teachers (NESTs)*, and *nonnative English-speaking teachers (NNESTs)*. The discussions around these terms occur at the following levels:

- ideological/ontological (e.g., identity, ownership, experience, expertise, authority, and superiority);
- discoursal (e.g., inclusivity-exclusivity, self-other, equity-inequity, privilege-marginalization);
- professional (e.g., teacher identity and legitimacy); and
- practical (e.g., division of labor in educational settings, privilege/marginalization in hiring practices and workplace settings).

Over the past couple of decades, critically-oriented scholars(hip) have problematized *standard* language ideology and orientation to the English language imposing an absolute adherence to the sociopolitically defined borders and boundaries traditionally defined, imposed, owned, and guarded by an idealized *NS* living in a homogeneous nation-state (Pennycook 2001, 2018). Informed by the broader issues of superdiversity and processes of glocalization and their sociohistorical manifestations in the form of (in)equity, privilege, and marginalization of identity and experience (see Selvi and Rudolph 2018), scholars revisited the fundamental aspects of the English language *per se* and its applications in language teaching, learning, and teacher education. Collectively, these analyses generated a set of profound questions for English language users and educators, including:

- Who owns English?
- Who is an ideal user of English?
- Who is an ideal teacher of English?
- Which English should we use/teach?
- Which culture is associated with English?
- Why do language learners learn English?
- Who is the target interlocutor?
- Which/whose norms do we rely on in using/teaching English?
- What is the source of instructional materials in English classrooms?
- What is the ideological basis of English language teaching?
- Who benefits from teaching English?
- What is gained/lost by teaching English?
- What is the role of other languages (and semiotic tools) in English classrooms/encounters?
- How do we define communicative/instructional success in and out of English classrooms?

What permeates through all these questions is the concept of "NS" and its corollaries—defined in terms of an expression of negation or absence, as in *non*native speaker (see Doerr 2009 for an ethnographic orientation, and Aneja 2016 for the constant reconstruction of personalities and subjectivities). Recent explorations of the transnational roles, forms, uses, users, functions, and statuses of English served as an intellectual stepping stone to a broader conversation on the validity, relevance, and applicability of NS and its legitimacy to language users and teachers. These concepts shape the mainstream and dominant discourses in the field of ELT and define some of the perceived and ascribed knowledge, skills, and dispositions traditionally predicated upon *native* and *nonnative* English-speaking professionals in ELT.

Despite ongoing critiques instigating change and transformation in our perspectives and practices (see Holliday 2015; Pennycook 2001; Phillipson 1992; Rudolph, Selvi, and Yazan, 2015, 2020; Selvi 2014, 2019), these labels continue to promote personal and professional discourses (e.g., inclusivity-exclusivity, self-other, equity-inequity, privilege-marginalization) undergirding the ELT profession and professionals therein. Departing from the earlier calls for the problematization and transformation of our *assumptions* in ELT (Pennycook 2001; Rudolph 2019), I first revisit the concept of *native speakerism* (Holliday 2006, 2015), extend it to *nonnative speakerism*, and finally discuss its ongoing resilience and persistence at the ideological, discoursal, professional, and practical levels. In conclusion, I point out some missing links and future directions in moving beyond juxtaposed binaries and the hegemony of *nonnative speakerism* in ELT and English language teacher education. Collectively, by contextualizing nonnative speakerism within language teacher education, this chapter responds to Uştuk and De Costa's (this volume) call for a sociopolitical agenda in language teacher education. Their call is particularly important and timely since "teaching and teacher education are inherently and unavoidably political" (Cochran-Smith 2005: 3) and they play "a substantial role and importance in promoting systemic pedagogical and professional responses for a refined understanding of teacher identity, ownership of language and instructional competencies" (Selvi 2019: 184). By problematizing the assumptions embedded in, manifested by, and reified through the concepts of *native speakerism* and *nonnative speakerism*, this chapter urges teachers and teacher educators to reexamine their lens in defining, assessing, and valuing teacher competency and legitimacy in ELT.

Towards Native Speakerism in ELT

Since the mid-1970s, several paradigms (e.g., World Englishes, English as an International Language, and English as a Lingua Franca), consolidated within the broader framework of *Global Englishes* (Galloway and Rose 2015), have been developed to examine the spread of English and the diverse roles, forms, uses, users, functions, and statuses of English in transnational contexts around the world. Even though each of these paradigms has some differences in terms of their research focus, they exhibit commonality in terms of their ideological foundation—destabilizing the prevalent idealization with the NS construct (as well as the power, authority, and the privilege associated with it) as a viable benchmark defining linguistic norms, pedagogical goals, and instructional success (Selvi 2019). As an extension of these paradigms focusing on the global spread of English (and its diverse ramifications) and in tandem with the growing interest in the notion of teacher identity, scholars in the 1980s (e.g., Medgyes 1983; Paikeday 1985), the 1990s (e.g., Braine 1999; Medgyes 1992, 1994; Phillipson 1992; Widdowson 1994), and the 2000s (e.g., Braine 2010; Doerr 2009; Kamhi-Stein 2004; Llurda 2005; Mahboob 2010) worked on the juxtaposed categories of identity traditionally predicated upon as *native* and *nonnative* English-speaking professionals in ELT.

In simple terms, the idealized NS (and therefore *NEST*) is characterized as White, Western, middle-class, monolingual, male, living in urban areas, and, more importantly, holding an uncontested linguacultural privilege and authority (Holliday 2005, 2006). In a world often constructed in binaries, this concept creates its *opposite* (i.e., *NNS*), who is defined as an individual whose linguacultural being and becoming as a language user are reduced into the prefix of *non-* and constructed in terms of the *other* (i.e., *NS*). For *the ELT profession*, this means not only idealization of/with *NS* as the absolute universal linguacultural target for acquisition and use but also as a powerful benchmark used in various aspects of language teaching practices (e.g., theory, research, curriculum, instructional materials, language assessment, and professional development) (Llurda 2016). For *ELT professionals* (often marked by their *nativeness* or lack thereof, as in *NEST* and *NNEST*), this means establishing a highly problematic causal relationship between their *nativeness* and pedagogical qualities. This "automatic extrapolation from competent speaker to a competent teacher based on linguistic grounds alone" (Seidlhofer 1999: 236) creates "a pervasive professional ideology serving as Damocles' sword hanging over the ELT profession(als)" (Selvi 2019: 186). Consequently, the idealized *NS* construct damages teachers' personal/professional identities (Ilieva 2010), self-esteem (Barratt 2010), and performance (Wang and Fang 2020), creates a professional milieu characterized by discrimination and marginalization (Jenkins 2017), and results in deprofessionalization of ELT (Kamhi-Stein 2016). Nevertheless, the ELT profession is still characterized by inequalities, discrimination, and discriminatory practices (both in hiring and workplace settings) directed at *NESTs* and *NNESTs* in various teaching contexts (Houghton and Rivers 2013a; Selvi 2014). For *language teacher education*, this means erecting, reifying, and perpetuating idealized and essentialized borders and hierarchies among ELT professionals and thereby missing the opportunity of building upon translinguistic/transcultural identity negotiations of ELT professionals for their immediate and/or future professional contexts.

This line of inquiry has become a fertile domain generating a plethora of perspectives with connections to prevalent professional discourses, ideologies, positions, and practices plaguing the ELT profession(als) for many years. As researchers dug deeper into these complexities, they came up with three realizations about the inequity, privilege, and marginalization:

1. They are not uniform *across* categories of identity, i.e., fluidly experienced not just by *NNESTs* but also by *NESTs*. In other words, it is impossible to make *a priori* universal generalizations about ELT professionals (e.g., "*NESTs* are privileged" and "*NNESTs* are marginalized") (Rudolph, Selvi, and Yazan 2015).

2. They are not uniform *within* categories of identity, i.e., fluidly experienced by both *NESTs* and *NNESTs* in a context-dependent fashion. In other words, rather than categories of identity, the context in which teachers live and work determines whether or not and the extent to which they experience these (Rudolph, Selvi, and Yazan 2015).
3. They are connected to so many different personal and professional traits (e.g., race, ethnicity, country of origin, gender, religion, sexual orientation, schooling, passport/visa status, physical appearance) and (perceived/ ascribed) "nativeness" is only one of many factors. Therefore, this should be "part of a larger complex of interconnected prejudices" (Houghton and Rivers 2013b: 14), initially operationalized through the theoretical lenses of "intersectionality" and, more recently, "assemblages" (Deleuze and Guattari 1987). This refined understanding complexifies the aforementioned categories and their contributions to the inequity, privilege, and marginalization by giving primacy to their hybrid, fluid, dynamic, and incomplete nature within and across time, space, and context.

In the meantime, scholars devised various pathways, structures, and initiatives of advocacy, collectively known as "the *NNEST* movement" (Braine 2010; Kamhi-Stein 2016) (see Figure 4.1). Resting upon theoretical, practical, and professional levels in ELT (Selvi 2014), "[t]he *NNEST* movement is critically situated at the nexus of TESOL and applied linguistics with a motivation to reconceptualize the value-laden, ideology-driven and professionally imposing discourses of 'native speakerism' defining the legitimacy in language learning and teaching" (Selvi 2019: 187).

It has been organized around developing individual and systemic responses against unethical and unprofessional practices in ELT and reinstating an egalitarian professional landscape sensitive to individuals' sociohistorical and contextualized negotiations of ethnic, racial, cultural, religious, gender, and linguistic identities. On one hand, the movement has contributed tremendously to the mainstream critically-oriented scholarship (and pertinent discourses and conversations) connected to institutionalized advocacy efforts and responses against inequity, marginalization, and discrimination. On the other hand, it has been criticized for capitalizing upon the most prevalent and problematic construct (i.e., *NNEST*), falling into the trap of promoting a particular approach to criticality and "fail[ing] to directly address both the neoliberal spread of English and the supremacy of English in discussions of bi-/trans-/multi-/

Figure 4.1 Three pillars of the *NNEST* movement (Selvi 2014, 2019).

plurilingualism" (Sánchez-Martín 2018: para. 20). In either case, the ELT profession is still characterized by inequalities, and the professionals therein (irrespective of their nomenclatures) experience marginalization and discrimination both in hiring and workplace settings in a hybrid and fluid manner.

Understanding Native Speakerism in ELT

As Kumaravadivelu argued, "any meaningful attempt to disrupt, and eventually dismantle, the unfair native-speaker dominance in ELT must begin with a clear understanding of what native-speakerism is and how it operates" (2015: viii). Our initial encounter with the term dates back to the late 1980s when Baumgardner, in his review of Braj Kachru's *The Indianization of English: The English Language in India* (1983), loosely used the term as a purely linguistic construct equating to "ambilingualism" (Baumgardner 1988: 340). Along the same lines, James referred to this as a "pseudo concept" and formulated it as "an assumed prejudicial deference to supposed linguistic infallibility of the NS" (1994: 193). Therefore, the first actual use of the term in relation to the ELT profession(als) was by Akoha et al. (1991), who recontextualized the obsession with the *NS*'s default authority, prestige, and supremacy in (foreign/second) language teaching as an ideology. During this time, other critically-minded scholars viewed the phenomenon (and its implications) in a broader context using different lenses and foci (see Lippi-Green 1997 for language subordination ideology, Phillipson 1992 for "linguistic imperialism" and "NS fallacy," and Widdowson 1994 for the "ownership of English"). This limited use and influence of the term continued in the early 2000s. For example, for Lasagabaster, it was just an extension of "the intolerance of nonnative speakers' linguistic limitations by some native speakers" (2004: 22) in the realm of foreign/second language teaching.

The conceptualizations revolving around *native speakerism* have undergone a theoretical transformation with the pioneering work of Adrian Holliday, who initially developed the concept of "culturism" (Holliday 2003), which later paved the way for "native speakerism" (Holliday 2005, 2006). Holliday purposefully situated his scholarship on this powerful construct because it encapsulated insights into the unequal ideological distribution of power connected to worldviews, ideologies, discourses, and practices creating a divisive landscape in the ELT world. For the first time, the term received complete and elaborate treatment by Holliday, who defined it as "a pervasive ideology within ELT, characterized by the belief that 'native-speaker' teachers represent a 'Western culture' from which spring the ideals both of the English language and English language teaching methodology (2006: 385). More recently, Holliday (2018) described native speakerism as a "neo-racist ideology" with wider implications that "stretch far beyond the classroom to attitudes and values that both pervade the whole ELT profession and extend to society as a whole, wherever English teaching and learning are considered to be an important activity" (2018: 4). Therefore, it could be argued that his greatest contribution was the advancement of the theoretically problematic and ideologically infused concepts of the *native speaker* and *nonnative speaker* (Davies 1991, 2013) and their recontextualization not as a linguistic but political/ideological question permeating into language, language teaching, and the language teaching profession and language teaching professionals.

Although the concept of, and scholarship around, Hollidayian "native speakerism" has gained traction over the years, it has also generated meta-critical accounts which seek to problematize and deconstruct categorical framings of identity, experience, (in)equity, and privilege/marginalization within critical scholarship building upon this framework (for an overview, see Rudolph 2022). What lies at the heart of the criticism that Holliday's work received in recent years was the (in)advertent utilization of "native speakerism" as a proxy for the idealization of *nativeness* in understanding manifestations of privilege and marginalization (Rudolph 2019, 2022). Furthermore, in his forceful critique of the inconsistencies embedded within critically-oriented ELT scholarship, Rudolph based his arguments on two major premises: (1) the problematic nature of the dichotomous treatment of categories of identity, and (2) the idealization of the *native speaker* construct leading to the perpetuation of the monolithic treatment of these categories. Collectively, this approach leads to the constructions of discourses and reification of *a priori* formulations of who individuals *were, are, will, could*, and/or *should* be and become as learners, users, and professionals of English in and beyond contextualized ELT (Rudolph 2019). Sharing similar concerns, Houghton and Rivers redefined the term to emphasize "prejudice, stereotyping, and/or discrimination, typically by or against foreign language teachers, on the basis of either being or not being perceived and categorized as a native speaker of a particular language" (2013b: 14). Situating sociohistorical negotiations and reducing complexities in binary oppositions of *native* and *nonnative* and their extensions (e.g., *us* vs. *them, local* vs. *expatriates, Western* vs. *non-Western*, knowledgeable vs. *non-knowledgeable, in* vs. *out*, and *Center* vs. *Periphery*) not only feeds dichotomously juxtaposed constructs of being, becoming, and doing but also serves as foundation research and advocacy efforts based on this problematic construction (Rudolph 2022). Despite these problems, in recent years, critically-oriented scholars have pushed the boundaries in this line of research by "(en)countering" (Swan, Aboshiha, and Holliday 2015), "tackling" (Lowe and Kiczkowiak 2021), "negotiating" (Galloway 2021), "redefining" (Houghton and Rivers 2013a), "reconceptualizing" (Matsuda 2021), "moving beyond" (Houghton, Rivers, and Hashimoto, 2018; Selvi and Yazan 2021), and "undoing" (Houghton and Bouchard 2020) "native speakerism" in diverse teaching contexts around the world. On one hand, I recognize the increasingly complex discussions revolving around Holliday's theoretical concept for valid reasons delineated above. On the other hand, I also acknowledge the judicious utilization of this concept as a critical ideological lens helping us to interpret bias, prejudice, stereotyp-e/-ing, (in)equity, discrimination, privilege, and marginalization embedded in political and cultural aspects of the ELT profession today. The idealized nativeness is not the only axis of discrimination in ELT (cf. race, ethnicity, country of origin, gender, religion/faith, sexual orientation, educational background, passport/visa status, and physical appearance, among others). However, it may be the most insidious and pervasive one—one that encapsulates gendered, classed, and raced essentializations and idealizations about being and becoming (Jenks and Lee 2019). Recognizing the pervasiveness of blatant discriminatory practices specifically using this term, I call for researchers, teacher educators, administrators, and policy-makers to engage in constant evaluation of the validity, reliability, and usability of this theoretical lens in understanding professional discourses, policies, and practices, when applicable.

Changing Perspectives: Understanding *Nonnative Speakerism* in ELT

The historical trajectory portrayed thus far serves as a useful orientation in approaching, understanding, and theorizing *nonnative speakerism*. In a traditional sense, the concept of the *nonnative* (as in *nonnative* speaker) emerged as a byproduct of its unmarked category (*native*, as in *native* speaker) in a mutually exclusive and juxtaposed manner. This highly problematic stance was cemented by the morphosemantic construction of the *non-* prefix, which not only defines one (i.e., *native* speaker) in terms of and less than the other (i.e., *nonnative* speaker) but also positions and reifies these categories of identities as static, monolithic, homogeneous systems (Doerr 2009) that are discursively (co-)constructed and fluidly experienced across time and space (Aneja 2016). Concomitantly, this ideological frame and divisive binary narrative permeate into ELT—as an activity, profession, and bona fide area of scholarly inquiry— and emerge again as *NESTs* and *NNESTs*, respectively. The dominant worldviews and mainstream discourses underpinning the ELT profession(als) traditionally defined the idealized *NEST* as White, Western, of the Global North, (often) male, a middle-class, monolingual individual residing in urban settings who is vested with a universal privilege of linguistic, cultural, and pedagogical authority to serve as the benchmark in all aspects of the ELT enterprise (anything ranging from theory to hiring practices). For *NNESTs*, this means perpetual entrapment in a pervasive professional ideology surrounding authority, superiority, and legitimacy and being subjected to inevitable discrimination and marginalization of professional identities and personas (e.g., Ruecker and Ives 2015; Selvi 2010). While this observation may be accurate and even critically compelling in understanding *certain* individuals, cases, contexts, and stories, organizing the fundamental pillars of the *NNEST* movement (research efforts, policy and advocacy initiatives, and teaching activities) only around this would afford, at best, a limited perspective, (in)equity, discrimination, privilege, and marginalization in ELT.

The term *nonnative speakerism* (or its hyphenated version, *non-native speakerism*) first appeared in Lengeling's (2010) work on becoming an English teacher, and it was used in tandem with *native speakerism* to describe the complexities embedded in the lived experiences of Spanish-English bilingual speakers who were born in Mexico but living in the United States for many years. A closer look at the subsequent uses of the term in the literature thereafter exhibited similar characteristics:

- used in contexts where its unmarked form (*native speakerism*) always occurs (e.g., Chaka 2021; Fithriani 2018);
- perpetuated the dichotomous juxtaposition with *native speakerism* by creating another duality (*NS-NNS, NEST-NNEST*, and *native speakerism-nonnative speakerism*) (e.g., Fithriani 2018);
- not operationalized and theorized (e.g., González 2020; Leonard 2019); and
- interpreted and used to mean "speaker*ness*" or "speaker*hood*" (e.g., Pietikäinen 2020; Tavares 2022).

However, I argue that the term deserves more detailed scrutiny and operationalization to make more substantial contributions to the growing critically-oriented scholarship and the discourses and practices it generates. The term *nonnative speakerism* refers to the idealization and promotion of teachers who are positioned or self-described as *nonnative speakers* as *more* viable models of learning and teaching. Similar to *native speakerism*, this ideology (and related discourses and practices) builds upon and extends (and even expands) the mutually exclusive binary categorization of teacher identity on the basis of "being or not being perceived and categorized as a native speaker of a particular language" (Houghton and Rivers 2013b: 14) and treats each of these categories as monolithic entities within which individuals and their identities, histories, experiences, characteristics, and skills are conflated and dissolved. However, different from *native speakerism*, which rests upon the "automatic extrapolation from competent speaker to competent teacher based on linguistic grounds alone" (Seidlhofer 1999: 236), *nonnative speakerism* establishes an automatic extrapolation from competent language learner to a competent teacher based on learning history alone. Departing from this premise, I have argued for the incommensurability of *nativeness* and/or *bi/multilingual* (speaker) identity as the primary (and often only) characteristics of effective second language educators:

> If we argue that "people do not become qualified to teach English merely because it is their mother tongue" (Maum 2002: 1), we should also argue that "people do not become qualified to teach English merely because it is their second language"

(Selvi 2014: 589). If the former is the *native speaker fallacy*, then the latter is the *nonnative speaker fallacy*.

Selvi 2019: 188

In the remainder of this chapter, I will first discuss the problematic assumptions embedded in nonnative speakerism and showcase its penetration into the critically-oriented scholarship focusing on teacher qualities, qualifications, and effectiveness. Then, I will explicate its relevance and significance in the construction of a sociopolitical agenda for language teacher education.

Resilience and Persistence of Discourses in ELT

In recent years, scholars working in (and beyond) the fields of ELT and applied linguistics have adopted various critical lenses, perspectives, and apparatuses to (re-)examine individuals' personal and professional identities, lived experiences, knowledge, and skills (see Rudolph, Selvi, and Yazan 2020; Yazan and Rudolph 2018). However problematic and limited they might be, these efforts and conversations have been instrumental in understanding the manifestations of (in)equity, discrimination, privilege, and marginalization (Rudolph, Yazan, and Rudolph 2019). In this section, I intend to establish the connection between *nonnative speakerism* and the assumptions it embodies and problematize the discourses it generates. These assumptions include (but may not be limited to):

1. It uses "value-laden, identity-shaping, and confidence-affecting *a priori* definitions and distributions of linguistic, cultural, and academic authority and superiority" (Selvi 2019: 185) and therefore perpetuates the juxtaposition of personal/professional identities. This, in turn, reifies borders of identity about who individuals *were, are, will, could,* and/or *should* be as language users and teachers of English (Rudolph, Yazan, and Rudolph 2019). Therefore, any calls or efforts to interrogate, destabilize, end, or move the perennial chasm between *NESTs* and *NNESTs* connected to this ideology may do more harm than good.
2. One of the growing trends within the *NNEST* movement and related scholarship and advocacy practices focuses on the relative (dis)advantages of *NESTs* and *NNESTs* (for a compilation of the literature on the advantages of *NESTs* and *NNESTs*, see table 1 in Selvi 2014: 588). Departing with discontent toward the mainstream discourses, practices, and scholarship underscoring the categorical *superiority* of idealized

NESTs, some scholars foregrounded the advantages of NNESTs to construe legitimacy. However, such efforts (a) make idealized and universalized generalizations about teachers, (b) perpetuate the juxtaposed dichotomous approach, and (c) establish a causal relationship between teachers and their teaching skills and competencies.

3. As an extension of the previous point, some scholars adopted alternative names in an effort to move beyond these binary categorizations and their consequences (for a summary of these alternatives and a comparison of advantages of the *NEST* and *NNEST* labels, see Selvi 2014). Oftentimes, the new nomenclature given to *NNESTs* has the ultimate motivation to erase and elevate the *non-* prefix (e.g., *bi/multilingual teachers*). However, it should be reminded that such efforts may inadvertently extend the juxtaposition (i.e., *bi/multilingual teachers* vs. *monolingual teachers*) where the latter is universally and perpetually monolingual (Rudolph 2019).

4. The propagation of *NNESTs* as a universal *better* option utilizes all the ideological entanglements that led to the emergence of *native speakerism* in a reverse direction. In other words, maintaining this position in the name of equity, equality, egalitarianism, and meritocracy is nothing more than subscribing to a reverse status quo.

Despite all these entanglements at the ideological, conceptual, semantic, professional, and advocacy levels, discourses, policies, and practices around these concepts still prevail and shape many aspects of the ELT enterprise, anywhere from knowledge-building to advocacy practices. Therefore, it is not uncommon to find scholars, research studies, blog posts, social media content, YouTube videos, or podcasts that still seek out the *better* teachers and claim to find the answer in concepts (i.e., *NESTs, NNESTs, bi/multilingual*, etc.) that have loose relevance with teacher qualities, qualifications, and competencies.

Missing Links and Future Directions: Towards a Sociopolitical Agenda for Language Teacher Education

Ever since we grasped the vitality of "teacher quality" on "student achievement" (e.g., Darling-Hammond and Bransford 2005), policy- and decision-makers embarked upon a series of education reforms with the intention to improve the qualities, attributes, and competencies of teachers, both at pre- and in-service levels. Within the scope of ELT (and second language teacher education), our perennial obsession with *speakerhood* (in the form of *NEST* and *NNEST*) seems to dominate the *teacher quality and effectiveness* discussions. Consequently, even though Medgyes (1992) argued three decades ago that the question of "Native or non-native: who's worth more?" is pointless, the mainstream scholarship, discourses, and practices are still under this juxtaposed binary ideology prioritizing *nativeness* (or lack thereof) over the sine qua non of teacher qualities, such as teacher education, teaching experience, continuous professional development, sense of professional identity, and motivation.

The fundamental premise of this chapter is simple and impactful—scholars in the fields of ELT and applied linguistics use a particular concept (*nonnative speakerism*) without fully describing its theoretical parameters and discussing its immediate implications. Departing from this need, I offered my reflections on the problematic concept of *nonnative speakerism*, showcased the discourses, policies, and practices around this term, and discussed its infusion into the critically-oriented scholarship shaping our understanding of teacher qualities, qualifications, and effectiveness. The common denominator of these discussions is the establishment of a substantiated connection between *speakerhood* and *teacherhood* based on value-laden, identity-shaping, and confidence-affecting essentialized categories of identity that homogenize contextualized and fluidly critical-practical negotiations of linguistic, cultural, and professional identity (Selvi and Rudolph 2017).

As Chimamanda Ngozi Adichie reminded us in her eloquent TED talk (Adichie 2009) on the dangers of a single story, such an exclusive approach to teacher identity (e.g., *native speakerism* or *nonnative speakerism*) may lead to a limited and restricted perspective of the real*ities* (in plural terms) surrounding the ELT profession(als). In a profession that values, celebrates, and draws upon pluralism and plurality, our approach to the broader concepts of (in)equity, discrimination, privilege, and marginalization necessitates theoretical, semantic, and practical expansions. Therefore, ELT professionals will continue witnessing (and even experiencing) discourses, ideologies, policies, and practices (both of hiring and workplace) of exclusion and inclusion at the same time. Advocating for and mainstreaming a participatory, inclusive, equitable, professional, egalitarian, and meritocratic professional landscape beyond contested values and idealizations of *NEST* and *NNEST* will be a long and arduous journey but one that will be a considerable gain for the professional stature of ELT and professionals therein.

In this picture, the language teacher education ecosystem (including teacher educators and teachers/teacher candidates from ethnolinguistically diverse backgrounds and professional practices) has a vital role in serving as a powerful catalyst in exposing, negotiating, interrogating, countering, destabilizing, and transforming the fundamental *assumptions* and practices undergirding ELT at the ideological, discoursal, professional, and practical levels. At a macro level, it underscores the development of a sociopolitical agenda (Uştuk and De Costa this volume) as an absolute necessity for experiences, values, and practices embedded in the ecosystem to serve as leverage for the negotiation and construction of critical, multifaceted, and agentive professional subjectivities for ELT professionals traditionally reduced to *NESTs* and *NNESTs* (Selvi 2016). At a micro level, it infuses "the explicit study of ideology and its role in teacher preparation" (Bartolomé 2010: 47), informed by post-structural approaches that conceptualize professional identity as "a socio-politically situated desire" (Norton 2013) and "a site of struggle" (Norton and Toohey 2011: 414) within the broader material conditions, pedagogical contexts, societal discourses and ideologies related to ELT. If we do not take the road less traveled, essentialized and undertheorized orientations to teacherhood (in the form of *native speakerism* and *nonnative speakerism*) will continue to reify and legitimize linguistic and professional borders, hierarchies, and subordination that underserve English learners, dehumanize the ELT professionals, and deprofessionalize the ELT profession.

Note

1 Echoing Holliday (2015), the term and its concomitant extensions are consistently used in italics to underscore the contested position over these labels and their ideological, discoursal, professional, and practical implications.

References

Adichie, C. N. (2009), "The Danger of a Single Story," *TEDGlobal 2009*. https://www.ted.com/talks/chimamanda_ngozi_adichie_the_danger_of_a_single_story (accessed December 1, 2021).

Akoha, J., Z. Ardo, J. Simpson, B. Seidlhofer, and H. G. Widdowson (1991), "Nationalism is an Infantile Disease. (Einstein) What About Native Speakerism," *BAAL Newsletter*, 39: 21–26.

Aneja, G. A. (2016), "(Non)Native Speakered: Rethinking (Non)Nativeness and Teacher Identity in TESOL Teacher Education," *TESOL Quarterly*, 50 (3): 572–596.

Barratt, L. (2010), "Strategies to Prepare Teachers Equally for Equity," in A. Mahboob (ed.), *The NNEST Lens: Non Native English Speakers in TESOL*, 180–201, Newcastle upon Tyne: Cambridge Scholars Publishing.

Bartolomé, L. (2010), "Daring to Infuse Ideology into Language-Teacher Education," in S. May and C. Sleeter (eds.), *Critical Multiculturalism: Theory and Praxis*, 47–59, New York: Routledge.

Baumgardner, R. J. (1988), "Contextualizing Indian English," *World Englishes*, 7 (3): 339–346. https://doi.org/10.1111/j.1467-971X.1988.tb00247.x.

Braine, G. (1999), *Non-Native Educators in English Language Teaching*, Mahwah, NJ: Lawrence Erlbaum Associates.

Braine, G. (2010), *Nonnative Speaker English Teachers: Research, Pedagogy, and Professional Growth*. New York: Routledge.

Chaka, C. (2021), "English Language Learners, Labels, Purposes, Standard English, Whiteness, Deficit Views, and Unproblematic Framings: Toward Southern Decoloniality," *Journal of Contemporary Issues in Education*, 16 (2): 21–37.

Cochran-Smith, M. (2005), "The New Teacher Education: For Better or For Worse?," *Educational Researcher*, 34 (7): 3–17.

Davies, A. (1991), *The Native Speaker in Applied Linguistics*, Edinburgh: Edinburgh University Press.

Davies, A. (2013), *Native Speakers and Native Users: Loss and Gain*, Cambridge: Cambridge University Press.

Deleuze, G., and F. Guattari (1987), *A Thousand Plateaus: Capitalism and Schizophrenia*, Minneapolis, MN: University of Minnesota Press.

Doerr, N. M. (2009), *The Native Speaker Concept: Ethnographic Investigations of Native Speaker Effects*, Berlin: De Gruyter.

Fithriani, R. (2018), "Discrimination Behind Nest and Nnest Dichotomy in ELT Profesionalism [sic]," *KnE Social Sciences*, 3 (4): 741–755. https://doi.org/10.18502/kss.v3i4.1982.

Galloway, N. (2021), "Negotiating Native-Speakerism in TESOL Curriculum Innovation," in Y. Bayyurt and M. Saraceni (eds.), *Bloomsbury World Englishes, Vol. 3: Pedagogies*, 93–106, London: Bloomsbury.

Galloway, N., and H. Rose (2015), *Introducing Global Englishes*, London: Routledge.

González, J. J. V. (2020), "Prospective English Teachers Reexamining Language Ideologies in Telecollaboration#," *Computer Assisted Language Learning*, 33 (7): 732–754.

Hammond, L. D., J. Bransford, and P. LePage (2005), *Preparing Teachers for a Changing World: What Teachers Should Learn and Be Able to Do*. San Francisco, CA: Jossey-Bass.

Holliday A. (2003), "Social Autonomy: Addressing the Dangers of Culturism in TESOL," in D. Palfreyman and R. C. Smith (eds.), *Learner Autonomy Across Cultures*, 110–126, London: Palgrave Macmillan.

Holliday, A. (2005), *The Struggle to Teach English as an International Language*, Oxford: Oxford University Press.

Holliday, A. (2006), "Native-Speakerism," *ELT Journal*, 60 (4): 385–387.

Holliday, A. (2015), "Native-Speakerism: Taking the Concept Forward and Achieving Cultural Belief," in A. Swan, P. Aboshiha, and A. Holliday (eds.), *(En)Countering Native-Speakerism: Global Perspectives,* 11–25, Basingstoke: Palgrave Macmillan.

Holliday, A. (2018), "Native-Speakerism," in J. I. Liontas (ed.), *The TESOL Encyclopedia of English Language Teaching*, Hoboken, NJ: Wiley-Blackwell.

Houghton, S. A., and J. Bouchard (2020), *Native-Speakerism: Its Resilience and Undoing*, Singapore: Springer Nature.

Houghton, S. A., and D. J. Rivers (2013a), *Native-Speakerism in Japan: Intergroup Dynamics in Foreign Language Education*, Bristol: Multilingual Matters.

Houghton, S. A., and D. J. Rivers (2013b), "Introduction: Redefining Native-Speakerism," in S. A. Houghton and D. J. Rivers (eds.), *Native-Speakerism in Japan: Intergroup Dynamics in Foreign Language Education*, 1–14, Bristol: Multilingual Matters.

Houghton, S. A., D. J. Rivers, and K. Hashimoto (2018), *Beyond Native-Speakerism: Current Explorations and Future Visions*, London: Routledge.

Ilieva, R. (2010), "Non-Native English-Speaking Teachers' Negotiations of Program Discourses in Their Construction of Professional Identities within a TESOL Program," *Canadian Modern Language Review*, 66 (3): 343–369.

James, C. (1994), "Don't Shoot My Dodo: On the Resilience of Contrastive and Error Analysis," *International Review of Applied Linguistics*, 32 (3): 179–200.

Jenkins, S. (2017), "The Elephant in the Room: Discriminatory Hiring Practices in ELT," *ELT Journal*, 71 (3): 373–376.

Jenks, C. J., and J. W. Lee (2019), "Native Speaker Saviorism: A Racialized Teaching Ideology," *Critical Inquiry in Language Studies*, 17 (3): 186–205.

Kachru, B. B. (1983), *The Indianization of English: The English Language in India*, Delhi: Oxford University Press.

Kamhi-Stein, L. D. (2004), *Learning and Teaching from Experience: Perspectives on Non-Native English-Speaking Professionals*, Ann Arbor, MI: University of Michigan Press.

Kamhi-Stein, L. D. (2016), "The Non-Native English Speaker Teachers in TESOL Movement," *ELT Journal*, 70 (2): 180–189.

Kumaravadivelu, B. (2015), "Foreword," in A. Swan, P. Aboshiha, and A. Holliday (eds.), *(En)Countering Native-Speakerism: Global Perspectives*, viii–xi, Basingstoke: Palgrave Macmillan.

Lasagabaster, D. (2004), "The Nativeness Factor: An Analysis of Students' Preferences," *International Journal of Applied Linguistics*, 147 (1): 21–43.

Lengeling, M. M. (2010), *Becoming an English Teacher: Participants' Voices and Identities in an In-Service Teacher Training Course in Central Mexico*, Guanajuato, Mexico: Universidad de Guanajuato.

Leonard, J. (2019), "Beyond '(Non) Native-Speakerism': Being or Becoming a Native-Speaker Teacher of English," *Applied Linguistics Review*, 10 (4): 677–703.

Lippi-Green, R. (1997), *English with an Accent: Language, Ideology, and Discrimination in the United States*, London: Routledge.

Llurda, E. (2005), *Non-Native Language Teachers*, New York: Springer.

Llurda, E. (2016), "Native Speakers, English, and ELT: Changing Perspectives," in G. Hall (ed.), *The Routledge Handbook of English Language Teaching*, 51–63, London: Routledge.

Lowe, R. J., and M. Kiczkowiak (2021), "Tackling Native-Speakerism through ELF-Aware Pedagogy," in Y. Bayyurt and M. Saraceni (eds.), *Bloomsbury World Englishes, Vol. 3: Pedagogies*, 143–156, London: Bloomsbury.

Mahboob, A. (2010), *The NNEST Lens: Non-Native English Speakers in TESOL*, Newcastle upon Tyne: Cambridge Scholars Publishing.

Matsuda, A. (2021), "Reconceptualizing '(Non-)Native English Speakers' Within the Paradigm of Teaching English as an International Language," in Y. Bayyurt and M. Saraceni (eds.), *Bloomsbury World Englishes, Vol. 3: Pedagogies*, 126–142, London: Bloomsbury.

Maum, R. (2002), "Nonnative-English-Speaking Teachers in the English Teaching Profession," Report No. EDO-FL-02-09. Washington, DC: Office of Educational Research and Improvement (ERIC Document Reproduction Service No. ED470982).

Medgyes, P. (1983), "The Schizophrenic Teacher," *ELT Journal*, 37 (1): 2–6.

Medgyes, P. (1992), "Native or Non-Native: Who's Worth More?," *ELT Journal*, 46 (4): 340–349.

Medgyes, P. (1994), *The Non-Native Teacher*, London: Macmillan.

Norton, B. (2013), *Identity and Language Learning: Extending the Conversation*, Bristol: Multilingual Matters.

Norton, B., and K. Toohey (2011), "Identity, Language Learning, and Social Change," *Language Teaching*, 44 (4): 412–446.

Paikeday, T. (1985), *The Native Speaker is Dead!*, Toronto: Paikeday Publishing.

Pennycook, A. (2001), *Critical Applied Linguistics: A Critical Introduction*, Mahwah, NJ: Lawrence Erlbaum.

Pennycook, A. (2018), *Posthumanist Applied Linguistics*, Oxford: Routledge.

Phillipson, R. (1992), *Linguistic Imperialism*, Oxford: Oxford University Press.

Pietikäinen, K. S. (2020), "On Second Language/Nonnative Speakerism in Conversation Analysis: A Study of Emic Orientations to Language in Multilingual/Lingua Franca Couple Interactions," *Journal of Pragmatics*, 169: 136–150.

Rudolph, N. (2019), "Native Speakerism (?!): (Re)considering Critical Lenses and Corresponding Implications in the Field of English Language Teaching," *Indonesian Journal of English Language Teaching*, 14 (2): 89–113.

Rudolph, N. (2022), "Narratives and Negotiations of Identity in Japan and Criticality in (English) Language Education: (Dis)Connections and Implications," *TESOL Quarterly*. https://doi.org/10.1002/tesq.3150.

Rudolph, N., A. F. Selvi, and B. Yazan (2015), "Conceptualizing and Confronting Inequity: Approaches Within and New Directions for the 'NNEST Movement,'" *Critical Inquiry in Language Studies*, 12 (1): 27–50.

Rudolph, N., A. F. Selvi, and B. Yazan (2020), *The Complexity of Identity and Interaction in Language Education*, Bristol: Multilingual Matters.

Rudolph, N., B. Yazan, and J. Rudolph (2019), "Negotiating 'Ares,' 'Cans,' and 'Shoulds' of Being and Becoming in English Language Teaching: Two Teacher Accounts from One Japanese University," *Asian Englishes*, 21 (1): 22–37.

Ruecker, T., and L. Ives (2015), "White Native English Speakers Needed: The Rhetorical Construction of Privilege in Online Teacher Recruitment Spaces," *TESOL Quarterly*, 49 (4): 733–756.

Sánchez-Martín, C. (2018), "An Interview with Nathanael Rudolph," *NNEST of the Month Blog*, November 22. https://nnestofthemonth.wordpress.com/2018/11/22/nathanael-rudolph/ (accessed December 1, 2021).

Seidlhofer, B. (1999), "Double Standards: Teacher Education in the Expanding Circle," *World Englishes*, 18 (2): 233–245.

Selvi, A. F. (2010), "All Teachers Are Equal, But Some Teachers Are More Equal Than Others: Trend Analysis of Job Advertisements in English Language Teaching," *WATESOL NNEST Caucus Annual Review*, 1: 156–181. http://sites.google.com/site/watesolnnestcaucus/caucus-annual-review.

Selvi, A. F. (2014), "Myths and Misconceptions about the Non-Native English Speakers in TESOL (NNEST) Movement," *TESOL Journal*, 5 (3): 573–611.

Selvi, A. F. (2016), "The Role of Teacher Education at a Crossroads of Tensions and Opportunities," *Asian Englishes*, 18 (3): 258–264.

Selvi, A. F. (2019), "The 'Non-Native' Teacher," in S. Mann and S. Walsh (eds.), *The Routledge Handbook of English Language Teacher Education*, 184–198, London: Routledge.

Selvi, A. F., and N. Rudolph. (2017), "Non-Native English Teachers' Professional Identities: Implications and Challenges for Teacher Education," in J. D. Martinez Agudo (ed.), *Native and Non-Native Teachers in English Language Teaching: Professional Challenges and Teacher Education*, 257–272, Berlin: De Gruyter.

Selvi, A. F., and N. Rudolph. (2018), *Conceptual Shifts and Contextualized Practices in Education for Glocal Interaction: Issues and Implications*, Singapore: Springer.

Selvi, A. F., and B. Yazan (2021), *Language Teacher Education for Global Englishes: A Practical Resource Book*, New York: Routledge.

Swan, A., P. Aboshiha, and A. Holliday, eds. (2015), *(En)Countering Native-Speakerism: Global Perspectives*, Basingstoke: Palgrave Macmillan.

Tavares, V. (2022), "Neoliberalism, Native-Speakerism and the Displacement of International Students' Languages and Cultures," *Journal of Multilingual and Multicultural Development*. https://doi.org/10.1080/01434632.2022.2084547.

Wang, L., and F. Fang (2020), "Native-Speakerism Policy in English Language Teaching Revisited: Chinese University Teachers' and Students' Attitudes Towards Native and Non-Native English-Speaking Teachers," *Cogent Education*, 7 (1): 1–22.

Widdowson, H. (1994), "The Ownership of English," *TESOL Quarterly*, 28 (2): 377–389.

Yazan, B., and N. Rudolph (2018), *Criticality, Teacher Identity, and (In)Equity in English Language Teaching: Issues and Implications*, Cham: Springer.

5

Critical Engagement with Achievement Gap Discourses and Data: Narrowing or Not?

Jamie L. Schissel and Nancy H. Hornberger

Introduction

The examination of achievement gaps on a variety of measures has been prevalent in educational research and used to inform educational policy for decades. A Google Ngram search (see Figure 5.1) shows a particularly dramatic rise in the occurrence of the term "achievement gap" from 1996 to 2008 with its prevalence beginning to decrease in 2009. Though there is not a definitive link in this move toward decreased use, one major political change that occurred at this time was the end of the Bush presidencies and the election of Barack Obama. In basic definitions, achievement gaps are generally understood as aggregated group differences in various markers of achievement such as standardized test score performance, graduation rates, or general vocabulary skills (e.g., the word gap). Achievement gaps focus on learners' outcomes (i.e., achievement) and how the outcome trends correlate with different group characteristics. In the United States, common comparisons include gender, race/ethnicity, socioeconomic status, disability label, and other demographic data categories commonly documented.

Yet as straightforward as these definitions may appear, Ladson-Billings (2006) has pointed to the extreme limitations of these perspectives on achievement gaps for understanding different educational experiences. She wrote, "this all-out focus on the 'Achievement Gap' moves us toward short-term solutions that are unlikely to address the long-term underlying problem" (2006: 4). Because of the persistent existence of achievement gaps under the definitions stated above despite decades of different initiatives and interventions, she challenges the overall framing of how we understand achievement from outcomes in isolation

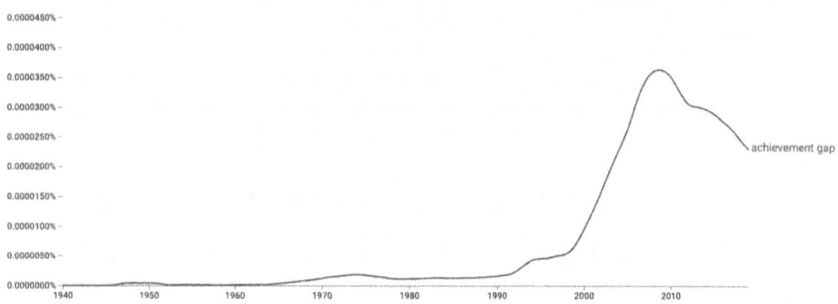

Figure 5.1 Occurrence of the term "achievement gap," 1940–2019.
Note: Graph created with Google NGram: https://books.google.com/ngrams/graph?content=achievement+gap&year_start=1940&year_end=2019&corpus=26&smoothing=2.

to broadening our perspectives. To do so, she posits a focus on *educational debt*, including historical, economic, sociopolitical, and moral debts that impact educational opportunities for all learners. This debt is accumulated over time and reproduces inequities in education, especially for historically minoritized and marginalized learners (e.g., minoritized/marginalized based on race, ethnicity, religion, sexual orientation). This *opportunity gap* (Ladson-Billings 2013) that learners face because of these different forms of educational experiences—or lack thereof—is absent from measures traditionally included in the achievement gap.

For students classified as English Learners (ELs), there has been a persistent focus on the achievement gap comparing test performance scores between students classified as ELs and non-ELs (Saunders and Marcelletti 2013). Large-scale, high-stakes, standardized tests play a prominent role in K-12 schools in the United States with respect to annual content area tests (e.g., mathematics, reading) and English proficiency tests (e.g., WIDA's ACCESS for ELLs 2.0). In attempts to reexamine differences in performances on tests, recent analyses have shifted the composition of comparison groups to combining students who are currently classified as ELs and students who have met state criteria to be exited from EL services (referred to as multilingual learners) and compare them with students who have never been classified as ELs (Kieffer and Thompson 2018). Further, some states also offer bilingual test versions in certain subjects. Yet issues remain with these attempts to better understand students' learning because of underlying issues with EL classification and with test construction.

In taking up these data and discourses framing inequities in educational opportunities and performance, we start with a rejection of prevalent perspectives on the achievement gap. The question of the narrowing of the achievement gap, we posit, functions as a discourse that overshadows the more nuanced understandings of the inequities that students classified as ELs face in US schools. Instead, the current discourses contribute to existing inequities and to creating new forms of oppression. In contrast, using this achievement gap framing, we focus on educational debt or the opportunity gap to unpack the longstanding, underlying factors realized within inequitable educational opportunities. For teacher education in TESOL specifically, unpacking different discourses and data of the achievement gap or opportunity gap is necessary to grapple with "historical, economic, political, and moral decisions that we as a society have made over time" (Ladson-Billings 2013: 13). For classroom teachers and teacher educators in TESOL, these analytical and questioning stances are vital to engaging critically with policies and pedagogical practices for the betterment of student learning.

Examining these phenomena within TESOL, we take up the question: What are the concerns around present discourses and data around the achievement gap? We highlight the issues that arise specifically with respect to an interpretive analysis of (1) EL classification and (2) test construction and score interpretation. We look to different analyses and data using the National Assessment of Educational Progress (NAEP) and Pennsylvania state assessment policies and practices as illustrative examples. We engage with flaws of relying on grand narratives of the narrowing or expanding of the achievement gap that serve to privilege aggregated data interpretations by blurring crucial contextual references. In applying our critical lenses on EL classification and test construction and score interpretation to direct examples, we aim to provide TESOL teachers and teacher educators with strategies for questioning how the achievement gap may be discussed or used to inform decisions in different instructional settings. We conclude with the implications of TESOL teacher education.

EL Classification

The first aspect of the achievement gap we focus on is *who* is being compared to *whom*. Who is considered to be a student classified as an EL? Federal and, to a certain extent, state policies in the United States largely shape these definitions. Federal policies stemming from the No Child Left Behind Act in 2001 and the Every Student Succeeds Act in 2015 largely dictate how classification processes are conducted by specifically stating which ways academic progress can be documented for the purposes of classification. In terms of achievement gap data, these policies dictate the measures with a particular focus on standardized tests in content areas such as English language arts and mathematics (for all students)[1] and the additional tests for English proficiency for students classified as ELs. Most of these standardized tests are used for high-stakes accountability purposes such as reporting progress of student learning for schools (e.g. school report cards), districts, states, and the national level, which can impact funding as well as incentivize teacher pay. These tests used for large-scale accountability purposes begin in grade 3 or around age eight and continue until grade 8 or age thirteen. In high school, all students must also take one additional standardized test for accountability purposes. However, in most schools, students in every grade level are also required to take standardized benchmark assessments, in particular in Kindergarten through grade 8 with varying accountability measures attached depending on the state. Requiring all students to take these tests means that there can be a delineation of group membership as connected to EL classification or not connected, creating the two groups to compare test score performance to describe "achievement gaps." Additionally, within these policies, students classified as ELs must take an annual standardized English proficiency exam. Achievement gap analyses are less common with regards to this type of testing.

EL classification up close

For students classified as ELs, content test scores and English proficiency test scores are used for large-scale accountability purposes as well as *individual educational decisions* around access to different educational opportunities. For example, all states are federally required to use the English proficiency test score to determine if a student who is classified as an EL can be reclassified as "fluent English proficient" and exited from EL educational services. As of 2015, 17 states also require content test scores in subjects such as English language arts and mathematics. Sixteen states require additional criteria such as final grades in courses, parent input, or input from teachers as well (Linquanti and Cook 2015). Thus the scale and scope of the use of these tests have real-life impacts within TESOL classrooms in addition to broad-reaching implications.

Being classified as an EL is generally conceived of as non-permanent group membership. Students are initially identified in a process by which parents report using a language other than English at home in a home language survey, followed by administering an English proficiency screening test to the student. Generally based on these criteria, districts, schools, and teachers make decisions about EL classification. Once classified as an EL, additional educational services are provided to these students by TESOL educators. The unifying characteristic across the United States for students classified as EL is that they have scored below the cut score(s) set by state educational agencies on an English proficiency test.

Students who are recently reclassified as "fluent English proficient" are monitored for four additional years, and their annual test scores are reported both with currently classified ELs and separately as their own category. Students in this monitored EL status may also have their academic achievement on standardized content tests reported according to the number of years since the student has been reclassified (e.g., year 1 of being reclassified, year 2 of being reclassified, etc.). Some states, such as Massachusetts, have a group of students they label "Ever Els," which includes students who are currently classified as ELs, students who are in their four years of monitoring status after exiting from EL services, and students who are more than four years past being monitored—ostensibly any student who has been or is classified as an EL.

In addition to the mandated high-stakes testing, a smaller group of students are selected to take low-stakes standardized tests in reading and mathematics in grades 4 and 8 each year. This test, the NAEP, is used for national-level tracking and comparison of student learning across states. The performance on these tests does not directly impact local decision-making. Data from the NAEP scores are often used as an indicator of trends in academic performance across the United States. NAEP test performance data quite often, however, is used for research around the achievement gap, which has the potential to impact policies and practices in the education of students classified as ELs.

Intragroup heterogeneity

Policies play a big role documenting and delineating what EL status is. For example, in the fall of 2018, the National Center for Education Statistics (NCES) reported that 10.2% or 5 million students in US schools were classified as ELs (NCES 2021). NCES further reports on students classified as ELs in relation to home language, country of origin, race/ethnicity, and socioeconomic status. Increasingly, attention is being given to students classified as ELs and identified as disabled. According to NCES, 15.3% of students classified as Els, or around 766,600 students, are also identified as disabled (NCES 2021).

Methods of capturing some of the EL intragroup heterogeneity are limited to the information that federal policies require schools to collect and report. For example, in research on testing and bilingual education for students classified as ELs, newcomers or recently arrived students are generally identified because they perform much lower on high-stakes standardized tests due to their limited experiences learning English or being enrolled in US schools. Yet even within this group of learners, such reporting misses many contextual factors that greatly impact students' educational experience.

For example, unaccompanied children have received politicized attention, especially over the past decade, yet are not included in NCES reports. Instead, the Office of Refugee Resettlement (ORR) documents the arrival of unaccompanied children since 2012. Unaccompanied children arrive in the United States seeking asylum. They primarily come from Honduras, Guatemala, El Salvador, and Mexico, leaving situations impacted by myriad glocal issues (e.g., climate change, violence, and political instability/upheaval). Their various educational and personal experiences are important to understand when thinking about educational opportunities made available once they have enrolled in US schools. Figure 5.2 shows the fluctuation in numbers of unaccompanied children documented by ORR by fiscal year from 2012 to 2021.

These available data are insufficient to make sense of how unaccompanied children are part of the broader national picture of students classified as ELs. The cumulative total of 486,195, whether they are currently or formerly enrolled in schools, represents a group of students with diverse needs that are not represented in our current policies around documenting students classified as ELs. We are not suggesting that unaccompanied children begin to be reported as a group so that they then would be compared to others via achievement gap analyses. Instead, in trying to understand unaccompanied minors' educational experiences in relation to educational opportunities they are—or are not—provided, we argue that more useful framings for understanding the myriad pathways and definitions of success within schools such as community involvement, leadership opportunities, building and sustaining meaningful partnerships, and other forms of success more focused on long-term relationship-building in contrast to individual outcomes can account for the life experiences that students bring to the classroom which are largely absent from achievement gap data and discourses and are urgently needed.

These discourses of the achievement gap center achievement of students classified as ELs in relation to others and fail to account for the ways in which such classifications can exacerbate or add to existing inequities in educational opportunities. There are many more ways in which the limits of our current documentation blur our understandings of the differences that exist within the broad category of students classified as ELs. It is important to note that EL classification policies themselves have now contributed to creating new

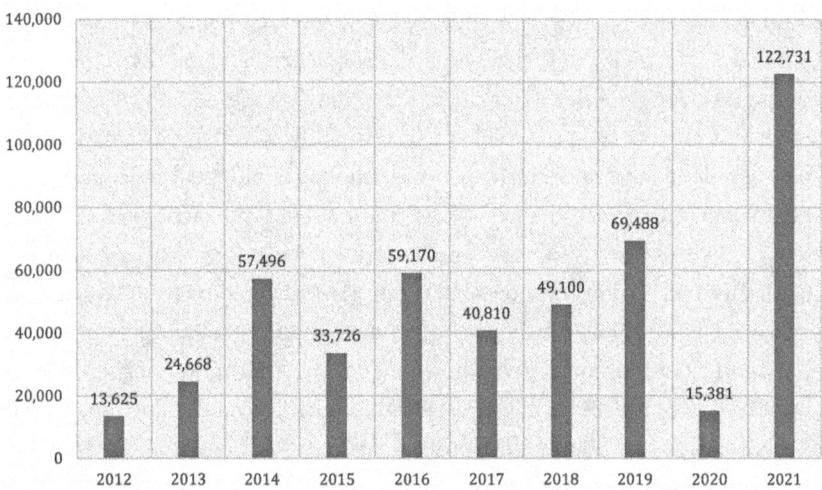

Figure 5.2 Number of unaccompanied children per fiscal year as reported by ORR.
Source: https://www.acf.hhs.gov/orr/about/ucs/facts-and-data.

subcategories of students classified as ELs, for example long-term ELs (LTELs). LTELs are students who have been classified as EL for more than six years. This categorization of learners centers around the premise that being classified as an EL is a non-permanent category, with the expectation that students should meet the benchmarks for reclassification within six years. The consequence of creating this subcategory in EL classification has meant a focus on LTELs' achievement through deficit lenses (Flores, Kleyn, and Menken 2015). Such self-created categories (e.g., LTELs) within other policy-created categories (ELs) point to intragroup heterogeneity but do so within the confines of policies and definitions that perpetuate deficit perspectives.

Further complicating understandings of this categorization is that many LTELs are also identified as having a disability. This disproportionately high number points to issues with not only EL classification but also the identification of disabilities among students classified as ELs (Kangas 2014). For example, Thompson (2015) identified that 35% of LTELs in one medium-sized school district in California were also identified as having a disability. NCES reports that approximately 14% of students have been identified with disabilities in the general school population. National data on the proportion of LTELs identified with disabilities, however, is not reported.

Relevant to these discussions of what it means to be a learner of English in these contexts remain theories of mono/bilingualism at odds with policy definitions. As stated earlier, the uniting characteristic of students classified as ELs is that they have failed to meet English proficiency benchmarks as measured by a standardized English proficiency test. Although some states have additional criteria, all states are required to have this testing threshold for (re)classification as part of federal requirements. In contrast, scholars in bilingual education in the United States and around the world have argued that such narrow constructs of language dismiss the dynamism and fluidity of language and language use, which transcend notions of monolingualism (Hornberger 1989, 2022; Otheguy, García, and Reid 2015). Further, scholars have argued that no person can be understood as monolingual given how language is a reflection of the different contact of different peoples that resist strict linguistic boundaries (Canagarajah and Liyanage 2012). The English proficiency tests focus on, for example, one sociopolitically defined variety of English broadly referred to as academic (American) English. Although much has been written about academic English in reference to instruction and assessment (Frantz et al. 2014), definitions remain vague or general, and the operationalization of academic English for English proficiency tests often becomes a narrow approximate. For TESOL professionals, these dynamic views of language and languaging serve to aid in understanding the complexities of teaching English and knowing that all persons who are engaged with English, even those since birth, are continuing to be taught and to learn English. Teaching English can also transcend viewing a standard variety of English as an isolated entity and instead build from how languages connect in ways that expand student learning opportunities and draw from students' experiences.

At this point, understandings have been complicated with respect to how comparison groups are determined for achievement gap research, or who is being compared to whom and some of the issues in finding group cohesion. The next section draws attention to the issues with the testing instruments that are used to represent student learning or achievement.

Test Construction and Score Interpretation

In the previous section, we focused on the *who* aspect of achievement gap analyses—that is, who is being compared to whom. In this section, we shift the focus to *what* is being compared, with a specific emphasis on standardized test scores. An important underlying issue here is the conceptualization of an achievement gap centered around test design and how test scores are interpreted.

In some very basic terms, the achievement gap as a concept is a realization of one way of interpreting test scores. Building on the issues brought up in the previous section about who is considered to be an EL or multilingual, we note that the unifying characteristic was their not performing at a predetermined cut score on a test. Thus, how the test was designed, and the purported ways of understanding test scores are crucial. In this section, we provide background in test construction and test use for TESOL professionals to encourage critical engagement with the tests that are often being used to make pedagogical decisions about students' learning. We then look more closely at analyses of the NAEP and uses of Spanish/English bilingual tests in Pennsylvania as illustrative examples of ways that achievement gap discourses have been used or could be altered to capture more of the broader issues surrounding how we define student learning for our students.

Test design essentials

Although all elements of test design and development are important to understand, TESOL professionals may, in particular, be interested in understanding (1) the theory of language used in constructing an assessment instrument, (2) the persons for whom the test has been developed and piloted with, and (3) the scope of proposed implications based on inferences about student learning from test scores.

For a theory of language, all language assessments (i.e., assessments of specific language skills) must specify how language and language learning are defined within the construct of the test. For example, the ACCESS for ELLs 2.0 suite of English proficiency tests developed by the WIDA Consortium that is used in over 30 states and territories reports to "draw on multiple theories and approaches in an effort to describe language use in academic contexts" (2014: 1) which are operationalized in the WIDA Standards. These explicit articulations of what and how language is understood within the test help to provide users with the constraints, limitations, and general aim and scope of the inferences that can be made from test scores. For this test, for example, there is a narrow definition or operationalization of what will be considered relevant or valuable as a representation of academic language.

Yet, as clearly as the Standards are written, scholars have also pointed out that the idea of an objective definition of "academic language" as a unit of language fails to capture how interpretations and applications of this concept with racialized, minoritized students—in particular, though not limited to, students classified as ELs—often reflect the bias of the individual making the inferences or interpretations. That is to say, rather than academic language representing an objective reality, it is instead interpreted through deficit lenses where two students from different racial-ethnic backgrounds who produce the same language are evaluated differently, dismissing the academic performance of minoritized students based on their perceived racial-ethnic identities (Flores 2020; García and Solorza 2020; Rosa 2016). In some studies (referred to as *matched-guise* studies), the same voice recording is played to two different groups, one group seeing a picture of the speaker as a white person, the other group seeing a picture of the speaker as from a racialized, minoritized background. In evaluating the quality of the content and language of the speaker, the group who saw a picture of a speaker from a racialized, minoritized background consistently stated that they had a problem understanding or with the clarity of the speech of the person, sometimes reporting a strongly accented English that they could not understand. Again, this is the same recording played to another group with the picture of a white speaker, where no such issues were reported (see Ball 1983; Lambert et al. 1960). Such interpretive biases around how academic language has been theorized and operationalized in assessment are important not only for language assessments but also content assessments. For TESOL professionals, it is important to understand these biases in test design and score interpretation and to examine their own potential biases when evaluating students.

Another aspect of language assessments is that they generally focus on one standard variety of a language, with little flexibility for any variation. Such foci are often referred to as a *monolingual* or *monoglossic* construct of a test, meaning that the test only recognizes the idealized standard language variety and disregards other varieties and multilingualism. This aspect of assessment design holds true for content assessments as well, though less explicitly. Often, content assessments do not have a clear theory of language articulated within the test design. For example, a mathematics test would focus on constructs related to math concepts, with a general assumption about the language of the test as the standard language variety that is most closely related to the medium of instruction. Instead, variations in language are treated as a potential measurement error. Often referred to as *construct-irrelevant variance*, tests are designed to reduce the ways that certain ways of wording items in a test item may "interfere" with the test-taker's ability to demonstrate what they know. Martiniello (2008) examined this issue with respect to mathematics tests. For example, she addressed how the use of the word "one" in a word problem as an indefinite referent (e.g., such as this *one* in the picture) rather than as the number one caused confusion for students classified as ELs taking the test.

In trying to reduce construct-irrelevant variance, test developers acknowledge two things: first, that linguistic bias exists and second, that it cannot be eliminated, only reduced. For score interpretation, it is important to note these inherent limitations within assessments that are using monolingual or monoglossic constructs. Teachers in TESOL classrooms can question if certain types of tests have been designed in ways that provide scores that are meaningful, and how much of the purported difference in achievement between different groups has to do with the limitations within the test design to utilize multilingualism as an important aspect of learning for students classified as ELs. In taking on these agentive professional stances, teachers are no longer passive consumers or implementers of top-down policies.

These theories of language underlying test design, and the implications for how test scores are interpreted, shed light on some of the underlying issues within the conceptualization of the achievement gap. For TESOL teachers and teacher educators of in-service and pre-service teachers alike, this essential information about testing provides the tools to engage with and interpret test scores based on their own expertise, rather than passively accepting a score or a score interpretation. Such skills or strategies lend themselves well to questioning research on the achievement gap.

Achievement Gap Discourses and Data

We apply our lenses around the complicated issues of EL classification and test construction/score interpretation to pose the question: How, if at all, are achievement gap discourses and data useful for TESOL teachers and teacher educators? We first look at achievement gap reports using NAEP data from NAEP reporting and Kieffer and Thompson (2018).

The Office of English Language Acquisition (OELA) in the US Department of Education publishes a report called "Fast Facts," which includes achievement gap analyses of NAEP data for students classified as ELs and non-ELs (OELA 2018). They look at mathematics and reading test scores for grades 4 and 8 for 2007–17. Across these different areas, they report slight increases in scores for students classified as ELs in grade 8 reading. The performance gap between these two groups remained relatively unchanged for the other comparisons. That is, for the 2007–17 span of NAEP data analyzed, the achievement gap data and discourse remain largely unchanged. There is no reflection of improved or changed educational opportunities for students in this type of comparison.

Many researchers have criticized that it is not possible to reflect different changes within the educational experiences of students classified as ELs (Umansky 2016, 2018; Umansky and Dumont 2021) and of the limits of the EL classification (Abedi 2008; Evans and Hornberger 2005; Schissel 2019). By definition, these are students who have not met a cut score for being considered "fluent English proficient." Presumably, students are performing well or not on these content assessments because of this aspect of their English language knowledge (Butler and Castellon-Wellington 2005). In keeping these groups categorized in these ways, the design of this comparison is premised on removing members from the EL group once they improve their performance, thereby sustaining the necessary conditions to maintain this gap consistently (Saunders and Marcelletti 2013).

Our lenses critiquing EL classification and test design provide us with score interpretations that reflect more clearly that the issues lie with classification and test design rather than student performance. Indeed, the students taking this test are performing "as expected" because their backgrounds put them together in this group classified as ELs, which is incongruent with the population for whom the test has been designed. And although test accommodations are available to improve accessibility, such accommodations have largely been ineffective in impacting the performance scores of students classified as ELs at a level of statistical significance (Kieffer, Rivera, and Francis 2012).

More recently, scholars have attempted to correct or adjust achievement gap analyses by changing the comparison groups. Kieffer and Thompson (2018) expanded the grouping of students classified as ELs to include students who have met state criteria to be exited from EL services—"ever-ELs." These multilingual learners are contrasted with students referred to as "never ELs." In their analyses of NAEP data from 2003 to 2015, Kieffer and Thompson report that multilingual students' scores on the mathematics and reading tests in grades 4 and 8 narrowed the achievement gap "by 24% and 27% in reading and 37% and 39% in math, in grades 4 and 8 respectively" (2018: 393). They posit that state and local changes, including the increase in dual language bilingual education programs, might account for this narrowing of the purported achievement gap.

This reported narrowing of the achievement gap is exciting to see. Kieffer and Thompson include a comparison of monolingual students, multilingual students (currently classified ELs and those exited from EL services), and students classified as ELs. As it stands, they are beginning to address the issues with EL classification but do not provide additional information to work toward questioning the ways in which achievement gap analyses may also contribute to decision-making about educational opportunities for students classified as ELs. By using an achievement gap model of analysis to try to report achievement of multilingual students, they fall prey to the same limitations of the existing structures, in particular monolingual or monoglossic measures in tests, which do not address who different practices may or may not be aiding in the learning opportunities of multilingual learners.

What is not addressed in these analyses are any changes that have been made to the NAEP test during this period. Beginning in 1996, the NAEP piloted the use of different test accommodations for students classified as ELs. This included the use of a Spanish test form for mathematics and later science. Currently, there are four accommodations specifically for students classified as ELs for the mathematics and science tests: bilingual translation dictionary without definitions in either language; directions-only read aloud in Spanish (also available for the reading test); Spanish/English version of the test; and test items read aloud in Spanish. Inclusion of students classified as ELs has also been a focus in NAEP test administration. Beginning in 2010, there has been a concerted effort to include as many students classified as ELs (and students with disabilities) as possible in NAEP testing. According to NCES, as of 2019, 90% of all students classified as ELs took the NAEP. Kieffer and Thompson report that "[d]ata suggest that current and former ELs comprise the substantial majority of multilingual learners, while never ELs constitute a small minority" (2018: 392). It is not possible to report on the exact number and proportions of test-takers in these different categories, mainly because the NAEP does not report a "formerly classified as EL" category. These limitations also cannot be factored into the interpretations. What we do know is that the NAEP test has a very high representation of students classified as ELs taking the test.

In examining the achievement gap, one area that we want to draw attention to with TESOL teachers and teacher educators is in relation to test construction. There is work being done where the design of the test, particularly the theory of language, is more aligned with multilingualism. Though there are many limitations in this area as well, such as requiring strict separation of languages in the test and test responses, multilingual approaches to language assessment for classroom TESOL assessments (e.g., Schissel, De Korne, and López-Gopar 2018; Schissel et al. 2018), multilingual approaches in classroom reading tests (Ascenzi-Moreno 2018), and within standardized content area assessments in multilingual South Africa (Heugh et al. 2017) provide an additional shift in our understandings of what is possible with assessments.

For standardized content tests in the United States that are often used for achievement data analyses, there remain some limitations regarding the access

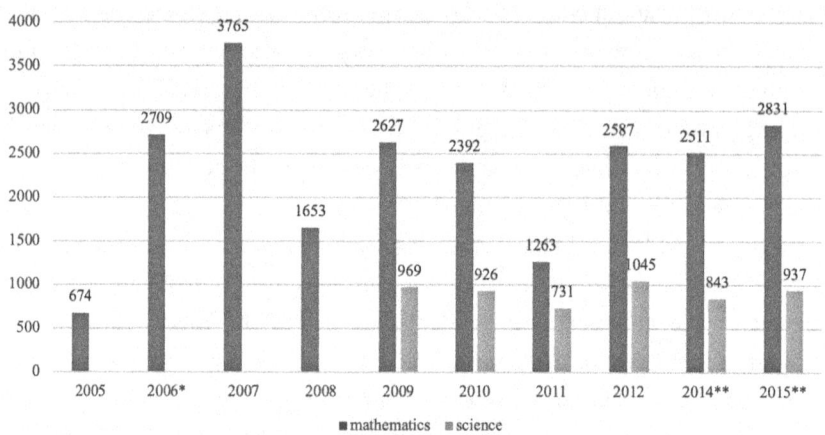

Figure 5.3 The number of Spanish-English test versions taken by subject and year.
*no grade 3 data, **no grade 11 data.
Source: Pennsylvania Department of Education (n.d.).

and feasibility of the use of these tests and how student performance is reported on these tests. In Pennsylvania, for example, there have been bilingual Spanish/English annual state benchmark tests available since 2005 for mathematics and since 2009 for science. Figure 5.3 shows the total number of students who have taken these required tests using the bilingual test forms from 2005 to 2015.

The figure shows a relatively steady number of students taking these exams. These test versions are recommended for a student classified as an EL who is "enrolled in US schools for fewer than three years and has not yet reached a level of English language proficiency … [and who is] literate in their native language" (Pennsylvania Department of Education 2016: 9–10). The requirements for this bilingual test form restrict its use based on the educational opportunities available to the student (e.g., literacy education in Spanish) and time. Comparing these numbers of students using test forms to all the reported students classified as ELs who are reported to come from Spanish-speaking families in Figure 5.4, we see what this policy means in practice.

Seeing these comparisons of the number of students potentially eligible to those actually taking the bilingual test version—approximately a ratio of 10 to 1—illustrates ways in which policies restrict access to bilingual tests directly and may indirectly reflect limited access to forms of bilingual education in the schools. In terms of student performance specifically on these tests, the scores are reported with all test scores for students classified as ELs. This bilingual version (and indeed all bilingual test versions in the United States) is a test

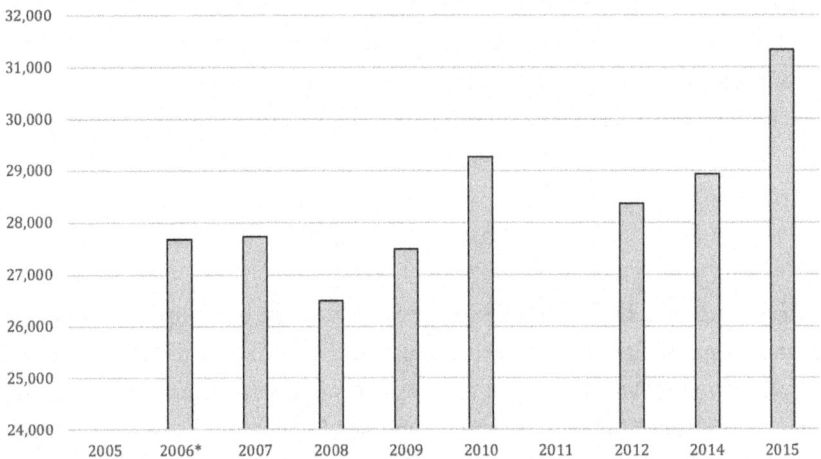

Figure 5.4 The number of Spanish-speaking students classified as ELs in Pennsylvania by year.
Source: US Department of Education (2006–15).

accommodation limited only to students classified as ELs. Thus, in the use of this test version, we see more evidence of issues related to opportunity gaps that are important for TESOL professionals.

There remain limitations of seeing a bilingual test version as a "solution" to understanding student learning. Indeed, standardized tests, in general, are seen as perpetuating inequities for minoritized groups (Au 2009). In talking about the UK context, but quite applicable for our look at the achievement gap in the United States, Gillborn has stated: "It is difficult to imagine a contrary situation where no action would be taken were a new assessment system to result in white children being out-performed by their peers in every minority group" (2006: 334). This statement points to central issues with using standardized testing to understand student learning. Testing has been in place as just one piece of a larger puzzle of different ways educational systems and institutions are set up to maintain inequities while often only paying lip service to addressing the current and longstanding history of those inequities in schools.

Thus, using our lenses of EL classification and test construction helps us see that the issues around EL classification impact how achievement gap analyses are conducted and thus the discourses around how students classified as ELs perform. Further, because little has been done to the testing instruments to impact their design for this group of learners and due to limitations with what has been done, inferences of score interpretation remain limited and problematic, especially for students classified as ELs. The consistent differences in performance between students classified as ELs and those not is a solid reflection of issues surrounding EL classification and test construction rather than any kind of meaningful indication of student learning.

Summary Thoughts

We have presented here how TESOL professionals can be equipped to question test use, in particular standardized test use, with their students. In questioning the utility of achievement gap analyses, we find little information in the conceptualization of the achievement gap that aids us in our work focusing on the teaching of English. Instead, we find flaws in trying to understand whose scores are being compared and what these scores can meaningfully tell us about students' performance. These flaws are especially relevant with respect to content tests, which are most often used to illustrate achievement gap data. The current ways of collecting and reporting data fail to serve TESOL professionals. Analyses such as those by Kieffer and Thompson (2018) hold promise but remain constrained by the limitations of the test design and the premise of comparison of achievement gap analyses. Differing sociopolitical contexts and experiences of students classified as ELs are largely absent from accountability-focused discussions about the achievement gap. What makes the focus on the achievement gap exceptionally harmful is the use of testing data that works against the educational and socio-emotional interests of students classified as ELs, precisely those who have been for too long systematically sidelined and neglected in our schools.

In returning to our initial framing of this topic, how to move from achievement gap to examine opportunity gaps or educational debt, we feel the critical lenses we have presented highlight how educators can move beyond the repetitive discourses of the achievement gap. Instead, we call for educators to focus on the rich intragroup heterogeneity of multilingual learners and their experiences and the limitations of making inferences based on tests that were designed largely without them in mind. For teacher educators, integrating opportunities for pre- and in-service teachers to engage with tests and testing data in applied scenarios— real or developed solely for training—is a vital step if TESOL teachers are to enact such practices in their schools. Creating activities within coursework that calls for this specific form of advocacy can provide educators the opportunity to troubleshoot different obstacles they may face within schools. One step further, teacher educators in TESOL can develop opportunities for teachers to question potentially biased assessment practices that they see in their own programs related to how testing data may be used. For example, not only could they question initial university English proficiency testing requirements (e.g., IELTS or TOEFL), but also post-admission testing given to international graduate teaching assistant candidates, currently required in several US states and other countries of the world such as Australia. Finally, although the achievement gap issues have largely been discussed here within the US context, teacher educators can focus on the ways in which these types of comparisons and reliance on standardized testing data are used across the globe often to perpetuate deficit perspectives of certain types of multilingualism, and the implications for the educational opportunities of multilingual learners worldwide. As an international discipline, including connections with contexts outside the United States will illustrate the broader impact of achievement gap data and discourses.

Note

1 For TESOL educators, standardized testing of these content tests also necessitates the assignment, use, and monitoring of test accommodations, or changes to the test administration, test response, or test itself (e.g., small group administration, bilingual test versions) for students classified as ELs.

References

Abedi, J. (2008), "Classification System for English Language Learners: Issues and Recommendations," *Educational Measurement: Issues and Practice*, 27 (3): 17–31.

Ascenzi-Moreno, L. (2018), "Translanguaging and Responsive Assessment Adaptations," *Language Arts*, 95 (6): 355–369.

Au, W. (2009), *Unequal by Design: High-Stakes Testing and the Standardization of Inequality*, Abingdon: Routledge.

Ball, P. (1983), "Stereotypes of Anglo-Saxon and Non-Anglo-Saxon Accents: Some Exploratory Australian Studies with the Matched Guise Technique," *Language Sciences*, 5 (2): 163–183.

Butler, F. A., and M. Castellon-Wellington (2005), "Students' Concurrent Performance on Tests of English Language Proficiency and Academic Achievement," in CSE Report No. 663, *The Validity of Administering Large-Scale Content Assessments to English Language Learners: An Investigation from Three Perspectives*, 47–83. http://cresst.org/wp-content/uploads/R663.pdf.

Canagarajah, S., and I. Liyanage (2012), "Lessons from Pre-Colonial Multilingualism," in M. Martin-Jones, A. Blackledge, and A. Creese (eds.), *The Routledge Handbook of Multilingualism*, 67–83, Abingdon: Routledge.

Evans, B. A., and N.H. Hornberger (2005), "No Child Left Behind: Repealing and Unpeeling Federal Language Education Policy in the United States," *Language Policy*, 4 (1): 87–106.

Every Student Succeeds Act (ESSA), Pub. L. No. 114-95 (2015).

Flores, N. (2020), "From Academic Language to Language Architecture: Challenging Raciolinguistic Ideologies in Research and Practice," *Theory into Practice*, 59 (1): 22–31.

Flores, N., T. Kleyn, and K. Menken (2015), "Looking Holistically in a Climate of Partiality: Identities of Students Labeled Long-term English Language Learners," *Journal of Language, Identity & Education*, 14 (2): 113–132.

Frantz, R. S., A. L. Bailey, L. Starr, and L. Perea (2014), "Measuring Academic Language Proficiency in School-Age English Language Proficiency Assessments Under New College and Career Readiness Standards in the United States," *Language Assessment Quarterly*, 11 (4): 432–457.

García, O., and C. R. Solorza (2020), "Academic Language and the Minoritization of US Bilingual Latinx Students," *Language and Education*, 34 (6): 505–521.

Gillborn, D. (2006), "Rethinking White Supremacy: Who Counts in 'White World,'" *Ethnicities*, 6 (3): 318–340.

Heugh, K., C. Prinsloo, M. Makgamatha, G. Diedericks, and L. Winnaar (2017), "Multilingualism(s) and System-Wide Assessment: A Southern Perspective," *Language and Education*, 31 (3): 197–216.

Hornberger, N. H. (1989), "Continua of Biliteracy," *Review of Educational Research*, 59 (3): 271–296.

Hornberger, N. H. (2022), "Researching and Teaching (with) the Continua of Biliteracy," *Educational Linguistics*, 1 (1): 1–26.

Kangas, S. E. (2014), "When Special Education Trumps ESL: An Investigation of Service Delivery for ELLs with Disabilities," *Critical Inquiry in Language Studies*, 11 (4): 273–306.

Kieffer, M. J., and K. D. Thompson (2018), "Hidden Progress of Multilingual Students on NAEP," *Educational Researcher*, 47 (6): 391–398.

Kieffer, M. J., M. Rivera, and D. J. Francis (2012), *Practical Guidelines for the Education of English Language Learners: Research-Based Recommendations for the Use of Accommodations in Large-Scale Assessments*, Portsmouth, NH: RMC Research Corporation, Center on Instruction.

Ladson-Billings, G. (2006), "From the Achievement Gap to the Education Debt: Understanding Achievement in US Schools," *Educational Researcher*, 35 (7): 3–12.

Ladson-Billings, G. (2013), "Lack of Achievement or Loss of Opportunity," in P. L. Carter and K. G. Welner (eds.), *Closing the Opportunity Gap: What America Must Do to Give Every Child an Even Chance*, 11–22, Oxford: Oxford University Press.

Lambert, W. E., R. C. Hodgson, R. C. Gardner, and S. Fillenbaum (1960), "Evaluational Reactions to Spoken Languages," *Journal of Abnormal and Social Psychology*, 60 (1): 44–51.

Linquanti, R., and H. G. Cook (2015), "Reexamining Reclassification: Guidance from a National Working Session on Policies and Practices for Exiting Students from English Learner Status," Washington, DC: Council of Chief State School Officers. https://ncela.ed.gov/resources/journal-re-examining-reclassification-guidance-from-a-national-working-session-on.

Martiniello, M. (2008), "Language and the Performance of English-Language Learners in Math Word Problems," *Harvard Educational Review*, 78 (2): 333–368.

National Center for Education Statistics (NCES) (2021), "English Language Learners in Public Schools," May, Washington, DC: NCES. https://nces.ed.gov/programs/coe/indicator/cgf.

No Child Left Behind (NCLB) Act of 2001, Pub. L. No. 107 (2002).

Office of English Language Acquisition (OELA) (2018), "Fast Facts: English Learner (EL) Trends from the Nation's Report Card," September, Washington, DC: OELA. https://ncela.ed.gov/sites/default/files/legacy/files/fast_facts/ELs-NAEP_Card.pdf.

Otheguy, R., O. García, and W. Reid (2015), "Clarifying Translanguaging and Deconstructing Named Languages: A Perspective from Linguistics," *Applied Linguistics Review*, 6 (3): 281–307.

Pennsylvania Department of Education (PDE) (n.d.), *PSSA Technical Manuals*. Harrisburg, PA: PDE.

Pennsylvania Department of Education (PDE) (2016), *PSSA and PSSA-M Accommodations Guidelines for English Language Learners*. Harrisburg, PA: PDE.

Rosa, J. D. (2016), "Standardization, Racialization, Languagelessness: Raciolinguistic Ideologies Across Communicative Contexts," *Journal of Linguistic Anthropology*, 26 (2): 162–183.

Saunders, W. M., and D. J. Marcelletti (2013), "The Gap that Can't Go Away: The Catch-22 of Reclassification in Monitoring the Progress of English Learners," *Educational Evaluation and Policy Analysis*, 35 (2): 139–156.

Schissel, J. L. (2019), *The Social Consequences of Testing for Language-Minoritized Bilinguals in the United States*, Bristol: Multilingual Matters.

Schissel, J. L., H. De Korne, and M. López-Gopar (2018), "Grappling with Translanguaging for Teaching and Assessment in Culturally and Linguistically Diverse Contexts: Teacher Perspectives from Oaxaca, Mexico," *International Journal of Bilingual Education and Bilingualism*, 24 (3): 340–356.

Schissel, J. L., C. Leung, M. López-Gopar, and J. R. Davis (2018), "Multilingual Learners in Language Assessment: Assessment Design for Linguistically Diverse Communities," *Language and Education*, 32 (2): 167–182.

Thompson, K. D. (2015), "Questioning the Long-Term English Learner Label: How Categorization Can Blind Us to Students' Abilities," *Teachers College Record*, 117 (12): 1–50.

Umansky, I. M. (2016), "To Be or Not to Be EL: An Examination of the Impact of Classifying Students as English Learners," *Educational Evaluation and Policy Analysis*, 38 (4): 714–737.

Umansky, I. M. (2018), "According to Plan? Examining the Intended and Unintended Treatment Effects of EL Classification in Early Elementary and the Transition to Middle School," *Journal of Research on Educational Effectiveness*, 11 (4): 588–621.

Umansky, I. M., and H. Dumont (2021), "English Learner Labeling: How English Learner Classification in Kindergarten Shapes Teacher Perceptions of Student Skills and the Moderating Role of Bilingual Instructional Settings," *American Educational Research Journal*, 58 (5): 993–1031.

WIDA (2014), *The WIDA Standards Framework and its Theoretical Foundations*, Madison, WI: Wisconsin Center for Education Research, University of Wisconsin-Madison. https://wida.wisc.edu/sites/default/files/resource/WIDA-Standards-Framework-and-its-Theoretical-Foundations.pdf.

Part Two

Setting the Sociopolitical Agenda

6

"Figuring Out My End Game": Supporting Novice ESOL Teachers' Emerging Identities as Humanizing Practitioners and Advocates through Peer Interaction

Megan Madigan Peercy, Danielle Gervais Sodani, and Wyatt Hall

Introduction

Teachers of minoritized student groups, including multilingual students, are often faced with challenges to enacting pedagogy that is equitable and just. This is particularly difficult for novice teachers who are finding their feet in new settings where they do not yet know the sociohistorical context, and where they hold little power or influence (Nieto 2000; Salazar 2013). At the same time, new teachers are still forging their identities as teachers: trying to determine who they are, who they will become, and what their context affords for their development (e.g., Athanases and Martin 2006; Buendía 2000). In this chapter, we argue that teacher induction represents a critically important site where novice teachers (NTs) might collectively work to forge identities as humanizing practitioners who are oriented to equity and justice, both in their mindsets and in their practices (Carter Andrews and Castillo 2016; Peercy et al. 2022b). Furthermore, we assert that NTs need collaborative spaces where they can cultivate the kind of agency necessary to develop their identities as humanizing practitioners and advocates, and this is particularly important for NTs of multilingual students, a group that is often marginalized (e.g., Le Cornu and Ewing 2008). In this chapter, we draw upon examples from a larger project in which we have worked collaboratively with 13 NTs of multilingual students over a period of seven years, and examine how NTs of multilingual students benefit from coming together in what they identify as "safe spaces"[1] with other NT practitioners. Specifically, we explore how their peer interactions within a supportive collaborative allowed them to position themselves and one another as advocates for multilingual students. We use prior work on humanizing teacher education, teacher identity development, and teacher agency as the lenses through which to consider NTs' opportunities to explore and challenge their pedagogy and develop emerging identities as humanizing practitioners.

Background and Theoretical Framework

Most approaches to NT induction focus on providing top-down support in the form of mentoring from experienced teachers and district-driven professional development programs to meet NTs' immediate needs to implement instruction (Feiman-Nemser 2010; Goldrick 2016). Less common is when NTs, among themselves or with more experienced teachers, leverage their own experiences, questions, dilemmas, doubts, and ideas to collaboratively examine problems of practice as equals (Geeraerts et al. 2015). However, when teachers are positioned as professionals who can understand and guide their continued growth over their careers, they can engage in both more self-directed and more collaborative development, readily drawing on the expertise of their colleagues (Kemmis et al. 2014). This perspective values teachers as capable and intelligent professionals who have meaningful ideas and contributions to make even as novices to the profession (Kemmis et al. 2014; Korhonen et al. 2017; Peercy et al. 2020), and is supported by scholarship regarding the positive impact of peer group collaboration among novices (e.g., Rogers and Babinski 2002; Tynjälä et al. 2021). Achinstein and Athanases (2009) further extend this perspective on NTs, noting that prior work on induction ranges from viewing NTs as workers who need to be managed to agents of change, and they illustrate that it is possible to support NTs as oriented to humanizing outcomes through teacher education, mentoring, and induction efforts that focus on NTs' pedagogical knowledge for equity. It is this understanding of NTs as having the potential for self-development through collaboration, and as capable of orientations for justice, in which we are interested.

Building upon perspectives that honor teacher agency in their approaches to induction, we argue that more humanizing approaches to induction may provide an important foundation for NTs' own emerging humanizing pedagogy. This foundation is especially important because NTs themselves often have not experienced humanizing education as students, throughout their PK-12 and higher education experiences. Instead, they are likely to have been socialized in a system of education that is rigid and controlling, producing winners and losers, and designed to reproduce inequality (Carter Andrews and Castillo 2016). We draw on scholarship in three areas to frame this study and to define humanizing induction: work on the importance of humanizing teacher education through collective experiences; work on the positioning of NTs as dynamically developing their identities as teachers; and work that identifies teacher agency as fundamental to developing NTs' capacity to advocate for students who are traditionally underserved.

Drawing from several theoretical models in the literature on teaching linguistically and culturally diverse learners, we define humanizing pedagogy as practice that aims for justice,[2] relies on mutually respectful relationships and dialogue, responds to the particulars of each context, and values all involved both as individuals and as community members. Teachers' humanizing pedagogy takes the form of caring, rigorous, trusting relationships characterized by active discovery of students' sociocultural resources and the purposeful integration of those resources in the classroom, as well as strengthening students' ethnic and linguistic identities, developing students' critical consciousness, and challenging inequitable systems (e.g., Bartolomé 1994; Ladson-Billings 1995; Peercy et al. 2022b; Peercy, Tigert, and Fredricks 2023; Salazar 2010, 2013). Carter Andrews and Castillo (2016) note that if NTs are going to engage in humanizing pedagogy with K-12 students, they must also experience it themselves. Grewal and colleagues (2019) similarly note that it is crucial for NTs to experience humanizing pedagogy so that they feel equipped to engage in the challenge of making their classrooms places where they and their students can be vulnerable. Grewal modeled and created a more humanizing space by repositioning pre-service teachers in her teacher education classroom as co-constructing the class curriculum and contents in her practicum course, and putting community at the center of her work. However, although there are these and other efforts to model and create humanizing spaces in *pre-service* teacher education experiences, which prepare NTs to be equity-minded advocates (see also Athanases and Martin 2006; Athanases and de Oliveira 2008; Price and Osborne 2000; Reyes 2016; Wynter-Hoyte et al. 2019), much of what happens during NTs' transition to their early years of teaching does not explicitly have humanizing aims, and much of what we know about their experiences does not reflect a humanizing approach to their induction (e.g., Artigliere and Baecher 2017; Farrell 2016). Therefore, NTs' transition from their pre-service coursework and practicum experiences to teaching in their own classrooms seems ripe with opportunity for newly imagined humanizing induction experiences. Through supportive peer interactions, NTs could nurture and reflect upon their own and each other's emerging identities as humanizing practitioners.

For induction to fruitfully support NTs' emerging identities as humanizing practitioners, we must better understand the conditions that foster such identity development during NTs' induction phase. Research has shown that when NTs are part of a pre-service program that centers equity, they are better equipped to be advocates for students, even in their early years of teaching (e.g., Athanases and de Oliveira 2008). As pre-service teachers become NTs with their own classrooms, Kayi-Aydar (2015) has found that the ways in which they claim agency to position themselves align closely with how they position their multilingual students; thus, if NTs position themselves and one another in humanizing ways, and as capable individuals, they may be more likely to do the same with their students. Furthermore, sustained engagement with colleagues—both other NTs and mixed groups of NTs and more experienced teachers—helps NTs significantly, as they struggle to identify who they are and who they want to become (e.g., Danielowich 2012; Yazan 2017). We draw upon this prior research to build a case that NTs' engagement with not only more experienced educators (e.g., teacher educators, mentors)—as is traditional during induction—but also *with one another* is an important means of developing their identities as capable, agentive, equity-oriented professionals (e.g., Geeraerts et al. 2015; Vangrieken et al. 2017). Extending Athanases and de Oliveira's findings that pre-service programs can support NTs' development as advocates, and their call for teacher induction that supports NTs' engagement in advocacy, we suggest that NTs can provide ongoing support to one another in developing emerging identities as advocates. We argue that when NTs have the opportunity to be part of a collective in which they have agency to construct an identity as contributing, capable, and equity-minded, they may be better able to develop their emerging humanizing practice.

Methods and Data Sources

Our findings come from a larger seven-year participatory design project with 13 NTs of multilingual students and eight teacher educators involved in teaching and supervising these NTs (e.g., Peercy et al. 2020b), as we examined the kinds of practices and supports that NTs of multilingual students use and need in their early years in the classroom. NTs in our collective had each been enrolled in an MEd in TESOL program at a large, Mid-Atlantic university in the US, and were in their student teaching internships or first year of teaching when data collection began. All were teaching in K-12 settings in which they were ESOL specialists and worked with "mainstream" grade level teachers in their schools. They taught in a variety of contexts, including elementary pull-out and plug-in ESOL (English for speakers of other languages) models, and secondary settings in which they taught content (e.g., ESOL science, ESOL math, ESOL English language arts) courses to multilingual students (see Table 6.1 for a list of NTs mentioned in this study; due to our focus on themes of advocacy and limitations in space, we highlight data from seven of the 13 NT participants in the larger dataset).

Teacher educators who worked on our team included one tenured faculty member, one clinical faculty member, and six doctoral students who worked with the NTs by teaching courses and/or supervising field placements. All specialized in the teaching and learning of multilingual students. The first author of this chapter was a teacher educator who taught each of these NTs while they were pre-service teachers in an ESOL literacy methods course; the second author joined the project for analysis and writing after the majority of data were collected; and the third author was one of the teacher educators involved in data collection and analysis in this project. The larger dataset includes classroom artifacts, audio- and video-recorded observation and interview data, postings to a discussion board and a closed group social media space, and data from meetings of the entire team (NTs and teacher educators). Here we focus on findings pertaining to the advocacy of the NTs from data transcribed from

Table 6.1 Study participants

Name	Years enrolled in MEd program	First year teaching as instructor of record	Race/ethnicity
Kendra	2013–15	2015–16	White
Hailey	2013–15	2015–16	Chinese American
Catherine	2014–15	2015–16	African American
Shannon	2015–17	2017–18	White
Breanne	2015–17	2017–18	White
Naomi	2013–17	2017–18	Chinese American
Sarah	2015–18	2018–19	White

19 team meetings that lasted approximately 1.5–2 hours each, and occurred at equal intervals approximately four times each school year, because they provide the most robust indication of how the specific needs and strengths of NTs are bolstered when they are part of a supportive collective.

Data analysis occurred in multiple phases. The focal point of the project was identifying and developing core practices that NTs identified as pivotal to their early teaching experiences (e.g., Kidwell et al. 2021; Peercy and Chi 2022; Peercy et al. 2019, 2020; Peercy, Tigert, and Fredricks 2023; Tigert et al. 2022). In our initial analysis, we employed the constant comparative method (Corbin and Strauss 2015) to identify emerging themes and patterns in the data for identification of the core practices NTs and the teacher educators collaboratively identified. This process also illuminated instances of our collective serving as a much-needed source of ongoing support for the NTs in our group. In the second phase of analysis, we used some of the codes identified in the first phase of analysis and ran reports from our analysis platform that highlighted instances in which NTs indicated the group as a means of support. We subsequently examined these key excerpts again inductively, looking more closely for instances of support. We initially identified four new codes (theory-practice connections, feelings of isolation, broad understanding of teaching, and sharing instructional resources), which we grouped into two larger themes (overcoming feelings of isolation, and NTs as valuable contributors). Here we focus specifically on how the NTs' positioning of one another as valuable contributors supported a more humanizing induction experience and their identity development as advocates as they embarked on the early part of their careers.

Supporting NTs' Emerging Humanizing Practice

Through our collective engagement, it became clear that a precursor to NTs' advocacy was a need to openly share their still-developing teacher identities, discussing their struggles, asking questions, admitting they were overwhelmed, and seeking support. In contrast to the stress and judgment they felt in their school settings, the NTs noted that they found our team meetings to be a "safe space" where they could be more fully themselves, reflect on their practice and their experiences, and be "very honest" without fear of negative repercussions. For this group of teachers, our time together was "safe" because it was characterized by the absence of pressure to perform and allowed time for them to grapple with challenging issues in and beyond their classrooms, such as practices they viewed as unjust. As we detail below, the teachers' collaborative engagement in our team's "safe space" humanized them, allowing them to claim agency and embody identities as advocates and emerging humanizing practitioners. For instance, Catherine (in her second year as a teacher) shared how the group had been an important source of support for her even when her school setting was not, and how important this was for her development as a NT. She described how she was able to maintain her identity as a capable teacher in part because of the touchpoint that was available to her in our team meetings:

> This year, we had a major change in administration, and that just threw everybody off kilter.... Both of my direct administrators were changed, and I didn't think I was going to feel any weight from that, I was like, you know, "I'm too cool, that can't affect me," but it did.... I had my routine down, so the kids were never a problem [Catherine had just described how academically challenging she had made her material, and that her students rose to the challenge in ways that she was very proud of]. It was just being able to find my place amongst the adults was very difficult, because I know, I am a teacher. I am "Miss Turner." But it's difficult to go to older, more experienced teachers and administrators and put my foot down, and let them know I'm here for the kids, not to be, bossed around. So that was, that was a challenge this year.... This group has really helped me figure out what my end game is, like what kind of a teacher I want to become.... I want to continue to learn, I don't want to be that teacher with all this experience and set in my ways.... I want to continue to be humble and learn from my fellow teachers no matter their experience. This group has really helped me with growing, and not only as a teacher, but emotionally, too, being able to know where I want to be overall.
>
> June 5, 2017 team meeting

Naomi, who had just finished her student teaching, expressed a similar sentiment and how important it was for NTs to have a group to engage with for several years:

> It's been a really great group.... The meetings from the beginning of the year were really helpful going into the internship, to talk about what were some of the concerns, and some of the things to look out for in the classroom before the internship started. And then, because you guys (referencing Shannon and Breanne) had started your internship first, that was also [this heads up that] these are things going into my internship, to look out for. Being in the conversation, we get to hear from first-year teachers, second-year teachers, and [about] the evolution of becoming a teacher. Insights, or noticing, things that I, without the heads up, it would be things that I would just encounter [with no

support], but I get the heads up, you know? ... I think this is something that all teachers would probably benefit from, for the first three or four years, like, what are you coming into.

June 5, 2017 team meeting

Breanne shared how important the opportunities to engage with NTs outside her own content area, grade level, and school context had been for her as she finished her student teaching and prepared to enter her first year as a teacher. She described how her learning had been enhanced by hearing from NTs in our group who had one or two years of experience in the classroom, in a variety of settings:

Shannon and Naomi and I all came in [to this group] with [other NTs] ahead of us.... It's been a huge resource and I feel like it prepared us for what the real classroom was like, and also being able to express our opinions on what we were seeing.

Shannon, a student teacher in the same cohort with Breanne, echoed this comment, suggesting the group was a great resource because of the ability to hear how teachers at the same early point in their careers "handled things and strategies and solutions and being able to workshop issues that [we're] encountering" (June 5, 2017 team meeting). For the teachers, this opportunity to come together gave them a venue where they could discuss issues that they did not feel they could raise in their school settings.

In this "safe space" where NTs were discussing problems of practice and co-creating solutions to those problems, we identified multiple kinds of advocacy emerging in the practice of these NTs. For the purposes of this chapter, we focus specifically on NTs' advocacy on behalf of students, which often begins within the classroom where NTs have the most agency, and then moves beyond the classroom when NTs seek help for providing more supports to their students and their families or seek to change school policies and practices affecting multilingual populations (e.g., Athanases and de Oliveira 2008). For example, when the group was asked by the first author what accomplishments they had experienced that week, Breanne, who was doing her student teaching in an elementary school, shared a tense, intimidating moment she had recently experienced when a classroom teacher had made a comment to her about an Indian student smelling like curry:

I was like, "Oh my god, what do I do? I have to do something, stand up for my student, this was not appropriate." ... My mentor teacher and the guidance counselor thought it warranted a discussion with the teacher. They had given me the option of do it myself, or let my mentor teacher address it with her. I was really nervous, I didn't want to start a conflict. They happened to be in the fourth grade team meeting, so all the teachers were there. I was really nervous and it was really stressful, but it was good to have this conversation with her.... I was proud of myself for standing up, for taking the first steps to try to stand up for a student.

December 15, 2016 meeting

Breanne's experience marked an emerging attempt to advocate for her students, especially at times when students and their families are not privy to the ways in which teachers may be characterizing them. Engaging in humanizing pedagogy is not merely a public orientation, but one that extends to the private interactions and collaborations with other educators outside of the classroom, in moments when students cannot advocate for themselves. By discussing this episode with other NTs and the teacher educators present, she communicated a growing sense of herself as a teacher who represented her multilingual students at all times, even when facing an unfavorable power differential as a student teacher.

Facilitation by the first author during that team meeting brought the conversation after Breanne's sharing to focus more explicitly on examples of advocacy that the NTs had experienced. Hailey shared a moment when she had pushed for her newcomer students to receive more challenging instruction from a third-grade classroom teacher with whom she partnered to provide instruction to multilingual students. Hailey's colleague had initially decided to have two third-grade newcomer students trace ABC letters because they did not speak English yet. Hailey described how she responded to this decision, using her understanding of students' existing home language literacy abilities:

I tested them and asked them the alphabet in their native language.... They could write letters just fine, they just didn't know them in English. I was trying to explain the difference between a beginner—somebody who's beginning in literacy—versus somebody with low English proficiency, and I could kind of see it click in her. She was like, "Oh, ok, so they understand these letters, so maybe the tracing isn't so helpful, but maybe if I'm giving them English words, then maybe that's at the level that would probably challenge them a little bit more than just tracing, copying." So I felt like the advocacy piece there was just trying to help her see the difference.

December 15, 2016 team meeting

During this meeting, Hailey expressed that "mainstream teachers with newcomers, they don't have the time to sit and talk with the student or see what they actually know in their first language" in order to develop appropriate instruction (December 15, 2016 team meeting). While Hailey could have pushed the conversation with her colleague further to highlight how these newcomers had literacy in their home languages that could be tapped into during instruction, and ways in which her mainstream colleague should also take responsibility to incorporate the newcomers' prior knowledge, interactions with her NT peers gave her an opportunity to try out her emerging understanding of how ESOL teachers can champion multilingual students with their colleagues. Hailey's description illustrates how language educators can use their expertise to view their multilingual students with an asset-based lens when others may not.

The NTs also shared examples of observing or being part of the advocacy that their mentor teachers engaged in on behalf of their students. For instance, Shannon shared how "it took a lot of pushing" on the part of her mentor to persuade the kindergarten teacher colleague with whom they co-taught to move a student to a higher challenge group (December 15, 2016 team meeting). Over time, they also discussed other aspects of advocacy, supporting each other's growing understanding of what it could entail, such as the importance of making sure multilingual students were not misidentified for special education services, the importance of valuing students' home languages, connecting with families in meaningful ways, and making sure they got sufficient instructional time with students to support their learning.

As the teachers moved through their induction, they brought more experiences to the group, often sharing resources, strategies for advocacy, and serving as sounding boards for one another. During a later meeting, Catherine, a secondary ESOL science teacher for students identified as having newcomer status and beginning proficiency in English, shared system-wide struggles with students being placed in classes that were inappropriate to their level of English language development, and Kendra and Sarah chimed in to unpack and affirm the challenges Catherine was articulating.

> **Catherine** In the beginning [the district] did not properly identify what [English proficiency] level [the students] were.... And [there were] some kids who were speaking [English] almost fluently and then some kids that were just like "Okay... I'm not understanding anything" [in the same class].
>
> **Kendra** And that wasn't an intentional...
>
> **Catherine** I don't know what they were thinking. We had to actually remove some of those kids and put them back into newcomer level because they were just not ready and we were setting them up for failure.

Sarah ... There's different models [for what your school is trying], but they're realizing that newcomer students are not getting enough focused attention ... newcomer students need so much intensive support ...

Catherine [overlapping]   Need that extra support.

June 7, 2018 team meeting

Kendra posing the question of whether such placements were intentional on the school administration's part demonstrates that this was a space to provide suggestive feedback to each other on how to advocate in this situation for her students. Sarah's comment further asserted that this was a valid concern, supporting Catherine in her frustrations as she developed her voice and her influence for her students, and suggesting that there were unaddressed systemic issues within the educational models that were shared among them as language educators. Even as a student teacher, Sarah was developing her emerging understanding of equitable instruction for newcomer students while also supporting Catherine's continued identity development as a third-year teacher when Catherine struggled to represent her students' needs to the school administration. This group was a space which afforded these NTs opportunities to engage in ideas and conversation that supported their emerging attempts at humanizing the academic experiences of multilingual students across the span of their induction period. Over time, this community of NTs became a place where they discussed advocacy beyond their classrooms as well, making their voices heard at school board meetings, supporting families concerned about immigration raids, and contacting state representatives with concerns.

NTs' opportunities to gather in a safe, non-judgmental space offered an opportunity to develop their identities as advocates. Through these interactions, they discussed their emerging humanizing practice and supported others as they strove to advocate for their students (see Peercy et al. 2019, 2020, 2022b) because their needs for self-development were fed through their engagement with a community of peers.

Discussion

Reeves has discussed the need for pre-service teachers of multilingual students to practice claims to legitimacy, developing identities that allow them to imagine "new possibilities" for themselves and their students (2018: 7). These "new possibilities" could include more humanizing approaches to practice with multilingual students; something that NTs can be more empowered to take on if they can find ways to challenge their own sometimes dehumanizing experiences as students and as NTs. One way of doing so seems to be through being in community with other NTs, where they feel safe enough to discuss their real issues, thus breaking free from their isolation and repositioning themselves and one another as important supports. As Catherine explained, our community was a place where she was able to figure out what kind of teacher she wanted to become: "This group has really helped me figure out what my end game is, what kind of teacher I want to become" (June 5, 2017 team meeting). Through interactions in our community, the NTs were able to claim agency and to construct themselves as someone of value, and who could direct their own path as an advocate and emerging humanizing practitioner of multilingual students. We argue that NTs need spaces where they can engage in peer interaction, and have their needs for relationship, community, and feeling seen and understood be met. Such interactions are fundamental to all human development, and to developing a humanizing outlook. These spaces allow NTs to consider and cultivate the resources to enact more powerfully humanizing practice with their students, creating similar spaces of belonging, acceptance, and validation.

Feiman-Nemser (2010) highlights a significant tension in NT induction, asking whether induction efforts should socialize teachers to "fit in" to schools as they currently are, or to become agents of transformation. This brings to the surface an important issue: schools are currently dehumanizing places for multilingual and other marginalized students and for many NTs who support them. Thus, it seems hard to argue that NTs should seek to fit in (e.g., Peercy et al. 2019). Instead, they need to be supported, like Sarah and Kendra supported Catherine, in creating important pedagogical and systemic transformation through humanizing practice. Teachers who begin their careers with a strong community of support, safe spaces to grapple with their problems of practice, and a solid sense of self will be more likely to claim agency to transform harmful systems and to stand in solidarity with marginalized students and their communities. As Achinstein and Athanases (2009: 578–579) note, we need to "understand what supporting new teachers to learn to teach against the (new) grain might mean in a growing educational climate of control (Cochran-Smith 2001)". Based on the data we have examined here, safe spaces in community with other NTs seem to be one important support that is not typically a part of most teacher induction programs.

Although much of the literature on formal induction efforts has emphasized the importance of experienced mentors in the same school who teach the same grade level and content, the NTs in our group used their time with peers from a variety of settings to foster identities as advocates for multilingual students. Such development aligns with growing scholarship about NT induction efforts, especially from European contexts, which suggest that peer groups can help create a space where NTs can share knowledge rather than only receiving it from experienced mentors (e.g., Heikkinen, Jokinen, and Tynjälä 2012), strengthen their professional identity (e.g., Geeraerts et al. 2015), share emotionally challenging experiences (e.g., Uitto et al. 2016), create personal networks, and broaden their perspectives (e.g., Estola, Heikkinen, and Syrjälä 2014; Hiltula et al. 2012). Our findings offer not only evidence of NTs using such a peer group to support each other in teaching multilingual students, but also in their efforts to humanize their pedagogy. Our study offers one example of bringing NTs together from their teacher preparation years through their induction to position each other as practitioners who advocate for their multilingual students, and develop an emerging humanizing pedagogy.

One important caveat to the findings from our study is that many of the NTs and teacher educators in our group were White females, who currently comprise the majority of US educators, despite growing numbers of language learners, students of color, and other minoritized groups in their classrooms. Here we focused on the emergence of a safe space for NTs in our group to explore and challenge their pedagogy, but we did not dig deeply into questions of the impact of White privilege, systemic racism, and their (and our) own racism on their classrooms. We recognize that these are crucially important conversations and questions for NTs and all educators to engage with. Thus, these safe spaces need to be spaces of challenge so that group members do not reinforce dominant discourses that are oppressive to marginalized students. Furthermore, creating spaces that support NTs of color is also critically important (Achinstein and Athanases 2009; Varghese, Daniels, and Park 2019). Future research should examine not only how to create and maintain safe spaces for all NTs to develop as educators, but also more specifically how to create safe preservice and induction spaces that support and challenge NTs to develop as critically engaged humanizing educators ready to enact equity-centered practices from the beginning of their careers.

Implications and Conclusion

Different approaches to induction—for instance, more supervisory and hierarchical versus more collaborative and dialogic—can make important differences in the ways in which NTs are received and supported as they join the profession (e.g., Kemmis et al. 2014), and can also have an impact on whether their future practice is more oriented to equity or to conformity and maintaining the status quo (e.g., Achinstein and Athanases 2009). We built upon previous research on the ways in which peer mentoring and collectives of NTs can support NT development to argue that in addition to formal induction and mentoring opportunities, NTs of multilingual students also benefit from interacting with one another in less hierarchical and formal ways. Given the many challenges that multilingual students often navigate inside and outside of the classroom and the related resources those same students bring to their classrooms (including language, race, immigration status, socioeconomic status, and religion), NTs of multilingual students represent a particularly revelatory case (Yin 2017) for induction experiences that might support the development of NTs' emerging identities as advocates in settings where students are typically underserved.

Given the potential benefits NTs can experience from gathering with one another, we suggest that future induction efforts seek ways to support organically formed NT groups, perhaps leveraging social media (e.g., Smith Risser 2013) to develop both dynamic and more stable groupings of NTs around topics of mutual interest. One way this might be achieved is through the kind of online support groups for NTs that Paulus and Scherff (2008) developed on discussion boards. Online or hybrid groups can also take advantage of new technologies that are now ubiquitous after the Covid-19 global pandemic, including meeting via online conferencing applications like Teams, Zoom, or Discord. Groups can also adopt practices from online supervision and coaching by recording video and then making time-stamped comments within the video for collaborative peer inquiry (Baecher et al. 2018), and by viewing examples of NTs enacting humanizing practice in video and other classroom data (e.g., Peercy and Chi 2022; Peercy, Hardy, and Crawford 2022a; Peercy et al. 2022b; Peercy, Tigert, and Fredricks 2023). Opportunities for interactions and activities aimed at helping NTs develop, understand, and integrate identities as advocates in their work with learners may help to humanize their teaching practices, and more readily welcome and affirm multilingual students' identities in their classrooms.

We also suggest that teacher education should prime the development of the NT community. One way this might occur is through earlier and more consistent partnerships with schools and districts while teachers are still pre-service, engaging pre-service teachers with in-service teachers when possible, and using mechanisms like participation in lesson study, rounds, or professional learning communities. This might have the dual effect of preparing pre-service teachers to look for and develop such communities, while also engaging practicing teachers in such work, possibly making a collaborative culture more normative in local districts. We can also learn from the strong work of peer mentoring groups in Finland, and incorporate hybrid peer mentoring between pre-service and in-service teachers to enhance the professional collaboration between the groups and allow for humanizing practices to be built across a career pathway (Kiviniemi et al. 2020; Korhonen et al. 2017). We need to find ways for universities and school districts to partner around the induction of NTs, creating greater continuity and opportunities for connection. Through our review of the literature that NT induction support that focuses on peer interaction in the US has generally emerged through grant-funded work (e.g., Durn 2010; Meyer 1999, 2002; Rogers and Babinski 2002), and the emphases on NT peer groups dissolve when grant funding ends. Given the importance our NTs placed on their opportunities to engage with one another as they developed their identities as advocates, and evidence from the teacher induction literature regarding how much NTs value collaboratively developing their identities as teachers in general, we wonder whether some of the funds that districts currently put toward induction could be used in ways that support NT groups.

Never has it been more urgent to offer learning opportunities and spaces that are humanizing for minoritized students and their teachers. NTs feel better equipped to teach minoritized students when they are positioned in ways that afford them agency and opportunities to develop identities related to advocacy, supporting them as they confront systems that are oppressive for multilingual and other minoritized students. University-based teacher educators and school-based administrators should explore ways to come together to meet this need by providing spaces where NTs can develop as humanizing educators. In doing so, we hope NTs can be prepared to inhabit and enact humanizing identities through the induction process and set the foundation for a long career as advocates for multilingual students.

Notes

1 It is important to note that we use the word "safe" because it is how NTs frequently described our collective. We acknowledge that these spaces need to challenge racial and other inequities, and not serve as a place in which systemic and individual racism is upheld, and that at times the notion of "safety" is used to maintain White dominance (e.g., Motha 2006).

2. Addressing issues of equity and justice are particularly important for NTs of multilingual students, who are often members of minoritized groups in US schools, due to factors such as socioeconomic status, race, ethnicity, language, religion, and prior school experience, among others.

References

Achinstein, B., and S. Z. Athanases (2009), "New Teacher Induction and Mentoring for Educational Change," in A. Hargreaves, A. Lieberman, M. Fullan, and D. Hopkins (eds.), *Second International Handbook of Educational Change*, 573–593, Dordrecht: Springer.

Artigliere, M., and L. Baecher (2017), "Sink or Swim: Aligning Training with Classroom Reality in ESL Co-Teaching," in T. S. C. Farrell (ed.), *Preservice Teacher Education*, 43–48, Alexander, VA: TESOL Press.

Athanases, S. Z., and K. J. Martin (2006), "Learning to Advocate for Educational Equity in a Teacher Credential Program," *Teaching and Teacher Education*, 22 (6): 627–646.

Athanases, S. Z., and L. C. De Oliveira (2008), "Advocacy for Equity in Classrooms and Beyond: New Teachers' Challenges and Responses," *Teachers College Record*, 110 (1): 64–104.

Baecher, L., S. Browne Graves, F. Ghailan, and H. College (2018), "Supervisor Learning through Collaborative Video Inquiry: It's Not Just for Teacher Candidates," *Contemporary Issues in Technology and Teacher Education*, 18(3): 556–577.

Bartolomé, L. (1994), "Beyond the Methods Fetish: Toward a Humanizing Pedagogy," *Harvard Educational Review*, 64 (2): 173–195.

Buendía, E. (2000), "Power and Possibility: The Construction of a Pedagogical Practice," *Teaching and Teacher Education*, 16 (2): 147–163.

Carter Andrews, D. J., and B. Castillo (2016), "Humanizing Pedagogy for Examinations of Race and Culture in Teacher Education," in F. Tuitt, C. Haynes, and S. Stewart (eds.), *Race, Equity and the Learning Environment: The Global Relevance of Critical and Inclusive Pedagogies in Higher Education*, 112–128, Sterling, VA: Stylus Publishing.

Cochran-Smith, M. (2001), "Learning to Teach Against the (New) Grain," *Journal of Teacher Education*, 52 (1): 3–4.

Corbin, J., and A. Strauss (2015), *Basics of Qualitative Research: Technique and Procedures for Developing Grounded Theory*, Los Angeles, CA: Sage.

Danielowich, R. M. (2012), "Other Teachers' Teaching: Understanding the Roles of Peer Group Collaboration in Teacher Reflection and Learning," *Teacher Educator*, 47 (2): 101–122.

Durn, J. L. (2010), "No Teacher Left Behind: Effectiveness of New Teacher Groups to Facilitate Induction," DEd dissertation, Indiana University of Pennsylvania (ProQuest AAT 365733484).

Estola, E., H. L. T. Heikkinen, and L. Syrjälä (2014), "Narrative Pedagogies for Peer Groups," in C. J. Craig and L. Orland-Arak (eds.), *International Teacher Education: Promising Pedagogies (Part A)*, 155–172, Bingley: Emerald Publishing.

Farrell, T. S. C. (2016), *Reflective Practice for Novice Language Teachers: From Trainee to Teacher*, Sheffield: Equinox Publishing.

Feiman-Nemser, S. (2010), "Multiple Meanings of New Teacher Induction," in J. Wang, S. J. Odell, and R. T. Clift (eds.), *Past, Present, and Future Research on Teacher Induction: An Anthology for Researchers, Policy Makers, and Practitioners*, 15–30, Lanham, MD: R&L Education.

Geeraerts, K., P. Tynjälä, H. L. T. Heikkinen, I. Markkanen, M. Pennanen, and D. Gijbels (2015), "Peer-Group Mentoring as a Tool for Teacher Development," *European Journal of Teacher Education*, 38 (3): 358–377.

Goldrick, L. (2016), "Support from the Start: A 50-State Review of Policies on New Educator Induction and Mentoring," Policy Report, Santa Cruz, CA: New Teacher Center.

Grewal, I. K., A. Maher, H. Watters, D. Clemens, and K. Webb (2019), "Rewriting Teacher Education: Food, Love, and Community," *Journal of Culture and Values in Education*, 2 (3): 44–60.

Heikkinen, H. L. T., H. Jokinen, and P. Tynjälä (2012), *Peer-Group Mentoring for Teacher Development*, London: Routledge.

Hiltula, A., L. Isosomppi, H. Jokinen, and A. Oksakari (2012), "Individual and Social Meanings of Mentoring," in H.L.T. Heikkinen, H. Jokinen, and P. Tynjälä (eds.), *Peer-Group Mentoring for Teacher Development*, 60–70, London: Routledge.

Kayi-Aydar, H. (2015), "Teacher Agency, Positioning, and English Language Learners: Voices of Pre-Service Classroom Teachers," *Teaching and Teacher Education*, 45 (January): 94–103.

Kemmis, S., H. L. T. Heikkinen, G. Fransson, J. Aspfors, and C. Edwards-Groves (2014), "Mentoring of New Teachers as a Contested Practice: Supervision, Support and Collaborative Self-Development," *Teaching and Teacher Education*, 43 (October): 154–164.

Kidwell, T., M. M. Peercy, J. Tigert, and D. Fredricks (2021), "Novice Teachers' Use of Pedagogical Language Knowledge to Humanize Language and Literacy Development," *TESOL Journal*, 12: e590. https://doi.org/10.1002/tesj.590.

Kiviniemi, U., P. Tynjälä, H. L. T. Heikkinen, and A. Martin (2020), "Running a Hybrid: Mingling in-Service and Pre-Service Teachers in Peer-Mentoring Groups," *European Journal of Teacher Education*, 44 (4): 555–571.

Korhonen, H., H. L. T. Heikkinen, U. Kiviniemi, and P. Tynjälä (2017), "Student Teachers' Experiences of Participating in Mixed Peer Mentoring Groups of In-Service and Pre-Service Teachers in Finland," *Teaching and Teacher Education*, 61 (January): 153–163.

Ladson-Billings, G. (1995), "Toward a Theory of Culturally Relevant Pedagogy," *American Educational Research Journal*, 32 (3): 465–491.

Le Cornu, R., and R. Ewing (2008), "Reconceptualising Professional Experiences in Pre-Service Teacher Education ... Reconstructing the Past to Embrace the Future," *Teaching and Teacher Education: An International Journal of Research and Studies*, 24 (7): 1799–1812.

Meyer, T. (1999), "Conversational Learning: The Role of Talk in a Novice Teacher Learning Community," DEd dissertation, Stanford University.

Meyer, T. (2002), "Novice Teacher Learning Communities: An Alternative to One-on-One Mentoring," *American Secondary Education*, 31 (1): 27–42.

Motha, S. (2006), "Out of the Safety Zone," in A. Curtis and M. Romney (eds.), *Color, Race, and English Language Teaching: Shades of Meaning*, 161–172, Mahwah, NJ: Lawrence Erlbaum.

Nieto, S. (2000), *Affirming Diversity: The Sociopolitical Context of Multicultural Education*, New York: Longman.

Paulus, T., and L. Scherff (2008), "'Can Anyone Offer Any Words of Encouragement?' Online Dialogue as a Support Mechanism for Preservice Teachers," *Journal of Technology and Teacher Education*, 16 (1): 113–136.

Peercy, M. M., and J. Chi (2022), "'Oh, I was Scaffolding!': Novice Teachers' Use of Scaffolding as Humanizing Practice with Multilingual Students," in L. De Oliveira and R. Westerlund (eds.), *Scaffolding for Multilingual Learners in Elementary and Secondary Schools*, 102–120, London: Routledge.

Peercy, M. M., J. Tigert, K. Feagin, T. Kidwell, D. Fredricks, M. Lawyer, M. Bitter, N. Canales, and A. Mallory (2019), "'I Need to Take Care of Myself': The Case for Self-Care as a Core Practice for Teaching," in C. R. Rinke and L. Mawhinney (eds.), *Opportunities and Challenges in Teacher Recruitment and Retention: Teacher Voices Across the Pipeline*, 303–325, Charlotte, NC: Information Age Publishing.

Peercy, M. M., T. Kidwell, M. DeStefano Lawyer, J. Tigert, D. Fredricks, K. Feagin, and M. Stump (2020), "Experts at Being Novices: What New Teachers Can Add to Practice-Based Teacher Education Efforts," *Action in Teacher Education*, 42 (3): 212–233.

Peercy, M. M., M. Hardy, and J. Crawford (2022a), "'Because We Bilingual': Examining an Early Career Teacher's Humanizing Perspectives on Academic Language," Paper presented at the Annual Meeting of the American Educational Research Association, April, San Diego, CA.

Peercy, M. M., J. Tigert, D. Fredricks, K. Feagin, W. Hall, J. Himmel, and M. Lawyer (2022b), "From Humanizing Principles to Humanizing Practices: Exploring Core Practices as a Bridge to Enacting Humanizing Pedagogy with Multilingual Students," *Teaching and Teacher Education*, 113. https://doi.org/10.1016/j.tate.2022.103653.

Peercy, M. M., J. Tigert, and D. Fredricks (2023), *Core Practices for Teaching Multilingual Students: Humanizing Pedagogies for Equity*, New York: Teachers College Press.

Price, J. N., and M. D. Osborne (2000), "Challenges of Forging a Humanizing Pedagogy in Teacher Education," *Curriculum and Teaching*, 15 (1): 27–51.

Reeves, J. (2018), "Teacher Identity," in J. I. Liontas (ed.), *The TESOL Encyclopedia of English Language Teaching*, Chichester: Wiley-Blackwell.

Reyes, R., III (2016), "In a World of Disposable Students: The Humanizing Elements of Border Pedagogy in Teacher Education," *The High School Journal*, 99 (4): 337–350.

Rogers, D. L., and L. M. Babinski (2002), *From Isolation to Conversation: Supporting New Teachers' Development*, Albany, NY: SUNY Press.

Salazar, M. D. C. (2010), "Pedagogical Stances of High School ESL Teachers," *Bilingual Research Journal*, Humanizing Pedagogy: Reinventing the Principles and Practice of Education as a 33 (1): 111–124.

Salazar, M. D. C. (2013), "A Journey Toward Liberation," *Review of Research in Education*, 37 (1): 121–148.

Smith Risser, H. (2013), "Virtual Induction: A Novice Teacher's Use of Twitter to Form an Informal Mentoring Network," *Teaching and Teacher Education*, 35 (October): 25–33.

Tigert, J., M. M. Peercy, D. Fredricks, and T. Kidwell (2022), "Humanizing Classroom Management as a Core Practice for Teachers of Multilingual Students," *TESOL Quarterly*, 56 (4): 1087–1111.

Tynjälä, P., M. Pennanen, I. Markkanen, and H.L.T. Heikkinen (2021), "Finnish Model of Peer-Group Mentoring: Review of Research," *Annals of the New York Academy of Sciences*, 1483 (1): 208–223.

Uitto, M., S. L. Kaunisto, G. Kelchtermans, and E. Estola (2016), "Peer Group as a Meeting Place: Reconstructions of Teachers' Self-Understanding and the Presence of Vulnerability," *International Journal of Educational Research*, 75 (January): 7–16.

Vangrieken, K., C. Meredith, T. Packer, and E. Kyndt (2017), "Teacher Communities as a Context for Professional Development: A Systematic Review," *Teaching and Teacher Education*, 61 (January): 47–59.

Varghese, M., J. R. Daniels, and C. C. Park (2019), "Structuring Disruption within University-Based Teacher Education Programs: Possibilities and Challenges of Race-Based Caucuses," *Teachers College Record*, 121 (4): 1–34.

Wynter-Hoyte, K., M. Muller, N. Bryan, G. Swindler Boutte, and S. Long (2019), "Dismantling Eurocratic Practices in Teacher Education: A Preservice Program Focused on Culturally Relevant, Humanizing, and Decolonizing Pedagogies," in T. E. Hodges and A. C. Baum (eds.), *Handbook of Research on Field-Based Teacher Education*, 300–320. Hershey, PA: IGI Global.

Yazan, B. (2017), "'It Just Made Me Look at Language in a Different Way': ESOL Teacher Candidates' Identity Negotiation through Teacher Education Coursework," *Linguistics and Education*, 40 (August): 38–49.

Yin, R. K. (2017), *Case Study Research and Applications: Design and Methods*, 6th edition, Los Angeles, CA: Sage.

Implementing an Intersectional Pedagogy in a TESOL Methods Course: A Narrative Approach

Hayriye Kayi-Aydar

Introduction

English language teacher education is not a neutral process. Just like English language teaching, TESOL teacher education is also a sociopolitical endeavor with social, cultural, historical, and political implications. A course that is commonly taught across almost all Teaching English to Speakers of Other Languages (TESOL) teacher education programs around the globe is TESOL methodology. While the course might be offered under slightly different names, it is typically included in both undergraduate and graduate curricula of TESOL programs, as noted in a recent volume on the preparation of teachers of English as an additional language in 11 countries (Polat, Mahalingappa, and Kayi-Aydar 2021). TESOL methodology courses usually aim to equip teachers with the professional knowledge, skills, and strategies necessary to teach English as an additional language to learners of all ages. While the courses traditionally focus on the teaching of various language skills (e.g., listening, speaking, grammar), they may also include the history of English language teaching methods (e.g., grammar translation, total physical response).

In the changing world we live in, it would be naïve to assume that the content of TESOL methodology courses remains the same. Major political developments around the globe, globalization, digital technologies, social movements, increased attention to (de)colonization, forced immigration, wars, global inequality, and the Covid-19 pandemic have repositioned the English language, English language learners and teachers, and English language teaching itself. As classroom teachers are often encouraged to consider the implications of such major global events and shifts for their students and teaching, we, as teacher educators, also need to situate and evaluate our practices within a sociopolitical context. A reconceptualization of TESOL methodology courses is particularly necessary because teaching methodologies, pedagogical decisions, teaching techniques and strategies, all of which TESOL teachers typically learn about in TESOL methodology courses, appear to have a direct influence on learning and teaching processes including learner and teacher identities (e.g., Song 2016; Steadman, Kayi-Aydar, and Vogel 2018; Wolff and De Costa 2017). Furthermore, TESOL teachers have the strong potential to contribute to positive change on various levels (e.g., individual, cultural, institutional, structural), and they can actively do so if they build the necessary competencies and attend to sociopolitical contexts of English language teaching.

Through critical reflections, teacher educators can understand how moral, political, and social issues impact practice (Farrell 2016), and it is through such reflections that they can make meaningful and positive changes in TESOL teacher education. The reflections I share in this chapter are an effort to contribute to those changes. Based on my reflective notes and course syllabi over the years, I present here an analysis of my *evolving* intersectional approach to teaching TESOL methods in the MA TESL programs that I taught in the United States between 2012 and 2022. The analysis presents my efforts and strategies in implementing a meaningful intersectionality-oriented practice in and through the TESOL methods course I have been teaching for a decade now. Intersectionality (Case 2017; Collins and Bilge 2020), as a theoretical lens, guides me as I make sense of my own narratives. In the rest of this chapter, after I describe my analytic framework and context, I demonstrate how intersectionality helps me (a) challenge the US centric knowledge and perspectives in TESOL methodology, (b) question naming and labeling in TESOL praxis, and (c) make invisible identities visible in TESOL teacher education.

Engaging in narrative inquiry

I am a woman who was born and raised in a middle-class Muslim family in Turkiye and who speaks English as an additional language. My identities as a White immigrant mother raising a bilingual child in the US and a college professor with a privileged social status often intersect in shaping my personal and professional life. While my own intersectional life experiences are not the focus of this chapter, they play a significant role in my understanding of intersectionality literature and praxis and implementing an intersectional pedagogy in my teaching. As I make sense of my own teaching experience and share it with readers of this chapter, I utilize the techniques of autobiographical narrative inquiry, which is "a methodology and a way of understanding experience narratively" (Clandinin 2016: 9). The notes I took over time, my course syllabi, and all related memories constitute the narratives. In re-creating and organizing my narratives, I first developed a chronology, which showed what I did in my TESOL methodology courses for the past 10 years. The course syllabi were particularly helpful in documenting the sequence of factual events. The chronology was necessary as I focused on the "development," "shifts," and "changes" in my experience over time. I then added reflective notes to the chronology; these notes were a combination of what I wrote in the past as well as what I wrote while I was reflecting on the past experience in the present. As I restoried my experiences, some narratives became less significant regarding my research focus for this chapter, and I eliminated them. Eventually, my chronologically and thematically restoried narratives led to one coherent full narrative, which I share here. The overall narrative I share is "temporal (reflecting on the past and looking to the future), emotive (positive and negative experiences, surprises), reflective (beliefs, expectations, and practices), strategic (plans and goals), and instructive (advice)" (Barkhuizen, Benson, and Chik 2013: 38).

A traditional approach to teaching TESOL methods

In 2012, I was hired as an assistant professor to teach in the Master of Education (MEd) TESOL program at the University of Arkansas. I was assigned to teach TESOL methods to a mixed group of students, which included the graduate students in the MEd TESOL program and elementary/secondary pre-service teachers enrolled in the Master of Arts in Teaching (MAT) program. The MAT students were required to take the class as part of their ESL endorsement. A large majority of my students were pre-service teachers in the elementary education program. Over 90% of the student body in my TESOL methods courses were White female monolingual domestic students.

The first TESOL methods course I taught at the University of Arkansas followed a traditional syllabus with a focus on teaching the language skills without paying much attention to the sociopolitical issues surrounding the practice or English language. The course was heavily prescriptive in nature, as I taught the teachers how they *should* teach English language learners (ELLs.) My lecture slides, for example, usually included an overview of the related terminology along with a set of guidelines, in the form of directives, for teaching a particular skill (e.g., L2 listening). The pre-service teachers appeared to appreciate content-mastery. At the end of the academic semester, however, I was unhappy with the content I taught as well as the way I taught it. As Hanstedt (2018) argues, while content and content mastery are both crucial, pure content coverage cannot fully prepare students to tackle real-life world problems. In the following year, I revisited my vision for the course and made some slight changes to the content. I continued to make further changes every year. The shift from the traditional approach to a critical one has happened gradually over time, though this shift will never be fully complete and there is and will always be work to do. The "story" I tell here therefore does not have an end and will continue to develop.

Intersectional pedagogy

Offered to understand and challenge inequity, discrimination, and exclusion, intersectionality is a lens or framework that shows how multiple social markers (e.g., race, gender, ethnicity) intersect and diversify human experience (Crenshaw 1989, 1991). It was first developed to understand the complexities and inequities experienced by Black women in the US. The intersections of race and gender positioned Black women differently. In other words, the oppressions Black women experienced were different from what Black men or White women experienced. It is important to stress that intersectionality is not only a term that describes the multiplicity of one's identities. Case argues that "characterization of intersectionality simply as a descriptive of multiple identities, rather than as a mechanism explaining inequality, does violence to the central idea that animates the concept" (2017: x). Case rather describes intersectionality as "fundamentally a theory of anti-subordination" (2017: x). In her study on a Korean teacher's identities and teaching in US elementary classrooms, Maddamsetti (2020) shows how intersectionality is beyond the notion of multiple identities. The "racialized, linguicized, and gendered experiences" (2020: 354) of the focal participant in the study led to privilege and marginalization simultaneously. For example, in efforts to negotiate her racialized body, she drew upon her privilege due to her upper-middle-class socioeconomic status.

For Collins and Bilge, intersectionality is also "a form of critical inquiry and praxis" and a "tool for empowering people" (2020: 37). Because intersectionality focuses on understanding "how race, gender, sexuality, age, ability, and citizenship relate in complex and intersecting ways to produce" (Collins and Bilge 2020: 16) privilege and subordination simultaneously, for the same individual or across groups of individuals, and ultimately inequality, it is highly relevant to the English language classroom where learners fit into multiple categories and experience (in)equality differently (Kayi-Aydar, Varghese, and Vitanova 2022). An intersectionality framework makes it possible to challenge the highly problematic perception of English language learners (or teachers) as one homogenous group, and it rather explains how various social markers position them otherwise. It allows us to ask: How can we move beyond the overemphasized "language learner identity" and recognize the multitude of identities in constructing TESOL methodology as well as identify and disrupt a variety of oppressions and inequalities embedded in TESOL practice? As a teacher educator, I see it as my responsibility to not only adopt an intersectional lens in training, teaching, and working with English language teachers but also teach about intersectionality to them. By learning how to approach their students and students' life experiences through an intersectionality lens, teachers can understand the complex social problems their students face, and learn to develop strategies to address social inequality in their classrooms and learning communities.

An intersectional approach to teaching TESOL methods

Applying intersectionality as a form of critical inquiry begins with being critical. Drawing on the work of Collins and Bilge, I understand "being critical" as "criticizing, rejecting, and/or trying to fix the social problems that emerge in situations of social injustice" (2020: 39). For the TESOL methods courses that I teach, this means identifying social problems and situations of social injustice and finding meaningful ways to tackle them in the context of English language learning and teaching. Towards this goal, I have incorporated the following changes into my teaching in the methods courses over time.

Challenging the US centric knowledge and perspectives

Since methodology is determined by knowledge, an intersectional approach to teaching TESOL methods demands an understanding of who the owners of that knowledge are. Sensoy and DiAngelo argue that

> One of the persistent myths of mainstream society is that the knowledge we study in schools is factual and neutral. Yet we know that knowledge evolves over time and is dependent on the moment in history and the cultural reference point of the society that accepts it.
>
> 2017: 23

Since knowledge is socially constructed, it is important to understand *who* produces it. A large majority of the books on TESOL methods currently available on the market are authored by White Western scholars who also happen to be native speakers of English. Their scholarship also indicates that only a few of them adopt a critical lens in their work. This does not mean that the 'quality' of those books is less or questionable; my aim here is not to evaluate the quality at all but to point out whose experiences and perspectives shape the knowledge acquired by language teachers and teacher candidates around the globe. Using those books, we get to see the field and construct the methodology of ELT via only or mostly White Western perspectives. For example, a commonly used textbook, *Teaching English as a Foreign or Second Language* (2017), authored by Jerry G. Gebhard, is built mostly on the author's own experience of teaching English. The methodology presented in the book is thus largely constructed through the author's experiences, voice, and perspectives. This is evident in Gebhard's frequent references to his own experience and ideas throughout the book, such as "I have observed particularly high levels of anxiety in many teaching settings" (2017: 66), "I have seen some teachers, including myself, circling ..." (2017: 81), "one thing that works for me ..." (2017: 81), and "simply paying attention to the name and face worked wonderfully for me when meeting individuals" (2017: 88). Such reflections that are tied to teaching strategies and techniques are plentiful.

I have often used Gebhard's textbook in my TESOL methods courses (and will probably continue to do so) along with many similar others, but I also often wondered how different the content and knowledge in the book would be if it had been written by, for example, a scholar of color from the Middle East, North Africa, or somewhere else. My domestic students (mostly White US students) appreciate the book, and if they have some teaching abroad experience, they relate even more easily. They draw connections often and identify with the author to a large extent because their intersectional identities are reflected and reconstructed while their experiences are centralized and privileged through Gebhard's voice in the book. How about the experiences of the other teachers in the classroom? What do they find from themselves and their lives in Gebhard's voice? In my current teaching context at the University of Arizona, most of the students who take my TESOL methods course happen to be ethnic/racial minorities. Likewise, most of the students to whom they will teach English as an additional language in the US, regardless of the setting (K-12, college, etc.), will also involve ethnically/racially diverse students who do not speak English as their first language. I feel morally and ethically responsible for ensuring that my students' experiences and identities in teaching ESL, and their prospective students' experiences and identities in learning it, not be constructed only by White scholars.

One of the initial changes I made to my TESOL methods courses was to include the work by the scholars who fall outside of the dominant scholar demographic profile but contribute to knowledge production in the areas of TESOL methodology. This was not to replace the texts or readings written by White Western scholars but to diversify the readings and provide space for scholars whose perspectives and stories are usually untold and unheard in the Western classroom. Surprisingly (or maybe not so), TESOL methods books written by non-Western or non-European scholars of color based in non-Western or non-European countries are almost non-existent. Fortunately, however, their work is available in academic journals and other academic venues. Also in efforts to highlight intersectionality and aim for a decolonial TESOL teacher education, my current TESOL methodology syllabus includes a student-led weekly discussion activity for which each class member must choose three articles to lead discussions in small groups. At least one of the articles must be written in a language other than English or published in a journal not based in the Global North. By integrating this work into my syllabi, course discussion, and assessment practices, my hope is that the audiences in my classrooms can see that there are scholars with different intersectional identities who are personally, academically, culturally, and sociopolitically positioned differently in relation to social inequalities that exist in the context of English language teaching. As the students engage with these readings, they have an opportunity to see what sociopolitical discourses are dominant (or ignored) across diverse contexts, how knowledges are built in and through the articles, and how power and ideologies are constructed in a wide variety of research and teaching settings. We can begin to understand the complexities associated with social inequality and all forms of -isms (e.g., racism) in relation to English language teaching/learning when we start paying attention to the knowledge produced by *all* in diverse sociopolitical contexts.

Questioning, naming, and labeling

As I stated earlier, an intersectional pedagogy allows us to challenge stereotypical understandings about, or homogeneous descriptions of, English language learners and teachers. It also allows us to understand the variety of inequalities that English language learners experience. Neither of these points is adequately addressed in most current TESOL methods books. Rather, English language learners are treated as one group of language learners, and the books usually present a "one-size fits all" methodology that the readers are encouraged to adapt in their own teaching contexts. There is usually an emphasis on individual differences but understanding and appreciating individual differences in the language classroom is not the same as understanding how social categories intersect and work together in marginalizing some learners while empowering others. Furthermore, the label "English language learner" itself is not intersectional in nature. It not only prioritizes English, but also capitalizes on the linguistic identity in isolation ignoring all other sociocultural assets as well as multicultural and multilingual identities English learners draw upon in the learning process (Colombo, Tigert, and Montecillo Leider 2019). In my initial years of teaching TESOL methods courses, just like the methodology textbooks, I treated English language learners as one learner group. I also realized that most of my students held certain, unchallenged beliefs about English language learners.

For several years now, I have begun the first day of class with a critical discussion of English language learners in the US and global TESOL contexts through an intersectional lens. Since the MA TESL students in my current program typically pursue diverse teaching career options (e.g., K-12 ESL, refugee/community ESL, English abroad), I avoid focusing on one particular context or learner group. I ask the class to define who English language learners are and then reflect on the definition. I ask teachers to consider how, even in the same ESL classroom, various intersections shape learners' access to resources differently as well as their ultimate educational experiences. As teachers consider multiple intersections (race and language; ethnicity, gender, and socioeconomic class; age and disability, etc.) they realize how those intersections complicate the identities and experiences of English language learners. Teachers I have worked with usually assume that English language learning immigrants come from low socioeconomic backgrounds, speak limited English, and have lower levels of education. While these assumptions are more or less accurate, as the current demographics show (see Pew Research Center 2020), digging a bit deeper and looking at the existing statistics actually offers a much more complex picture. Within the immigrant population in the US, there are stark differences among the nation's immigrant groups in terms of educational attainment, citizenship status, economic status, English proficiency, and so on. I ask the teachers to think about the local ESL non-profit community program in our town where volunteers teach English to individuals from different backgrounds, but mostly immigrants and refugees. A wealthy Asian female who holds citizenship, a White European male on an F-1 visa, and a Black Muslim with fluent English in the same ESL classroom will all experience privilege and subordination differently, and their access to educational resources within and outside the classroom will possibly look very different too.

Race, ethnicity, and linguistic background intersect often in describing English language learners (Motha 2014). It is therefore a useful practice to think about the ethnic/racial labels we use in describing certain groups of English language learners and consider them in broader sociopolitical contexts. For example, Vásquez Jiménez argues that

> Bluntly stated, "Hispanic" erases our Blackness, Africanness and Indigeneity by centering whiteness. How so? Well as seen in the previous section when we were grounding the term "Hispanic", in one of its most simplistic form, it means "as of Spain"; therefore, it is actually then solely inclusive to people's connection to Europe, Europeanness, white, whiteness and essentially Euro-whiteness. As a result, since the discourse of "Hispanic" includes solely identities that are Eurocentric, it then is exclusionary to anything that is not of a Eurocentric identity.
>
> 2018: 115

Salinas and Lozano acknowledge that the alternative term Latinx, on the other hand, "challenges the ideologies of language, culture, and gender, and is a way to recognize the importance of the intersectionality of social identities" (2019: 303). They claim that the term is "inclusive in that it recognizes the intersectionality of sexuality, language, ethnicity, culture, geography, and phenotype" but also note the critique offered by numerous scholars for the use of the term. For some, the term Latinx is "a blatant form of linguistic imperialism, that it is being used in the United States only, and that its use cannot be considered as 'speaking Spanish'" (2019: 306) as well as its failure in representing intersecting areas of privilege and oppression.

In engaging in the discussions of naming and labeling, my goal is not to dictate how individuals should self-identify, but to show that the commonly used, taken-for-granted labels that we use to describe English language learners are never neutral, and the labels we choose in describing them serve to understand and reproduce certain discourses, ideologies, and intersectional identities. Approaching labels through an intersectional lens allows us to unpack the complexities in learner and teacher identities as well as their experiences.

Making invisible identities visible

In the early years of my teaching TESOL methods courses, there was a disconnect between what I was teaching and what I was researching. Over time, I have begun to integrate my research on identity and agency and other relevant identity literature into the content of my TESOL methods courses. Inspired by

Kist (2017), who describes how he integrated a multimodal autobiography assignment into his teaching, I included a similar assignment for my students. For teachers to be able to understand intersectional identities of their students, they should be able to analyze and understand their own intersectional identities first as well as the privileged and subordinate positions that they might hold in certain contexts. The assignment required the course participants to create their language-oriented memoirs and narrate them as multimodal texts. This was also a useful way for the classroom community to get to know each other at the start of the semester and build a close learning community.

The initial experience with this assignment showed to me two things. First, many students had not learnt about intersectionality, and their analysis of their own experiences lacked criticality. Adopting a critical lens seemed to be more challenging for those who came from historically oppressed communities or minoritized backgrounds. Second, some course participants could make connections between their language learning/teaching experiences in relation to other identity aspects, but they focused only on their minoritized identities. However, an intersectionality lens places the emphasis not only on subordination or oppression but also privilege. To encourage them more in their critical thinking, I added an explicit item to the assignment guidelines, which prompted the teachers to think about and more explicitly express their own social class, ethnicity, race, age, etc., in relation to English language teaching and learning.

An intersectionality lens pushes the teachers to more critically reflect on their experiences and go beyond the typical remarks, such as "I learned English because it was mandatory in the school curriculum" or "I learned other languages because I had such a strong interest and talent at a very young age." It helps them make their invisible intersectional identities visible. For example, a White American Muslim teacher narrated her experience of often being asked "where are you from?," especially by her ESL students. Clearly, the scarf she was wearing positioned her *less* American in the eyes of her students, despite the fact that she was born and raised in the US and spoke English as her mother tongue. The autobiography assignment serves as an introduction to intersectionality, and over time, many teachers learn how to connect course readings and discussions to intersectionality. Another assignment, ESL class observation reports, is also an opportunity for teachers to engage in an intersectionality analysis and "interrogate their own assumptions about others' behavior and to reflect on what they were drawn to observe" (Grzanka 2017: 71). They also better understand the shifts that they and their students experience "in belonging to dominant and subordinate groups depending on location" (Greenwood 2017: 33). This is especially eye-opening for international or transnational student-teachers, as they make sense of the shifting meanings of their ethnic, racial, linguistic identities and the intersectionality of all those in a new country. These vulnerable and sometimes uncomfortable narratives are important to be heard so that teachers can understand that English language teaching is beyond teaching the language itself; it is rather identity work and a sociopolitical act.

Push-back

Designing and teaching a course through an intersectional framework has many benefits, but it is not always a smooth process. At various times, I myself have experienced several "push-backs" from the teachers in my classes. Some teachers insist on perceiving their students all the same regardless of their differences and intersectionalities. Similar perceptions are widely reported in the scholarly literature (e.g., Mellom et al. 2018; Reeves 2004; Ullucci and Battey 2011). There are also teachers who understand the TESOL curricula through firm boundaries and believe that the issues of identity, intersectionality, -isms, and other forms of oppression or subordination should not be addressed in a TESOL methods course but rather in other courses, such as multicultural education or English sociolinguistics. It is also common that some teachers perceive a TESOL methodology constructed through an intersectional lens as "opiniated" or as a "political agenda," an observation also noted by Sensoy and DiAngelo (2017). Some of these teachers acknowledge the minoritized experiences of others, but they claim that such inequalities would not exist in their own classrooms and do not think an intersectional approach would be relevant to their own teaching contexts.

While individual or group experience is essential in intersectionality and intersectional pedagogy supports the integration of personal experience to academic content, such an approach does not make the methodology or pedagogy a personal, political agenda. I often point out that the inequalities and privileges experienced by individuals with certain intersectional identities are systematically documented across time and settings through empirical evidence in publications. The empirical studies as well as the statistical data (e.g., governmental, educational) that show inequalities in educational attainment in relation to certain social categories clearly demonstrate that these sociopolitical issues, which affect every aspect of our profession and practice, are neither an opinion nor a personal agenda. By doing so, perhaps unwillingly, I realize and acknowledge that I reproduce the highly problematic discourse in regard to knowledge production— the very same discourse that I resist being part of and am critical of in this chapter. As I offer "evidence" for substantiating the well-known, longstanding sociopolitical forms of oppression, I strive to put the human experience and narratives under the spotlight. Nevertheless, this conflicting practice is still something I struggle with and work on.

An important element in intersectional pedagogy or any kind of critical praxis is "change" or "transformation." Most often, some teachers push back because what they are presented with does not match with their core beliefs about learners or teaching or even themselves. The "change" or "transformation" may make them feel uncomfortable. I do not see my role as a teacher educator or course instructor through these terms either. I am not in the classroom to change teachers' beliefs or practices, nor do I ever expect us to hold the same beliefs about the English language, English language learners and teachers, and TESOL teacher education. Rather, I present the different ways of approaching "knowledge" and different ways of knowing, but what teachers do with the *knowledges* they are presented with is completely up to them.

Moving Forward

As stated early in this chapter, we live in a changing world. Various communities have racial, ethnic, gendered, or socioeconomic struggles that are exacerbated due to increasing global inequality almost on a daily basis. As Hanstedt asserts, "the parameters are changing. The tools and technologies are changing. We live in a wicked world, and unpredictable world. We need wicked graduates with wicked competencies" (2018: 4). He then asks, "this is an ambitious goal, one that some might see as problematic. After all, is it really our job as academics to engineer social, political, and economic change?" (2018: 4). His response is one I fully agree with: "perhaps this is not our job. But neither is it our job to create mindless individuals who simply do as they are told" (2018: 4). Indeed, the teachers and teacher candidates whom we train in TESOL programs will be prepared to tackle the consequences of the global issues in their classrooms, and understand and work with their students better, when they are not only passive receivers of knowledge but also sociopolitically aware, culturally sensitive, and critically responsive. It is thus necessary to situate the English language and English language teaching always in a sociopolitical context and implement an intersectional pedagogy in TESOL teacher training.

In this chapter, I describe three major ways of integrating intersectionality into my teaching of TESOL methodology. First, I argue that the construction of a teaching methodology through White Western perspectives alone offers a limited sociopolitical view and is therefore problematic. Like Case, I feel "professionally and ethnically responsible for making sure students from a broad range of backgrounds feel represented in the course materials and get the message that their identities are worthy of academic study" (2017: 2). I aim for a complex pedagogy or methodology that introduces different ways of knowing through diverse voices of scholars and researchers with varying intersectional identities, diverse experiences, and from different geographical locations. Such methodology is necessary and useful in understanding intersecting forms of power, the status quo, and oppression manifested differently in different contexts. I also encourage teachers in my classes to approach English language learner groups intersectionally so that they can understand complexities of the self and "invisible within-group diversity" (Case 2017: 2). Challenging taken-for-granted identity labels frequently used in the TESOL methodology as well as personal biases and assumptions about learner groups is a crucial step toward this goal. Furthermore, I believe that teachers can approach this complexity by understanding how intersectionality works in their own lives first and a careful consideration of how the intersectionality that they experience influences their perceptions, beliefs, professional interactions, and classroom pedagogy and practices.

Intersectionality capitalizes on the oppressive sociopolitical realities in diverse contexts and the role of the many social categories and intersecting forms of power in creating and sustaining such realities. It aims for change and transformation, for which, besides theory and research, meaningful actions (e.g., course design, community engagement, professional development) for disrupting oppressive realities are necessary. Given this complexity, an intersectional pedagogy is neither simple nor does it have straightforward guidelines. Mistakes are inevitable in its implementation, and resistance from the student audience can be discouraging. Along with critical self-reflections and discipline-wide engagement with intersectionality, an intersectional framework will, in my opinion, help advance TESOL methodology. As Case emphasizes, "more publications of innovative ideas and outcomes are essential across disciplines and within interdisciplinary spaces" (2017: 19).

Conclusion

Johnson argues that:

> if the goal of L2 teacher education is to prepare the individual teacher to function in the professional world of L2 teaching, then it is critical to account for how an

individual's activities shape and are shaped by the social, cultural, and historical macro-structures which constitute that professional world.

2009: 77

This understanding is important as these structures also contribute to inequalities and injustices in educational environments. If we want to truly advocate for English language learners as teachers and teacher educators, we cannot pretend that social injustices do not exist in our classrooms. Intersectionality is a lens that we can use to make sense of those injustices and develop the necessary tools, skills, and strategies to question, challenge, and change them. I am encouraged and inspired by Greenwood's remarks, by which I would like to conclude this chapter:

> In the classroom, privilege has many sources: white privilege, male privilege, heterosexual privilege, class privilege, and others. Each comes with its own set of invisible, unearned advantages (McIntosh 1988) that facilitate comfort and performance in educational contexts and confer attributions of intellectual competence to some but not others. Although these privileges arise from different sources, all operate to create, sustain, and legitimate inequalities in the classroom. Raising intersectional awareness about the ways these intersections operate in the classroom is not easy because privileged students may be defensive and resistant, but it is a vital component of social justice curriculum in any discipline.

2017: 37

References

Barkhuizen, G., P. Benson, and A. Chik (2013), *Narrative Inquiry in Language Teaching and Learning Research*, New York: Routledge.

Case, K., ed. (2017), *Intersectional Pedagogy: Complicating Identity and Social Justice*, New York: Routledge.

Clandinin, D. J. (2016), *Engaging in Narrative Inquiry*, New York: Routledge.

Collins, P. H., and S. Bilge (2020), *Intersectionality*, 2nd edition, Hoboken, NJ: Wiley.

Colombo, M., J. M. Tigert, and C. Montecillo Leider (2019), "Positioning Teachers, Positioning Learners: Why We Should Stop Using the Term English Learners," *TESOL Journal*, 10: e432. https://doi.org/10.1002/tesj.432.

Crenshaw, K. (1989), "Demarginalizing the Intersection of Race and Sex: A Black Feminist Critique of Antidiscrimination Doctrine, Feminist Theory, and Antiracist Politics," *University of Chicago Legal Forum*, 1989 (1): 139–167.

Crenshaw, K. (1991), "Mapping the Margins," *Stanford Law Review*, 43 (6): 1241–1299.

Farrell, T. S. C. (2016), "Anniversary Article: The Practices of Encouraging TESOL Teachers to Engage in Reflective Practice: An Appraisal of Recent Research Contributions," *Language Teaching Research*, 20 (2): 223–247.

Gebhard, J. G. (2017), *Teaching English as a Foreign or Second Language: A Teacher Self-Development and Methodology Guide*, Ann Arbor, MI: University of Michigan Press.

Greenwood, R. M. (2017), "Intersectionality Foundations and Disciplinary Adaptations: Highways and Byways," in K. A. Case (ed.), *Intersectional Pedagogy: Complicating Identity and Social Justice*, 26–45, New York: Routledge.

Grzanka, P. R. (2017), "Undoing the Psychology of Gender: Intersectional Feminism and Social Science Pedagogy," in K. A. Case (ed.), *Intersectional Pedagogy: Complicating Identity and Social Justice*, 62–81, New York: Routledge.

Hanstedt, P. (2018), *Creating Wicked Students: Designing Courses for a Complex World*, Sterling, VA: Stylus Publishing.

Johnson, K. E. (2009), *Second Language Teacher Education: A Sociocultural Perspective*, New York: Routledge.

Kayi-Aydar, H., M. Varghese, and G. Vitanova (2022), "Intersectionality for TESOL Education: Connecting Theory and Justice Pedagogy," *CATESOL Journal*, 33: 1. http://www.catesoljournal.org/wp-content/uploads/2022/08/CJ33-1_Kayi-Aydar_Varghese_Vitanova.pdf.

Kist, W. (2017), "Life Moments in Texts: Analyzing Multimodal Memoirs of Preservice Teachers," *English Journal*, 106 (3): 63–68.

Maddamsetti, J. (2020), "Intersectional Identities and Teaching Practice in an Elementary General Classroom: A Case Study of a Plurilingual Teacher Candidate," *Journal of Language, Identity & Education*, 19 (5): 342–358.

McIntosh, P. (1988), "White Privilege and Male Privilege: A Personal Account of Coming to See Correspondences through Work in Women's Studies," Working Paper No. 189, Wellesley, MA: Wellesley Centers for Women.

Mellom, P. J., R. Straubhaar, C. Balderas, M. Ariail, and P. R. Portes (2018), "'They Come With Nothing': How Professional Development in a Culturally Responsive Pedagogy Shapes Teacher Attitudes Towards Latino/a English Language Learners," *Teaching and Teacher Education*, 71: 98–107.

Motha, S. (2014), *Race, Empire, and English Language Teaching: Creating Responsible and Ethical Anti-Racist Practice*, New York: Teachers College Press.

Pew Research Center (2020), "Key Findings about U.S. Immigrants," August 20, Washington, DC: Pew Research Center. https://www.pewresearch.org/fact-tank/2020/08/20/key-findings-about-u-s-immigrants/.

Polat, N., L. Mahalingappa, and H. Kayi-Aydar (eds.) (2021), *The Preparation of Teachers of English as an Additional Language Around the World: Research, Policy, Curriculum and Practice*, Bristol: Multilingual Matters.

Reeves, J. (2004), "'Like Everybody Else': Equalizing Educational Opportunity for English Language Learners," *TESOL Quarterly*, 38 (1): 43–66.

Salinas, C., Jr., and A. Lozano (2019), "Mapping and Recontextualizing the Evolution of the Term Latinx: An Environmental Scanning in Higher Education," *Journal of Latinos and Education*, 18 (4): 302–315.

Sensoy, O., and R. DiAngelo (2017), *Is Everyone Really Equal? An Introduction to Key Concepts in Social Justice Education*, New York: Teachers College Press.

Song, J. (2016), "Emotions and Language Teacher Identity: Conflicts, Vulnerability, and Transformation," *TESOL Quarterly*, 50 (3): 631–654.

Steadman, A., H. Kayi-Aydar, and S. M. Vogel (2018), "From College Composition to ESL: Negotiating Professional Identities, New Understandings, and Conflicting Pedagogies," *System*, 76: 38–48.

Ullucci, K., and D. Battey (2011), "Exposing Color Blindness/Grounding Color Consciousness: Challenges for Teacher Education," *Urban Education*, 46 (6): 1195–1225.

Vásquez Jiménez, A. (2018), "Dismantling the White Supremacist Term and Discourse of 'Hispanic,'" in G. J. Sefa Dei and S. Hilowle (eds.), *Cartographies of Race and Social Difference*, 103–121, Cham: Springer.

Wolff, D., and P. I. De Costa (2017), "Expanding the Language Teacher Identity Landscape: An Investigation of the Emotions and Strategies of a NNEST," *Modern Language Journal*, 101 (S1): 76–90.

8

Teacher Identity in Critical Autoethnographic Narrative: Making Sense of the Political in the Personal

Bedrettin Yazan

Introduction

Language teacher identity (LTI) research has repeatedly suggested strong connections between teachers' identities, learning, and practices, and identity work is conceptualized as an inevitable part of teaching and learning to teach languages (Clarke 2009; Danielewicz 2001). Recent scholarship has revised this suggestion by further centering identity and maintaining that teacher learning is identity learning (Beijaard 2019). One of the major implications of research on LTI is to integrate identity into the curriculum of teacher education practices and center teacher learning activities on teachers' identity work (De Costa and Norton 2017; Kanno and Stuart 2011; Lindahl and Yazan 2019; Varghese et al. 2016). Responding to that research implication as a language teacher educator and researcher of teacher education, I decided to make LTI a central component in one of my teacher education courses. I designed an assignment for that purpose which I called "critical autoethnographic narrative" (CAN) (Yazan 2019a, 2019b) and incorporated it in my graduate level linguistics class in Spring 2018 (Yazan 2018). The current study, which I report on in this chapter, draws upon the data of one teacher candidate, Kateryna,[1] from the implementation of CAN that semester. I address the following research question in Kateryna's case: *How does Kateryna construct her language teacher identity in her semester-long CAN writing process?*

What is teacher identity?

In this study, I combine Olsen's (2016) definition of teacher identity with Varghese's critical perspective (Varghese et al. 2016) to LTI. Olsen foregrounds the complex and dynamic nature of teacher identity as a process and defines it as

> the collection of influences and effects from immediate contexts, prior constructs of self, social positioning, and meaning systems (each itself a fluid influence and all together an ever-changing construct) that become intertwined inside the flow of activity as a teacher simultaneously reacts to and negotiates given contexts and human relationships at given moments.
>
> 2016: 139; parentheses in original

Although Olsen's definition is a very comprehensive one, it would better capture teacher identity's complexity if it were to explicitly include teachers' imaginations and aspirations about their future self, in addition to "prior constructs of self." Therefore, I rely on the theorization of imagined teacher identity that was offered by earlier scholars (Barkhuizen 2016; Kanno and Norton 2003; Yazan and Peercy 2018) using the seminal work of Anderson (1991) and Wenger (1998). Wenger's (1998) theorization of imagination as part of identity construction and becoming part of a community of practice helps understand the role of imagination in language teacher identity. That is, through imagination, language teachers

> include in [their] identities other meanings, other possibilities, other perspectives, ... recognize [their] own experience as reflecting broader patterns, connections, and configurations, ... see [their] practices as continuing histories that reach far into the past, and ... conceive of new developments, explore alternatives, and envision possible futures.
>
> Wenger 1998: 178

As part of their ongoing professional growth, teachers re-negotiate identities with possible new dimensions across time and space which orient their current engagement in teaching practice (see also the concept of "visioning" in Duffy 2002 and Hammerness 2003).

Additionally, Olsen's (2016) theorization focuses on "social positioning" and "meaning systems" which allude to the discursive dimension of teacher identity. Yet, for the purpose of the current study, the discursive dimension should be further articulated with a critical approach to explain the connection between micro, mezzo, and macro levels of language teaching. Therefore, I rely on Varghese's critical theorization of LTI as discursive construction "within hierarchically organized racial, gendered, linguistic, religious, and classed categories and processes within teachers' personal lives as well as in and through their teacher education programs, classrooms, schools, disciplines and nation-states" (Varghese et al. 2016: 546). Varghese's theorization unpacks the "meaning systems" and "immediate contexts" (in Olsen's definition) that influence teacher identity construction.

Background literature on language teacher identity

Identity can serve as "a research frame" to explore teachers' learning situated within sociocultural contexts and "a pedagogical tool" to orchestrate teacher education practices to provide identity-oriented teacher learning experiences (Olsen 2008). In second language teacher education (SLTE) research, scholars have used LTI as "a research frame" considerably more than "a pedagogical tool" since the late 1990s. That is, LTI has presented SLTE researchers with new dimensions as a research framework to understand how language teachers learn to teach and grow as professionals with beliefs, values, and priorities which are inseparable from their personal biographies. Utilizing the LTI framework, scholars have constructed an extensive research base that theorizes and explores, in varying contexts:[2] (a) the relationship between language teachers' professional identities, learning, and practice (Martel 2015; Varghese 2006); (b) the relationship between professional identities and other social identities (language, culture, race, gender, sexual orientation, class, religion/faith) with corresponding privilege/marginalization (Duff and Uchida 1997; Golombek and Jordan 2005; Motha 2006; Park 2017; Sánchez-Martín 2021); (c) the relationship between LTI and teachers' emotions (Benesch 2017; Song 2016), agency (Kayi-Aydar et al. 2019), investment (Barkhuizen 2016), and immunity (Hiver and Dörnyei 2017); (d) the influence of ideologies/discourses on LTI, with asymmetrical power relations (Rudolph, Yazan, and Rudolph 2019; Sayer 2012); (e) the influence of (imagined) professional community membership on LTI (Yazan and Peercy 2018); (f) the individual construction/customization of professional discourses as part of LTI (Ilieva 2010); and (g) the contradictory nature of LTI with corresponding tensions (Menard-Warwick 2014). This research base largely converges on the premise that LTI is an ongoing, fluid, dynamic, and contextual-bound process which involves undulations through human interactions with colleagues, administrators, students, and parents (Barkhuizen 2017; Yazan and Lindahl 2020).

Despite the extensive use of LTI as a research frame, there are not many studies in SLTE which report on the ways LTI can be used as a pedagogical tool (Olsen 2008: 5), pedagogical intervention (Morgan and Clarke 2011), or pedagogical innovation (Martel 2018; Trent 2014). Most of the above-cited research studies concluded their reports with emphatic calls for LTI to become an explicit goal in SLTE practices. However, the research that uses LTI as a pedagogical frame has yet to grow. Potential reasons for that dearth of research include: (a) such practice-based research would need recalibration of teacher education activities to situate LTI as the main focus, which may not be possible in all teacher education programs; (b) teacher educators would need to be introduced to the pertinent LTI research that explains the relationship between teacher learning and identity with potential benefits of an identity approach to teacher education; and (c) identity could resist modularizing and curricularizing (Morgan 2004) since it does not lend itself to integration into standards-based teacher education infused with neoliberal ideologies. Also, the fact that there are not many published studies does not mean that teacher educators are not actually integrating identity-focused teacher learning activities in their practices. Below, I briefly review the studies that report on the design and use of identity-oriented activities for teachers.

Two of these studies focus in particular on the relationship between teacher candidates' language identities and professional identities. Canagarajah (2020) relies on the concepts of transnationalism and translingualism and designs literacy autobiography as a writing genre and research method for teachers of literacy. He uses this narrative-based teacher-learning activity for student teachers to negotiate their transnational and translingual identities which are inseparable from their professional teacher identities. Lindahl, Fallas-Escobar, and Henderson (2021) use the multimodal, metaphorical activities of "language ideology trees" and "language portraits" (Busch 2012; Coffey 2015) in their undergraduate ESL methods courses with elementary and secondary teacher candidates. Here the teacher educators' goal was to support teacher candidates' understanding of the relationship between language ideologies and their professional identities through reflections mediated by those two activities. One study describes the use of an extracurricular learning design, namely race-based caucuses (Varghese, Daniels, and Park 2019). The teacher educators constructed communities of elementary teacher candidates and met with them informally outside the usual teacher education program over a semester. In such meetings, the teacher educators facilitated conversations around race and racialization, and teacher candidates were invited to share their pertinent experiences. Varghese and colleagues explicitly designed these caucuses to help teacher candidates see the relationship between their racialized identities and teacher identities, both of which are conceived as part of their professional growth.

Additionally, two studies integrated LTI in a teacher education course over the semester. Yazan (2019b) used "critical autoethnographic narrative" as a semester-long writing activity for teacher candidates in a graduate-level linguistics course. The teacher educator provided feedback over four installments of this narrative to help teacher candidates story and analyze their past and recent experiences with language learning and teaching. Based on autoethnography's methodological affordances, the main goal was to support teacher candidates' understanding of their professional identities situated in sociocultural and sociopolitical contexts. Lastly, Martel and Yazan (2021) redesigned an entire language-teaching practicum course to infuse an identity approach into each course activity throughout the semester, from CV preparation to teaching observations and feedback conferences. The goal was to help teacher candidates develop an identity lens to understand their learning through this course, in which one teacher candidate, Dave, started constructing his social justice teacher identity.

The activities above represent strategic integration of LTI in teacher education practices. LTI conceptually spans across micro, meso, and macro levels or layers of language education. If teacher candidates can gain a better understanding of their own identity development and construct an identity lens to view teaching and learning, they could better make the connection between the language classroom and sociocultural discourses in their professional lives. Thereby, the integration of LTI can make a significant contribution to strengthening a critical, sociopolitical agenda in SLTE and pushing toward social justice language education.

Description and Implementation of Critical Autoethnographic Narrative

Back in 2018, I designed CAN as my response to the calls in the research on LTI for making identity one of the main foci of teacher education practices (Kanno and Stuart 2011; Morgan and Clarke 2011). This response was reflective of and characterized by my identity as a teacher educator and as a researcher of language teacher education, and I view the period of design and implementation of CAN as identity work for myself (in relation to agency, emotions, and commitment/investment) which I have explored in my writings (Yazan 2018, 2019c, 2022). Theoretically, I built CAN upon prior scholarship I had been following in educational linguistics: critical language teacher education (Hawkins 2011; Hawkins and Norton 2009), autoethnographic writing as critical identity work (Canagarajah 2012; Park 2013; Solano-Campos 2014), narrative as teacher learning (Johnson and Golombek 2011), and narrative as identity construction (Barkhuizen 2016). I articulated the goal of CAN as follows: to provide language teacher candidates with discursive and experiential space to narrate and analyze significant past and recent language-related incidents and to explore their own identity construction as a language learner, user, and teacher *vis-à-vis* other pertinent social identity categories situated within sociopolitical and sociocultural discourses (Yazan 2019b). Following the methodological affordances of autoethnography (see Holman Jones, Adams, and Ellis 2016; Hughes and Pennington 2017; Sughrua 2020), teacher candidates author their identities by examining the relationship between self, others, and cultures. They use "personal experience to examine and/or critique cultural experience" (Holman Jones, Adams, and Ellis 2016). More specifically, the following four characteristics make CAN projects autoethnographic, different from "autobiographical narratives" (West 1995), "literacy autobiographies" (Canagarajah 2020), and "recurrent storying" (Golombek and Johnson 2021): "(1) purposefully commenting on/critiquing of culture and cultural practices, (2) making contributions to existing research, (3) embracing vulnerability with purpose, and (4) creating a reciprocal relationship with audiences in order to compel a response" (Holman Jones, Adams, and Ellis 2016: 22).

CAN is a semester-long scaffolded teacher learning activity of writing and researching identities which is completed with four installments of writing ensued by one-on-one feedback sessions from the instructor (see Table 8.1 for the timeline). In the initial installments, I encourage the teacher candidates to focus on writing as many stories as they can recall from past or recent experiences and to talk to their family members and friends if they see it fitting. I review each installment and give written feedback before I meet with every teacher candidate individually to go over the written feedback and discuss next steps in their writing. These individual feedback sessions give me the opportunity to clarify my expectations, help the teacher candidates understand what an autoethnographic writing is, and collaboratively discuss how they would like to construct their CAN. What makes their work autoethnographic is the focus on the analysis of their stories or storied experiences to understand and discuss the complex ways in which ideologies circulate in societal discourses, construct and normalize hierarchies in our day-to-day language interactions, and attempt to shape our beliefs, priorities, values, and practices (see Pavlenko and Blackledge 2004). My main expectation is for teacher candidates to identify those ideologies in their stories and critique/resist/subvert them discursively and performatively (Sughrua 2016, 2020) as they engage in the writing of their CAN.

Table 8.1 Implementation of CAN in Spring 2018[3]
Source: Adapted from Yazan (2019a).

CAN activity	Timeline	Length
Installment 1 submission	February 1, 2018	6–10 pages
Installment 1 feedback session	February 8–10, 2018	41–61 minutes
Installment 2 submission	February 23, 2018	11–25 pages
Installment 2 feedback session	March 8–12, 2018	52–73 minutes
Discussion board post	March 29, 2018	899–1,576 words
Installment 3 submission	April 13, 2018	24–72 pages
Installment 3 feedback session	April 19–20, 2018	29–69 minutes
Mapping out CAN	April 19, 2018	20 minutes
Rubric construction pair work	April 19, 2018	20 minutes
Individual presentation	April 26, 2018	15–40 minutes
Installment 4 submission	April 30, 2018	21–88 pages
Installment 4 feedback session	May 1–7, 2018	50–93 minutes

What I have observed so far in the earlier stages of this assignment is that as teacher candidates keep writing their stories, they keep remembering more to tell. I always frame the scope/criterion for inclusion broadly, by telling them to story any language-related experience of theirs or others around them. When they share an experience in class as part of a large group conversation, I ask them to consider storying that experience to include in their CAN. The same occurs in individual feedback sessions—that is, I encourage the teacher candidates to consider incorporating the language-related experiences they remember during our conversations.

Later in the semester, we discuss potential readings where they can find theoretical approaches that they can use to analyze their stories. Most of those readings are part of our syllabus, but I create a separate folder that includes further readings in case the ones on the syllabus do not directly pertain to the focus of their CAN. Additionally, we devote class sessions to practice the analysis of their stories. I bring in unidentified data from prior research projects and we conduct collaborative data analysis in the class by using the following questions:

- Who is involved? What are the actors/agents?
- What has happened or is happening?
- What decisions are made?
- Who makes those decisions?

- What is the justification for those decisions?
- Who is expected to act on those decisions?
- What identity positions are assumed/enacted?
- What is the imagined/future decision, action, and identity?

Toward the end of the semester, I ask students to draw a concept map of their CAN in progress to practice visualizing and sharing their stories in multimodal texts. They can choose to modify that visual representation as they progress in their CAN writing, but the ultimate visual goes in their final submission. They also work in pairs to create a rubric in the class. Then, I construct one based on the ones they have co-created. I share that rubric (see an example in the Appendix) with the teacher candidates to receive their feedback and make sure we all have a clear understanding of what their final submission should include. Finally, in the last class meeting, I have the teacher candidates present their CAN to their classmates, and I encourage them to submit proposals to present at professional conferences.

Methods

In this study, I followed a qualitative research design which uses the data constructed in the pedagogical implementation of CAN in a teacher education course. I use a teacher candidate's (Kateryna's) data from the first iteration of the CAN project in Spring 2018 to address the following research question: *How does Kateryna construct her language teacher identity in her semester-long CAN writing process?* For that purpose, I analyze a qualitative dataset composed of four installments: one-on-one feedback sessions (FBS), discussion board posts (DBP), visual map of CAN, pair work conversation of rubric co-construction, and CAN presentation. My analysis was informed by Olsen's (2016) definition of teacher identity, Kanno and Norton's (2003) application of Anderson's (1991) and Wenger's (1998) concepts, imagination in language (teacher) identity construction (see Barkhuizen 2016), and Varghese's (2006) critical discursive approach to language teacher identity. That is, I used deductive analytical codes based on those scholars' theorization of teacher identity: "influence/effect from immediate contexts (i.e., personal lived experience, school, nation-state)," "prior construct of self," "future aspirations/imaginations," "social positioning," "meaning system," "response to/negotiation of context," "response to/negotiation of human relationship," and "hierarchically organized categories/processes."

Participant

Kateryna comes from an immigrant family that always consciously encouraged her preservation of home languages against the dominance of English through her schooling (see Figure 8.1 for her visual map of CAN). Her parents migrated from Ukraine to the USA when she was four years old. She grew up and went to school in the Miami (Florida) metropolitan area. She identifies herself as "a speaker of Ukrainian, Russian, English and Spanish" (CAN Installment 4) and stresses that her family's language policies and her motivation afforded her "this good language maintenance" (CAN presentation). "[M]y parents had established the norm that in the home I would speak only Ukrainian to them ... with Russian television on as daily exposure, listening to old Soviet and 90's music as well as indulging in old Souz-Multfilm cartoons" (Installment 1). Kateryna studied Russian as her major in college and completed TEFL (teaching English as a

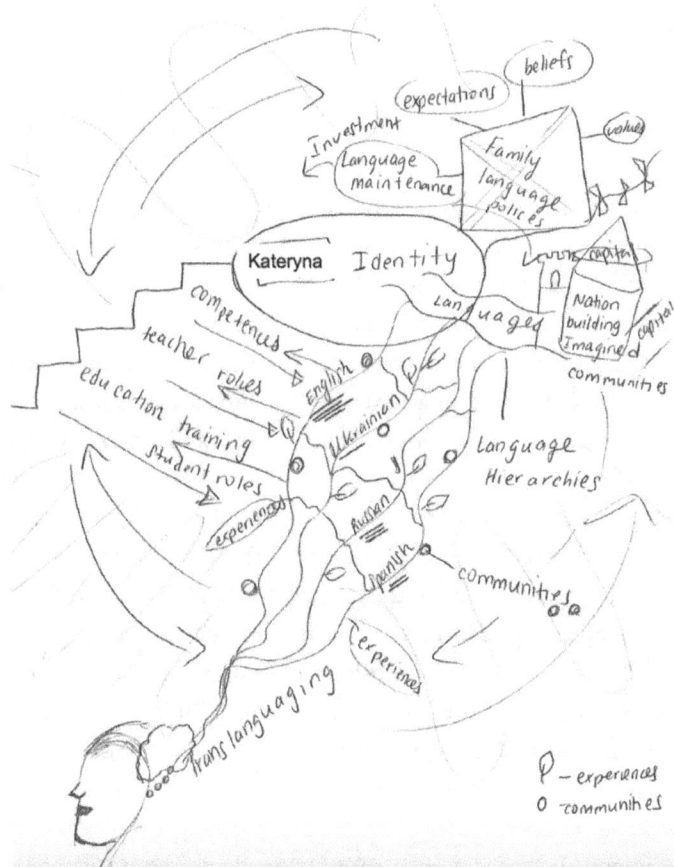

Figure 8.1 Visual map of Kateryna's CAN.

foreign language) certificate afterwards. As part of that certificate, she volunteered as a teaching assistant in K-12 ESL classes in Orlando, Florida. After that, she was awarded a Fulbright English Teaching Assistantship, through which she spent a year teaching English in Ufa, the capital of the Russian Republic of Bashkortostan.

At the time of the study, Kateryna was a graduate student in her second year of the MATESOL program at a large research university in the Southeast US. As part of the funding from the program, she received a stipend as a teaching assistant, whereby she worked in the intensive English program of the university, teaching writing to international college students in first-year composition classes. After completing the MATESOL program, she was hired as an adjunct instructor to keep teaching those composition classes.

Findings

Authoring her CAN, Kateryna constructs a language teacher identity with a critical perspective on linguistic and cultural diversity in schools. By making "the personal political" (Holman Jones 2005: 765) in the analysis of her lived experiences and observations, she (a) discusses the imagined nature of national identity and borders and positions herself as a crosser of "those nation-state borders both as a translingual and a transnational" (CAN Presentation); (b) unpacks complexities involved in her multilingual language use characterized by translanguaging; (c) problematizes the binaries (e.g., nativeness) in language education and argues "in negotiating those translingual and transcultural spaces, really none of the sort of binaries kind of apply to me and a lot of my experiences" (CAN Presentation); (d) examines the role of language in community membership (e.g., when becoming part of a local community thanks to her proficiency in Russian); (e) explores the relationship between language and sociopolitical forces (e.g., in the lack of Russian subtitles on Bashkir TV); (f) discusses and critiques ideologies involved in English-only schooling in the US (e.g., in first-year college composition classes) and in language hierarchies (e.g., between Bashkir and Russian, Creole and 'standard' English). In these analyses of her lived experiences, Kateryna enacts an identity of a language teacher with a critical perspective to language and its situatedness within sociopolitical discourses.

In the interest of space, I will share two excerpts here to demonstrate her critical language teacher identity that she constructs in her CAN writing. The first excerpt[4] comes from her Installment 1 and Kateryna discusses an observation from her field experience in a public elementary school which was part of her TEFL certificate program. She has added the second excerpt[5] to her Installment 3 in which she discusses a more recent tension from her classroom co-teaching which was part of her MATESOL program assistantship. As part of her making sense of autoethnography as a researcher and writing genre, she first shared that recent tension with me during our second face-to-face feedback session and asked if it would be appropriate to write about that tension in her CAN assignment.

"[H]er parents spoke Creole"

In this story, Kateryna shares a first-grade teacher's instructional decision in a classroom of multilingual and multicultural students. Kateryna discusses how that decision represents the teacher's subscription to and perpetuation of the ideologically-laden hierarchical relationship between Creole and English.

Excerpt 1

I observed and taught a lesson for a first-grade class in a public school county in Orlando. The class was a mix of races and ethnicities but overall no students had intentional English Second Language support. One student whose family is from Haiti was that week's Star Student. If a student was chosen to be a Star Student then throughout the course of the week the student would participate in various reward activities highlighting their accomplishments as a model learner. One of these activities included a letter from the student's parents praising their accomplishments and their child. After telling me about the letter, the first-grade teacher then swiftly proceeded to regard the opportunity as inaccessible to [student's name] since her parents spoke Creole. I smiled and remained silent, still not aware of how I was internalizing her comment. Now the more and more I recount this story in my mind and sometimes speak about it, the more enraged I become. This teacher, despite her well intentions, completely shut down an opportunity for her student to feel valued in both languages and possibly translate her parent's thoughts.

Furthermore, just because her parents do not write the letter in English does not mean that they cannot validate their daughter in their home language. I am sure that those hardworking immigrants are not illiterate and even if they are they can still speak to their daughter. These small invalidations, now categorized as microaggressions, are exactly how and why bilingual education is not fully integrated in the United States Education System.

CAN Installment 1

The analytical codes that I used for this excerpt were "response to/negotiation of human relationship," "response to/negotiation of context," and "hierarchically organized categories/processes." At the time of her observation, Kateryna "smiled and remained silent, still not aware of how I was internalizing her comment." As she told this story to herself and others multiple times, she kept thinking about her responses to and negotiation of what she observed on that day, and the human relationship between the teacher and herself and between the teacher and the student whose multilingual identity was invalidated in the classroom. What she wrote in her CAN is her most recent response to this observation. That is, she discusses the hierarchization of languages as she believes the teacher's decision discredited the legitimacy of Creole in her classroom. Kateryna explains what the teacher should have done or what she herself would have done if she were a teacher. Her explanation and response to what the teacher did are indexical of her teacher identity with a devotion to inclusivity of all languages that students bring to the school and help students preserve and claim ownership of their languages. Enacting that critical teacher identity in her writing, she closes her story with a response to and negotiation of the broader macro context of the US public school education that is shaped by dominant sociopolitical forces.

"[M]ulti-layered struggle of teaching academic writing"

In the story below, Kateryna brings in a contentious professional interaction (and ideological tension) between her mentor teacher and herself when teaching first-year college composition to international students. They had an instructional disagreement about whether or not multilingual students should be allowed to use "source materials" published in languages other than English when writing their papers.

> **Excerpt 2**
>
> We bring our ideologies as teachers into the classrooms. Even if we are not conscious or reflective of our beliefs, they reflect our teaching practices. These values and teaching dynamics are compounded in a co-teaching environment. In this case teachers need to be able to acknowledge and negotiate their teaching beliefs and ideologies. I was faced with a multi-layered struggle of teaching academic writing to non-native speakers and negotiating proper source usage. Some of my students wanted to use foreign language resources as some of their source materials and references. After the solvable problem of understanding

"what is a good source?" was tackled, the question of the language of the source material came to a point of contention between my co-teacher and I. My co-teacher believed that since this class is an English class the sources should be in English and we should not rely on Google translate for accuracy. From my perspective, I believe that as a second language learner it takes significantly more time to read, process and digest various academic articles which already have their own genre complexity and jargon in addition to the added complexity of working in the English language. I could relate to my own experiences of writing a diploma paper in Russian, for which I used both Russian language sources and English language sources. I would also play portions of written text on the Google Translate audio files in order to read faster and absorb information. When I asked other professors about what the best course of action would be, they replied, "well why can't you use foreign language materials?" In my own class, as an instructor and not a graduate student whose teaching depends on my assistantship as well as is influenced by my co-teacher, I would do just that. In this scenario I felt limited by the academic pecking order, unsure of exact curriculum requirements or deviations, and limited by my cooperation with my co-teacher. In the end we did compromise but I still felt as though my classroom authority was dominated by both the co-teacher but largely and more importantly by English Language Ideologies.

CAN Installment 3

I used the following codes when analyzing this excerpt for Kateryna's teacher identity: "influence/effect from immediate contexts," "prior construct of self," "social positioning," "response to/negotiation of human relationship," and "hierarchically organized categories/processes." Because this excerpt comes from Installment 3, I assume that her opening sentences and explicit reference to the role of ideologies are indicative of the class meetings and one-on-one feedback sessions which included discussions of ideologies and identities. She explicates the relationship and tensions between the English-only language policies in writing composition classes and her language teacher identity and practice. She relies on her lived experience as a second language learner/writer (prior construct of self) and explains her perspective as a language teacher. She acknowledges the complicated nature of this decision-making in a co-teaching setting. She is clearly certain about what classroom policies she would have in her classes if she were the instructor of the record, which is guided by her teacher identity. Although she felt disempowered by how institutional discourses position her as a graduate student dependent on her teaching assistantship, she asserted agency within the contextual constraints in order to learn "the best course of action" from her professors. This agency is indexical of her critical language teacher identity with resistance to English-only policies that seem to dominate the program without "exact curriculum requirements."

Discussion and Conclusion

In this chapter, I showcased my efforts as a teacher educator to contribute to the sociopolitical agenda in SLTE. These efforts are undergirded by the conceptual approach that focusing on identity in teacher education can provide a more nuanced understanding of the interconnection between micro, meso, and macro layers of language education (De Costa and Norton 2017; Douglas Fir Group 2016). CAN, as an identity-oriented teacher learning activity, has worked for me to help teacher candidates capture that nuance in understanding the sociopolitical situatedness of (a) languages, (b) language learning and teaching, and (c) themselves as teachers and users of languages. In the case of Kateryna, she particularly constructed a teacher identity with a critical perspective to language education. She parsed out the interplay between ideologies, teacher identity, and instructional policies, decisions, and actions. Observant of the "social positioning" in the classroom shaped by macro-level "meaning systems," she brought her past experiences into her current teacher identity construction (Olsen 2016), critiqued the hierarchical organization of languages which always positions English at the top (Varghese et al. 2016), and shared her imagined teacher identity by envisioning democratic, multilingual practices in her *own* future classroom (Barkhuizen 2016). In the two excerpts I presented above, she problematizes the dominance of English as the only legitimate language in the classroom and advocates for opportunities for students to deploy all their language resources as part of their learning in school settings. Kateryna justifies and bolsters this advocacy by bringing in her multilingual identity and corresponding past experiences. In the remainder of her CAN, she maintains this critical language teacher identity (see the cases of Mr. Martinez in the study by Shin and Rubio 2022 and Dave in Martel and Yazan 2021) as summarized in the initial section of findings.

This small-scale study reported in this chapter responds to the calls for the intentional integration of LTI in the practices of SLTE. It contributes to the critical language teacher education guided by "a view of situated language usage that is shaped through pervasive social, cultural and political ideologies and forces that serve to empower some people while marginalizing others" (Hawkins

2011: 2). My study findings corroborate the earlier studies which investigated language teachers' negotiation of identities in relation to dominant ideologies and those which examined teacher candidates' use of identity-oriented activities of teacher education. For example, Kateryna constructed her critical language teacher identity by resisting the teaching practices that perpetuate the ideologically-laden hierarchization of languages. This construction is similar to how language teachers in earlier studies (see Menard-Warwick 2014; Rudolph, Yazan, and Rudolph 2019; Sayer 2012; Varghese 2006) negotiated their identities through their agentive responses to the dominant ideologies in various socio-educational contexts. Additionally, Kateryna used CAN as an experiential, discursive, and performative (Sughrua 2016) space in which she re-storied and analyzed her lived experiences to construct her teacher identity in her writing. Over the semester, she asserted agency to engage in purposeful identity work and directed the contours of her identity construction in that writing. This use of storying and analysis of own experience confirms the effectiveness of such use of narrative in supporting identity-oriented teacher learning in earlier research (see Canagarajah 2020; Lindahl, Fallas-Escobar, and Henderson 2021; Martel and Yazan 2021; Varghese, Daniels, and Park 2019), which also relied on identity as a "pedagogical tool" (Olsen 2008). Lastly, writing her CAN, Kateryna worked toward developing her ideological clarity (Bartolomé 2004; Lindahl, Fallas-Escobar, and Henderson 2021) as an indication of her critical teacher identity. She identified ideologies that are influential upon her future professional practice, compared them to her own ideological orientation, and reflected on how those ideologies shape the asymmetrical power relations in the socio-educational context in which she will serve minoritized language learners.

Closing this chapter, I would like to share three caveats for the use of CAN based on the challenges I have had. First, whoever uses CAN should be aware that their identities as a teacher, teacher educator, and researcher will inform the implementation of CAN. For instance, how they believe learning, teaching, and teacher learning can/should occur will influence the direction of how they will use CAN in their teacher education courses. Second, teacher educators might find themselves having to alternate or shuttle between identities of teacher educator and researcher as they support the teacher candidates' CAN writing process. They might need to enact their researcher identity to support teacher candidates' analysis of lived experience. However, foregrounding their identities as teacher educators throughout the entire process could help them keep the identity-oriented purpose of CAN as the focus of their teacher education practices. Lastly, one full semester (*c*. 14–15 weeks) might not be sufficient for teacher candidates to understand the purpose of CAN, narrate all their stories about the nature, use, learning, and teaching of languages, and analyze those stories. Teacher candidates should always be encouraged to keep adding to their CAN as they take more teacher education courses and teach languages, as well as present and publish their work to share their stories with the broader community of language practitioners.

Acknowledgments

I am grateful to the editors, Peter De Costa and Özgehan Uştuk, for inviting me to contribute to this collection. Also, I am thankful to Peter Sayer who provided feedback on the presentation of this chapter in the AAAL 2021 online conference and to the peer reviewer and Amanda Giles who did a very careful read of my chapter and helped me strengthen it with their insightful comments. Lastly, I gratefully acknowledge Kateryna and all teacher candidates in my teacher education course in Spring 2018 for sharing their stories and using critical autoethnography as their teacher learning activity.

Notes

1. All names are pseudonyms.
2. Although I lay out the strands of LTI topics distinctly here, they tend to overlap to varying degrees in research studies cited.
3. Adapted from Yazan (2019a).
4. Interestingly, Kateryna kept this story (as is with minor edits) in her CAN until the third installment, but she chose not to include it in the final installment.
5. Kateryna kept this excerpt as is in Installment 4 of her CAN.

References

Anderson, B. (1991), *Imagined Communities: Reflections on the Origin and Spread of Nationalism*, London: Verso.
Barkhuizen, G. (2016), "A Short Story Approach to Analyzing Teacher (Imagined) Identities Over Time," *TESOL Quarterly*, 50 (3): 655–683.
Barkhuizen, G., ed. (2017), *Reflections on Language Teacher Identity Research*, New York: Routledge.

Bartolomé, L. I. (2004), "Critical Pedagogy and Teacher Education: Racializing Prospective Teachers," *Teacher Education Quarterly*, 31 (1): 97–122.

Beijaard, D. (2019), "Teacher Learning as Identity Learning: Models, Practices, and Topics," *Teachers and Teaching: Theory and Practice,* 25 (1): 1–6.

Benesch, S. (2017), *Emotions in English Language Teaching: Exploring Teachers' Emotion Labor*, New York: Routledge.

Busch, B. (2012), "The Linguistic Repertoire Revisited," *Applied Linguistics*, 33 (5): 503–523.

Canagarajah, A. S. (2012), "Teacher Development in a Global Profession: An Autoethnography," *TESOL Quarterly*, 46 (2): 258–279.

Canagarajah, A. S. (2020), *Transnational Literacy Autobiographies as Translingual Writing*, New York: Routledge.

Clarke, M. (2009), "The Ethico-Politics of Teacher Identity," *Educational Philosophy and Theory*, 41 (2): 185–200.

Coffey, S. (2015), "Reframing Teachers' Language Knowledge through Metaphor Analysis of Language Portraits," *Modern Language Journal*, 99 (3): 500–514.

Danielewicz, J. (2001), *Teaching Selves: Identity, Pedagogy, and Teacher Education*, Albany, NY: SUNY Press.

De Costa, P. I., and B. Norton, eds. (2017), "Transdisciplinarity and Language Teacher Identity," *Modern Language Journal*, 101 (S1). https://doi.org/10.1111/modl.12368.

Douglas Fir Group (2016), "A Transdisciplinary Framework for SLA in a Multilingual World," *Modern Language Journal*, 100 (S1): 19–47.

Duff, P. A., and Y. Uchida (1997), "The Negotiation of Teachers' Sociocultural Identities and Practices in Postsecondary EFL Classrooms," *TESOL Quarterly*, 31 (3): 451–486.

Duffy, G. G. (2002), "Visioning and the Development of Outstanding Teachers," *Reading Research and Instruction*, 41: 331–344.

Golombek, P. R., and K. E. Johnson (2021), "Recurrent Restorying through Language Teacher Narrative Inquiry," *System*, 102: 102601. https://doi.org/10.1016/j.system.2021.102601.

Golombek, P., and S. R. Jordan (2005), "Becoming 'Black Lambs' not 'Parrots': A Poststructuralist Orientation to Intelligibility and Identity," *TESOL Quarterly*, 39 (3): 513–533.

Hammerness, K. (2003) "Learning to Hope, or Hoping to Learn? The Role of Vision in the Early Professional Lives of Teachers," *Journal of Teacher Education*, 54 (1): 43–56.

Hawkins, M. R., ed. (2011), *Social Justice Language Teacher Education*, Bristol: Multilingual Matters.

Hawkins, M., and B. Norton (2009), "Critical Language Teacher Education," in A. Burns and J. Richards (eds.), *Cambridge Guide to Second Language Teacher Education*, 30–39, New York: Cambridge University Press.

Hiver, P., and Z. Dörnyei (2017), "Language Teacher Immunity: A Double-Edged Sword," *Applied Linguistics*, 38 (3): 405–423.

Holman Jones, S. (2005), "Autoethnography: Making the Personal Political," in N. K. Denzin and Y. S. Lincoln (eds.), *The SAGE Handbook of Qualitative Research*, 763–791, Thousand Oaks, CA: Sage.

Holman Jones, S., T. E. Adams, and C. Ellis (2016), *Handbook of Autoethnography*. New York: Routledge.

Hughes, S. A., and J. L. Pennington (2017), *Autoethnography: Process, Product, and Possibility for Critical Social Research*, Thousand Oaks, CA: Sage.

Ilieva, R. (2010), "Non-Native English-Speaking Teachers' Negotiations of Program Discourses in their Construction of Professional Identities within a TESOL Program," *Canadian Modern Language Review*, 66 (3): 343–369.

Johnson, K. E., and P. R. Golombek (2011), "The Transformative Power of Narrative in Second Language Teacher Education," *TESOL Quarterly*, 45 (3): 486–509.

Kanno, Y., and B. Norton (2003), "Imagined Communities and Educational Possibilities: Introduction," *Journal of Language, Identity, and Education*, 2 (4): 241–249.

Kanno, Y., and C. Stuart (2011), "Learning to Become a Second Language Teacher: Identities-in-Practice," *Modern Language Journal*, 95 (2): 236–252.

Kayi-Aydar, H., X. Gao, E. R. Miller, M. Varghese, and G. Vitanova, eds. (2019), *Theorizing and Analyzing Language Teacher Agency*. Bristol: Multilingual Matters.

Lindahl, K., and B. Yazan (2019), "An Identity-Oriented Lens to TESOL Teachers' Lives," *TESOL Journal*, 10: 506. https://doi.org/10.1002/tesj.506.

Lindahl, K., C. Fallas-Escobar, and K. I. Henderson (2021), "Linguistically Responsive Instruction for Latinx Teacher Candidates: Surfacing Language Ideological Dilemmas," *TESOL Quarterly*, 55 (4): 1190–1220.

Martel, J. (2015), "Learning to Teach a Foreign Language: Identity Negotiation and Conceptualizations of Pedagogical Progress," *Foreign Language Annals*, 48 (3): 394–412.

Martel, J. (2018), "Three Foreign Language Student Teachers' Experiences with Content-Based Instruction: Exploring the Identity/Innovation Interface," *Innovation in Language Learning and Teaching*, 12 (4): 303–315.

Martel, J., and B. Yazan (2021), "Enacting an Identity Approach in Language Teacher Education," in M. Bigelow and K. Paesani (eds.), *Diversity and Transformation in Language Teacher Education*, 35–62, Minneapolis, MI: University of Minnesota, Center for Advanced Research on Language Acquisition.

Menard-Warwick, J. (2014), *English Language Teachers on the Discursive Faultlines: Identities, Ideologies and Pedagogies*, Bristol: Multilingual Matters.

Morgan, B. (2004), "Teacher Identity as Pedagogy: Towards a Field-Internal Conceptualisation in Bilingual and Second Language Education," *Bilingual Education and Bilingualism*, 7 (2–3): 172–188.

Morgan, B., and M. Clarke (2011), "Identity in Second Language Teaching and Learning," in E. Hinkel (ed.), *Handbook of Research in Second Language Teaching and Learning*, Vol. 2, 817–836, New York: Routledge.

Motha, S. (2006), "Racializing ESOL Teacher Identities in U.S. K-12 Public Schools," *TESOL Quarterly*, 40 (3): 495–518.

Olsen, B. (2008), "How Reasons for Entry into the Profession Illuminate Teacher Identity Development," *Teacher Education Quarterly*, 35 (3): 23–40.

Olsen, B. (2016), *Teaching What They Learn, Learning What They Live: How Teachers' Personal Histories Shape Their Professional Development*, New York: Routledge.

Park, G. (2013), "'Writing is a Way of Knowing': Writing and Identity," *ELT Journal*, 67 (3): 336–345.

Park, G. (2017), *East Asian Women Teachers of English: Narratives of Where Privilege Meets Marginalization*, Bristol: Multilingual Matters.

Pavlenko, A., and A. Blackledge, eds. (2004), *Negotiation of Identities in Multilingual Contexts*, Bristol: Multilingual Matters.

Rudolph, N., B. Yazan, and J. Rudolph (2019), "Negotiating 'Ares,' 'Cans' and 'Shoulds' of Being and Becoming in ELT: Two Teacher Accounts from One Japanese University," *Asian Englishes*, 21 (1): 22–37.

Sánchez-Martín, C. (2021), "Teachers' Transnational Identities as Activity: Constructing Mobility Systems at the Intersections of Gender and Language Difference," *TESOL Quarterly*, 56 (2): 552–581.

Sayer, P. (2012), *Ambiguities and Tensions in English Language Teaching: Portraits of EFL Teachers as Legitimate Speakers*, New York: Routledge.

Shin, J., and J. W. Rubio (2022), "Becoming a Critical ESL Teacher: The Intersection of Historicity, Identity, and Pedagogy," *TESOL Quarterly*, 57 (1): 191–212.

Solano-Campos, A. (2014), "The Making of an International Educator: Transnationalism and Nonnativeness in English Teaching and Learning," *TESOL Journal*, 5 (3): 412–443.

Song, J. (2016), "Emotions and Language Teacher Identity: Conflicts, Vulnerability, and Transformation," *TESOL Quarterly*, 50 (3): 631–654.

Sughrua, W. M. (2016), *Heightened Performative Autoethnography: Resisting Oppressive Spaces Within Paradigms*, New York: Peter Lang.

Sughrua, W. M. (2020), "The Core of Critical Performative Autoethnography," *Qualitative Inquiry*, 26 (6): 602–632.

Trent, J. (2014), "Innovation as Identity Construction in Language Teaching and Learning: Case Studies from Hong Kong," *Innovation in Language Learning and Teaching*, 8 (1): 56–78.

Varghese, M. (2006), "Bilingual Teachers-in-the-Making in Urbantown," *Journal of Multilingual and Multicultural Development*, 27 (3): 211–224.

Varghese, M., S. Motha, J. Trent, G. Park, and J. Reeves, eds. (2016), "Language Teacher Identity in Multilingual Settings," *TESOL Quarterly*, 50 (3): 545–571. https://doi.org/10.1002/tesq.333.

Varghese, M., J. R. Daniels, and C. C. Park (2019), "Structuring Disruption Within University-Based Teacher Education Programs: Possibilities and Challenges of Race-Based Caucuses," *Teachers College Record*, 121 (4): 1–34.

Wenger, E. (1998), *Communities of Practice: Learning, Meaning, and Identity*, Cambridge: Cambridge University Press.

West, L. (1995), "Beyond Fragments: Adults, Motivation and Higher Education," *Studies in the Education of Adults*, 27 (2): 133–156.

Yazan, B. (2018), "TESL Teacher Educators' Professional Self-Development, Identity, and Agency," *TESL Canada Journal*, 35 (2): 140–155.

Yazan, B. (2019a), "Towards Identity-Oriented Teacher Education: Critical Autoethnographic Narrative," *TESOL Journal*, 10: 388. https://doi.org/10.1002/tesj.388.

Yazan, B. (2019b), "Identities and Ideologies in a Language Teacher Candidate's Autoethnography: Making Meaning of Storied Experience," *TESOL Journal*, 10: 500. https://doi.org/10.1002/tesj.500.

Yazan, B. (2019c), "An Autoethnography of a Language Teacher Educator: Wrestling with Ideologies and Identity Positions," *Teacher Education Quarterly*, 46 (3): 34–56.

Yazan, B. (2022), "Language Teacher Educator's Identity Work in Using Critical Autoethnography as a Teacher-Learning Activity," in K. Sadeghi and F. Ghaderi (eds.), *Theory and Practice in Second Language Teacher Identity*, 151–164, Cham: Springer.

Yazan, B., and K. Lindahl (2020), "Language Teacher Learning and Practice as Identity Work," in B. Yazan and K. Lindahl (eds.), *Language Teacher Identity in TESOL: Teacher Education and Practice as Identity Work*, 1–10, New York: Routledge.

Yazan, B., and M. M. Peercy (2018), "'Pedagogically Speaking, I'm Doing the Right Things': Three ESOL Teacher Candidates' Professional Identity Development," *Teacher Learning and Professional Development*, 3 (1): 1–18.

Appendix: Co-constructed Rubric for Critical Autoethnographic Narrative Assignment

Criteria	Weight
Assignment/audience/purpose	15%
Follows the guidelines specified in the syllabus	
Constructs the narrative in an expected genre, i.e., language autoethnography	
Considers an audience and provides adequate and clear information in the narrative	
Content/process/investment	
Narrates the pertinent experiences with language use, learning, and teaching by providing adequate details, (i.e., generates data)	15%

Criteria	Weight
Discusses and utilizes a theoretical framework informed by the literature to construe these experiences by clearly showing the connection between narration and analysis, (i.e., analyzes data)	15%
Completes each installment/draft on time and actively participates/engages in the one-on-one feedback sessions	15%
Attends and responds to the feedback by making necessary changes in the manuscript across drafts	15%
Organization	15%
Includes clearly written introduction and conclusion/implications sections	
Narration and analysis of experiences follows the synthesis of theoretical framework	
Sections are clearly labeled by (sub)headings	
Conventions and writing	10%
Follows APA conventions in in-text citations and references section	
Includes clear and compelling writing with smooth transitions between sentences and paragraphs	
Uses punctuation and capitalization appropriately throughout	

Adapted from Yazan (2019c).

Developing Decolonizing Language Teachers in Colonial Sociopolitical Contexts

Mario E. López-Gopar, Vilma Huerta Cordova, William M. Sughrua, Juan Ignacio Martínez Martínez, and Denisse Zárate Ríos

Introduction

Mexico presents a unique case for language teacher education programs, whereby multilingualism includes complexities of the historical marginalization of Indigenous peoples and social inequalities that impact language teaching and learning. In terms of the current socioeconomic situation faced by the whole of Mexican society, comprised mostly of *mestizos* (Spanish-speaking people with a mixed Spanish/European and Indigenous ancestry) and 68 Indigenous ethnic groups, this reality is highly problematic and complex. Of the OECD countries, Mexico has one of the widest gaps between rich and poor. In fact, Carbajal (2021) reports that 46.9% of the wealth in Mexico is controlled by 1% of the population and that the annual income of wealthy people is 141 times that of those considered to be of low socio-economic status (SES), or 50% of the population. Within this current scenario, the teaching of English accentuates social inequalities, as the teaching of English does not begin until the secondary level in public schools (students 12 years of age and older) and only 5% of the population in Mexico can afford private language institutes or elite bilingual schools where English instruction begins in kindergarten (López-Gopar and Sughrua 2014).

During the last two decades, however, the Mexican government has joined the neoliberal world-trend to bring English into elementary schools and kindergartens (Sayer 2015), which promises "progress," "development," and "equality," while excluding other foreign languages and *othered* Indigenous languages. Due to recent national school reforms, English is now part of the Mexican national curriculum in elementary schools and kindergartens and is being implemented in some schools in different states around the country. This has created a great demand for English teachers (Ramírez Romero, Sayer, and Pamplón Irigoyen 2014). ELT classes in elementary schools and kindergartens, however, typically include critical curricular content as well as decontextualized materials and textbooks, sending the message that English is *the* language to learn (López-Gopar et al. 2009). Another problem is that English language teaching preparation programs in Mexico do not focus on preparing language teachers for young students.

In order to counteract this reality through the development of sociopolitically aware and decoloniality-minded pre-service language teachers equipped to work with young learners, the purpose of this chapter is two-fold: (1) to describe the two-year language-teaching preparation curricular journey of two student teachers, Denisse and Juan (co-authors of this chapter), who were enrolled in a language teaching preparation program in a Mexican public university and who decided to work with young learners during their teaching praxicum; and (2) to present Denisse and Juan's reflections regarding their teaching praxicum conducted in a low-SES elementary school located in Oaxaca. Based on data generated from participant observations, ethnographic field notes, and audio and video recordings of classes and reflective writing pieces (an ethnographic portrait and a critical analysis about their teaching praxicum) written by Denisse and Juan, and utilizing a decolonizing language teaching (López-Gopar 2016) and social justice (Hawkins 2011) theoretical lens, Denisse and Juan's reflections are divided into three succinct sections: (a) learning about, and from, the community; (b) learning about, and from, the children; and (c) gaining critical praxicum insights related to decoloniality. To accomplish this purpose, we first introduce our context, followed by a section on the theories that guide our praxis and the focus of this chapter. We then present the six-stage curricular journey, followed by Denisse and Juan's reflections intertwined with our discussion.

Our colonial sociopolitical context

Mexico's current social division between rich and poor has its origin in its colonial past. Mexico endured colonialism for 300 years under Spanish rule (1521–1821) and looting of its natural resources by Europeans who used Indigenous peoples and African slaves to work the mines. Galeano (1992) argues that the richness of the land in the Americas resulted in the poverty of its people. Colonialism also determined the stratification of social classes dictated by ethnicity and race (e.g., Spanish/Creoles [the children of Spanish peoples born in Mexico]/Mexicans;

White/Brown/Black). López-Gopar and Sughrua (2014) argue that due to *mestizaje* (the mixture among races) and the colonial difference (the remaining state of coloniality in the present day, as ingrained in Mexican people's minds and social practices), Mexico's current social-class stratification is complex, with language proficiency playing a part. According to López-Gopar and Sughrua:

> Social class in Mexico can be defined as the interplay between economics, language, racial features, schooling, and ways of being, acting and consuming. In other words, social status seems determined by whether or not one is rich or poor (economics); whether one speaks Spanish, another "modern" language such as English, or an indigenous language (language); whether one is White, Brown, or Black (race); whether one has been formally educated (education); whether one has attended or is attending a private or public school or an urban or rural school (schooling); and whether or not one behaves, acts, and consumes "modernly" (ways of being).
>
> 2014: 105–106, parentheses in original

Social stratification and inequalities are exacerbated in poor states like Oaxaca, where Denisse and Juan conducted their teaching praxicum. Oaxaca is not only the most culturally and linguistically diverse state in Mexico, it is also the second poorest. Most Oaxacans are part of the 95% of Mexicans who face economic hardship. The economic situation is even worse for Indigenous groups in Oaxaca, which struggle financially, more so than the rest of the *mestizo* population. Many Indigenous families have to meet their basic needs with a minimum wage of US$6 for eight hours of work (Enciso and Camacho 2013). As a result of low-paying jobs, 76% of Indigenous children and young adults in Oaxaca live in poverty and have a nutritionally poor diet (Enciso 2013). English in this case most likely will not make a difference to Oaxaca children's lives in terms of economics. In fact, López-Gopar and Sughrua (2014) report that even Mexican English teachers in Oaxaca receive low pay, making on average US$4 per hour with no benefits or job security. This is also the case in other Mexican states, according to Ramírez Romero, Sayer, and Pamplón Irigoyen (2014). Within this colonial sociopolitical context, why should English be a part of children's lives if it won't make a difference and might even exploit teachers like Denisse and Juan? Having pondered this, we acknowledge that English *is* already in Mexico and will continue to feed into more and more elementary schools in Oaxaca and other states in Mexico, and so we realize that as language educators we can either do nothing about the situation or try to make the teaching of English on our terms and for our own purposes, having a social justice and decolonizing agenda, with (student) teachers like Denisse and Juan at the forefront.

Our visioning of Denisse and Juan as torchbearers of a decolonial-minded ELT is congruent not only with the post-colonial context of Mexico and Oaxaca (as described above) but also with the curriculum of the BA program in ELT where we work as teacher educators and from where Denisse and Juan graduated. Housed at the state public university of Oaxaca, this BA in ELT, like similar programs at public universities across Mexico, has been designed locally as to its course offerings while conforming to general guidelines, such as an eight-semester program, as required by the national Ministry of Education. The main goal of the Oaxaca BA, similar to that of the other BA programs in Mexico, is to prepare Mexican teachers of English as an additional language at the primary, secondary, high school, university, and adult continuing education levels. The BA program in Oaxaca, with a current cohort of 790 students, has experienced two curricular reforms, one in 2001 and the other in 2013. The 2001 reform made the curriculum more flexible through a credit-hour scheme and elective course offerings, while the 2013 reform complemented its existing language-proficiency, linguistics, culture, pedagogy, and research foci with a critical perspective in the sense of seeking social equity (e.g., Freire 2005; Madison 2012; Rawls 2003), including the decolonial awareness that English holds sway over Indigenous languages and Spanish.

This criticality of the Oaxaca BA sets it apart from most other BA ELT programs in Mexico which have a mostly or exclusively linguistic and didactic orientation. For instance, presenting three representative BA ELT programs in Mexico, Goodwin Seadler et al. (2015) explain that ELT preparation in Mexico typically centers on teaching skills and English proficiency. This is facilitated by courses grouped according to three areas: *linguistics*, as related to the acquisition of English; *pedagogy*, as related to teacher training on matters such as lesson plan design and student assessment; and *research*, as related to the writing of a final project or paper in order to obtain teacher certification (Goodwin Seadler et al. 2015). In contrast, our BA ELT program in Oaxaca, while including the same type of linguistic, pedagogic, and research-oriented courses, also incorporates a critical approach in that it promotes language teaching as an act that not only offers students and their communities' linguistic development but also contributes to their social wellbeing and empowerment, especially in the case of low-SES and marginalized communities facing social injustice (López-Gopar 2016). Because the schools located in such communities in Oaxaca and other Mexican states will most likely employ our student graduates from the Oaxaca BA, we consider it paramount that the students are critically aware. This awareness will be significant and lasting because, as Kemmis (2002) notes, the key decisions that pre-service teachers make now will likely impact their future lives in the academic, family, and social spheres.

To that end, our BA program in Oaxaca, as mentioned, complements its general linguistics and pedagogic approach with a critical perspective that includes a sub-focus on decolonizing the hegemonic nature of English. This criticality dominates the courses that are grouped in the curricular areas labeled *critical applied linguistics* (eight courses) and *research* (five courses), while having minimal presence in the other areas labeled *language* (eight courses to develop students' English; six courses to develop Spanish, which is most students' first language; and five courses in another language, which can be a Oaxacan Indigenous language), *teaching and practice* (10 courses), and *elective* (16 courses). As a result, we admit that the criticality is somewhat "isolated" or "departmentalized" in the BA program, being mostly restricted to the *critical applied linguistics* and *research* areas, and to particular course offerings in the *elective* area, and to the third-language option in the *language* area for those students opting to study an Indigenous language. For that reason, and in order to more fully achieve the program goal of preparing critical language teachers, we as teacher educators in our own classes have attempted to make the critical perspective more transversal in the other areas of the program, without jeopardizing the linguistic and didactic foci of the particular classes. More specifically, and as related to this present study, we have relied on different theories on social justice and decolonizing pedagogies in those courses within the *research* area which lead to the students' teaching praxicum. That praxicum and those courses we describe later in the chapter. For now, let us turn to the critical-oriented theories underlying the praxicum and courses.

Social justice and decolonizing pedagogies

In this chapter, social justice and critical/decolonizing perspectives are adopted as theoretical lenses to analyze "processes of unfairness or injustice within a particular lived domain" (Madison 2012: 5), which is the case for most low-SES people in Mexico, so as "to make a contribution toward changing those conditions toward greater freedom and equity" (ibid.). In terms of second language teacher education, Hawkins (2011) argues that this field has been influenced by psycholinguistic, communicative, sociocultural, and critical approaches. However, Hawkins calls for a social-justice approach to language teacher education that highlights the role of both language-teacher educators (e.g., Mario, Vilma, and Bill, co-authors of this chapter) and language (student) teachers (e.g., Denisse and Juan) as agents of social change. Acknowledging that social injustice involves gender (Banegas, Jacovkis, and Romiti 2020), immigration (Kitsiou et al. 2019), and bilingualism (Warren 2021), among other issues, teacher educators and/or researchers have implemented changes or proposed courses in second-language teaching preparation programs and worked with student teachers to develop a critical, responsive, and inclusive stance in their teaching praxis (Morgan 2016; Sharma and Phyak 2017; Yazan 2019). In our case, as part of the final two years of Denisse and Juan's four-year teaching preparation program, we have created a six-stage process to work closely with them and their classmates before, during, and after their teaching praxicum in public elementary schools in order to enact an agentive role pursuing social justice and decolonization.

Since our view of social justice follows Rawls' (2003) argument that social justice is a shared belief system that disqualifies and looks beyond *colonial* inheritance of social and cultural/*colonial* differences, we also rely on *decolonial* theories to inform our work with student teachers. Mexico, like most Latin American countries, endured hundreds of years of colonialism. Latin American thinkers, such as Mignolo (2000) and Quijano (2007), argue that even though Mexico's colonial period apparently ended with the country's independence in 1821, the colonial logic (coloniality) has remained, positioning European ontologies and epistemologies as the goals that all Mexican people should aspire to should they want to leave their "lowliness" behind. Nowadays, following this colonial "aspiration," the English language has been positioned as the most "desired" language in Mexico (Motha and Lin 2014). English is advertised as the language that will "open doors" (Sayer 2015) to brighter futures and that will change people's lives; this implies the discriminatory message that most Mexicans are dissatisfied with their current lives. Part and parcel of the enactment of these colonialist discourses are ELT student teachers' future roles. Granados Beltrán argues that "[c]oloniality may also influence student-teachers' beliefs, their everyday behaviors, and their expectations in relation to the course of study" (2016: 7). Hence, language-teaching preparation programs should engage student teachers in conversations around decolonizing pedagogies.

Being aware of the colonial discourses present in English language teaching in Mexico, teacher educators and (student) teachers have attempted to challenge these discourses; in other words, "to decolonize" English language teaching (Calderón 2016; Granados Beltrán 2016; López-Gopar 2016). Decolonization does not mean the end of coloniality, but it represents people's struggle to challenge coloniality and "marks the[ir] postures, positionings, horizons, projects, and practices of being, thinking, sensing, and doing that resist and re-exist, that transgress and interrupt the colonial matrix of power" (Walsh 2020: 606). Approaching pedagogy from a decolonial stance, "[t]he goal of decolonial pedagogy is to question, displace, and subvert of concepts and practices left by colonial inheritance with the purpose of intervening, constructing, creating, and liberating by means of a decolonizing practice" (Granados Beltrán 2016: 10). Focusing on ELT and addressing language teacher education programs specifically, Kumaravadivelu argues that a decolonial approach involves "restructuring the existing teacher education programs so that prospective teachers are helped to develop the knowledge, skill, and disposition necessary to become producers, not just consumers, of pedagogic knowledge and pedagogic materials" (2016: 81). This restructuring must be done at the local level since working with a decolonial lens involves "the particularity/singularity of settings and phenomena" (Toohey and Smythe 2022: 122–123). Hence, decolonializing language-teaching preparation programs should be locally grounded; "if [they are] to be useful and useable, [they have] to be formulated and implemented by local players who are knowledgeable about, and sensitive to, local conditions" (Kumaravadivelu 2016: 81).

In the next section, we describe how we structured the last two years of our language teaching preparation program in order to engage student teachers, like Denisse and Juan, in "critical and reflexive dialogue," which is a pillar of decolonizing paradigms (Diversi and Finley 2010: 15), and which thus keeps us "vigilant of the ways we might unintentionally reproduce colonialist regimes of knowledge" (Calderón 2016: 5).

Denisse and Juan's Six-Stage Reflexive Journey

Denisse and Juan are now graduates of a four-year language teaching BA program housed in a public state university in Oaxaca. As mentioned previously, and as we further describe below in this section, the main goal of this program is to provide the Oaxacan and larger Mexican community with critical language teachers who are aware of the hegemony of English and other so-called modern languages (e.g., French and Italian) over Indigenous languages and Spanish. Like Denisse and Juan, most undergraduate students enrolled in the BA program are from middle-class and working-class backgrounds. Along with the rest of their cohort of 40 student teachers, Denisse and Juan, during the last four semesters of their BA program, worked with Mario, Vilma, and Bill, who acted as their teacher educators and supervisors of their teaching praxicum. In order to engage student teachers in a critical, decolonizing, and reflexive journey, we developed six stages that they go through during the last two years of their BA program. We describe these stages here not necessarily as a blueprint to be followed in other contexts, as we agree with Toohey and Smythe that because working with a decolonial approach acknowledges the particularity of every setting, "making recommendations for universal or context-free teacher education programs and practices is contrary to [this] approach" (2022: 1–2). Therefore, these six stages served as a way to maintain a reflective dialogue with undergraduate students Denisse and Juan, within the educative context of Oaxaca.

Stage 1: Writing autobiographies

The first stage is a childhood autobiographical writing project undertaken at the beginning of the fifth semester. During this stage, the student teachers focus on their childhood from birth to 12 years of age. For pre-writing activities, the student teachers spend many sessions telling each other stories they remember from their childhood in connection with their family and friends, their school experiences and teachers, their mischiefs, accidents, successes and failures, and any other topics they care to bring up. After this, they take part in a digital brainstorming with the help of a partner, asking each other questions in order to dig deeper into their childhood memories and to create stronger bonds as new classmates. The actual writing of the autobiographies is done individually, and the student teachers include photos of special moments in their childhood. These autobiographies not only reposition the student teachers as children, but also remind them about the "little" but important things in children's lives. Most importantly, these autobiographies challenge the generic treatment of teachers and students within coloniality. According to Asher, autobiographies are decolonizing texts since they are (re)generative, transformative, and self-reflexive "narrative[s] of the self not contained by colonialism" (2009: 5). Finally, the student teachers do a peer review of their autobiographies both to polish their writing and to "meet" a child similar to the ones they will encounter in their upcoming praxicum.

Stage 2: Dialoguing with decolonizing theories in language teaching

The second stage involves the development of a historically situated theoretical framework, which the student teachers use to critically analyze their future praxicum. This stage takes up the remainder of the fifth semester, during which the student teachers dialogue with one another so as to appropriate decolonizing theories on their own terms. Following López-Gopar, who argues that decolonizing projects should be historically grounded should one want to "understand children's backgrounds and take that as a starting point in the curriculum" (2016: 195), this stage begins with a critical reflection of Mexico's 300 years of colonialism perpetrated by the Spanish and the remaining state of coloniality (Mignolo 2000; Quijano 2014). We share a critical view of history with the student teachers, since in Mexico's basic education curriculum the teaching of history has a Eurocentric slant, which starts with the "discovery of America" by Christopher Columbus and the invisibilization and anonymity of Indigenous groups.

During this stage, the student teachers appropriate five main theoretical concepts: (1) *modernity/coloniality*—the grand narrative that emerged from the expansion of European colonialism and capitalism, imposing Eurocentric models of subjectivity, authority, economy, and knowledge (Mignolo 2000; Quijano 2007); (2) *colonial difference*—the discourse that transforms otherness into inferiority, whereby some human beings, cultures, languages, nations, etc. are considered to be superior to others based on, for example, race, gender, social class, and linguistic proficiency (Mignolo 2009); (3) *coloniality of being*—the de-humanization or the non-existence of people when they are treated generically (Walsh 2007), which began at the onset of colonialism when there were discussions as to whether the peoples of the Americas were in fact "people" (Mignolo 2000, 2009); (4) *geopolitics of knowledge*—the understanding that all knowledge is produced at local levels and is "provincial" in Grosfoguel's terms (2013), which challenges the universal valence given to one single knowledge (Eurocentric) and the erasure of the *othered* ways of knowing produced in other places; and (5) *decoloniality*—the ongoing struggle to delink ourselves from coloniality, to challenge colonial difference, and to validate local knowledges and languages (López-Gopar 2016; Mignolo 2007; Walsh 2020).

These five concepts are appropriated by the student teachers when analyzing their personal experience of confronting, or imposing on others, colonial difference. The appropriation of these concepts also involves collecting and analyzing memes, videos, texts from social media, as well as language textbooks. Furthermore, the student teachers reflect on the local knowledge produced by their own families and communities that are often dismissed as old wives' tales, myths, or *creencias* (so-called popular and non-scientific beliefs). Through this introspective analysis based on the above five concepts, the student teachers conclude not only that coloniality is connected to language teaching and part of daily living, but also that people engage in decolonial struggles on a daily basis.

Stage 3: Becoming critical ethnographers

During the sixth semester, the student teachers are introduced to critical ethnography and ethnographic methods in order to conduct an ethnographic research project about the community where they will undertake their teaching praxicum. A *critical* approach is adopted in order to acknowledge that ethnography has also been used to (re)position marginalized groups as the "colonial other" (Smith 2012). Thus, the student teachers do not engage in ethnographic research to *learn about* the community, but to *learn from and with* the community. They also take an embodiment approach (Ng 2018) as their data collection is deeply connected with their feelings. During their first visits to the community, Denisse and Juan kept diaries in which they recorded their first impressions and their feelings while there. In their journal entries, they also compared and contrasted this community to their own. Besides journaling, Denisse and Juan took photographs of the linguistic landscape, zooming in on the use of Spanish and English in public signs. They were also attentive to the use of Indigenous languages, which are almost never heard in urban neighborhoods. As part of their critical ethnographic research, Denisse and Juan also engaged in conversations with members of the community (adults, young people, and children) through semi-structured interviews focusing on social issues, politics, economics, religion, education, history, language(s) in the community, and the presence or influence of the English language. With all this information, Denisse and Juan wrote an ethnographic report in which they identified topics that might be relevant to children's lives in this particular community in order to develop a critical thematic unit, which is the next stage in the process.

Stage 4: Authoring a critical thematic unit

At the end of the sixth semester, based on their critical ethnographic analysis, the student teachers identify social problems highlighted by community members. Examples include water shortages, which are a major problem in some neighborhoods; pedestrian safety, which relates to a lack of street lighting, proper sidewalks, and street signage; gang violence; and health issues, including the availability of health services, people's diets and obesity, especially among children. One of these issues is adopted as the theme or topic of the student teacher's critical thematic unit. The *critical* aspect of this thematic unit starts with choosing a social issue identified by the community members and observed by the student teachers. Furthermore, the main goal of these critical thematic units is not linguistic *per se*; rather, they have a social justice and decolonizing agenda.

For Denisse and Juan, their chosen theme was health care. Their critical thematic unit objectives, or messages to the children, were: (1) we have to take care of our body; (2) it is important to know and to have good healthy habits; (3) it is important to share with people around me the healthy habits I have learned; and (4) we can learn about health in any language as all languages are important. In order to meet these objectives, the student teachers work on creating identity texts (Cummins and Early 2011), co-created by the student teachers and children, which not only display what the children have learned, but also demonstrate the intelligence and creativity of the children, proving that knowledge is co-created everywhere (geopolitics of knowledge). In the case of Denisse and Juan, they co-created with the children a daily timeline to record the healthy habits that the children already engaged in as well as any new ones they had learned from one another or from Denisse and Juan. This timeline included drawings made by the children with accompanying sentences in Spanish and English. From this theme and the identity texts, Denisse and Juan set their linguistic goals, both grammatical and lexical, along with the language abilities they would focus on (speaking, listening, reading, and writing). In our critical thematic units, learning English is not the end goal but the conduit to address a social issue present in the children's lives. As part of the development of their critical thematic units, the student teachers select different teaching strategies (for example, based on games, songs, or puppets) and different teaching methods, while connecting their theme to other school subjects (math, science, geography, etc.). Finally, assessment is done through the creation and sharing of the identity texts.

Stage 5: Conducting the praxicum

The fifth stage commences at the beginning of the seventh semester, when the student teachers begin their teaching *praxicum* in pairs, like Denisse and Juan, working with children from low-SES backgrounds in public elementary schools, pre-schools, and non-governmental organizations. The concept of "praxicum," instead of practicum, is used to highlight the praxis orientation (action plus reflection) proposed by Freire (2005). We regard student teachers as reflective practitioners who engage critically with their own and the children's context, who adapt their methods and strategies to better meet the needs and learning styles of the children, who develop their own theories while engaging their students in their classes, who co-create knowledge with their students, and who negotiate affirming identities for themselves and the children, which speaks back to coloniality. During this stage, which lasts the whole semester, the student teachers take turns leading the class while the other documents the teaching praxicum, takes photos, videos, audio recordings of activities in the class, and collects samples of the children's work. Throughout the praxicum, we also hold reflective debriefings with the entire cohort of 40 student teachers. In these debriefings, the student teachers share their successes, frustrations, and any other feelings they are experiencing in their teaching praxicum. These sessions supportive yet critical, as we regard critical self-reflexivity to be necessary in decolonizing pedagogies (Diversi and Finley 2010).

During this stage, the student teachers, including Denisse and Juan, keep a diary for every class they teach, and each diary entry consists of three things, or episodes, that occur in the class. Each episode includes four components. The first component is the "narrative," which explains in detail what the episode is all about. The second component is "asking genuine questions" about this episode: things that the student teachers ponder in order to critically reflect on their praxicum. In the third component, "making connections," the student teachers connect the episode to their own experiences as children and as language learners, to the experiences of their friends and classmates, to other research studies, to the five decolonial theoretical concepts explained in stage 2, and to any other theories they think may speak to their episodes. The last component is "drawing conclusions." This is the space where the student teachers come up with theories in situ; in other words, their conclusions become theories supported by empirical evidence. In this manner, the student teachers are not only consumers of theories developed elsewhere, usually in Eurocentric places (Kumaravadivelu 2016), but also generators of theories which they will develop as part of their teaching experience. The student teachers' diaries focus on their class in general and on a child in particular. Two of the student teachers' episodes focus on critical moments in their class and one episode focuses on a specific child they select as a case study. The diaries and all the data collected by Denisse and Juan become the foundations for the next stage.

Stage 6: Writing as a reflexive process

Stage 6 takes place during the eighth semester, the last in the student teachers' BA program. While continuing with their teaching praxicum, the student teachers refrain from collecting data and writing diaries as rigorously as they had done during the previous stage, and instead focus on writing two documents in pairs (in this case, Denisse with Juan): (1) an ethnographic portrait of the child they focused on during the teaching praxicum, and (2) a critical analysis of their teaching praxicum. Before writing up these two documents, we spend several sessions with the entire cohort of student teachers, sharing stories and insights regarding their case study and their class in general. Hence, the analysis of their case study and their teaching praxicum is an intersubjective and collective endeavor. Case studies and praxicum experiences are compared and contrasted, looking for evidence of (de)coloniality. As part of their ethnographic portrait, the student teacher first writes the "story of their student," focusing on different themes emerging from their diary. In the case of Denisse and Juan, they wrote about their students' competitiveness, their behavior, their relationships with other children, and their feelings expressed in class. The story is followed by an in-depth analysis connecting the personal, theoretical, and societal levels. In terms of the critical analysis of their teaching praxicum, this document begins with an overview of the student teacher's praxicum and critical thematic unit. Then, they reflect on achieving the objectives or messages in their thematic unit and analyze the children's identity texts. The student teacher also evaluates the children's linguistic development in the languages used in class. The second part of this document focuses on critical moments in the teaching praxicum and a discussion of the themes that emerged from the student teacher's analysis of the data and their diary.

In the case of Denisse and Juan, the first themes to emerge were focused on feelings experienced both by themselves and the children, followed by a theme on "creativity" and another on "from failure to success." This piece of writing concludes with an analysis of how modernity/coloniality and colonial difference were either re-created or challenged during their praxicum and their role in this process, zooming in on student teachers' social responsibility as decolonial agents of change. In the next section, based on Denisse and Juan's experience as critical ethnographers and the two documents described here, we focus, albeit succinctly, on the written reflections of Denisse and Juan regarding their felt connection to the community and the children as well as their insights on decoloniality.

Learning About, and From, the Community

Denisse and Juan conducted their teaching praxicum in a low-SES neighborhood in the city of Oaxaca. Typically, such neighborhoods are believed to be dangerous, inhabited by "colonial others." Hence, simply setting foot in such a neighborhood is a learning and decolonial experience. Denisse and Juan had similar impressions and feelings about this community. They both noted the "kindness of their inhabitants" (our translation).[1] In his journal, Juan wrote: "While I was walking, I could tell that people know each other, and greet each other from faraway …which tells me that they are kind people." Denisse also perceived people's kindness and willingness to talk to "strangers" about their community: "We approached and asked them if we could interview them and record it. The woman agreed in a very natural and kind way." In Denisse and Juan's terms, they both felt "comfortable" in this community. Juan wrote: "When we arrived, I noticed that it was a small neighborhood. I walked around without feeling afraid. There were not that many cars, and people greeted each other, which made me feel very comfortable." Similarly, Denisse commented: "I felt very comfortable because I realized that this community is similar to my own neighborhood." They both even felt peaceful, as noted by Juan in his journal. "Walking in the streets of this neighborhood gives you tranquility and peace. I forgot about my worries and I felt as if I lived here." Denisse and Juan's realizations about the kindness of the people and their feelings of comfortableness and peacefulness challenge coloniality and colonial difference. Colonial difference places *othered* people together with their neighborhoods toward the bottom of the hierarchy with traits typically assigned to the "colonial other": primitive, needy, barbaric, dangerous (Mignolo 2000, 2009). Even though Denisse and Juan both come from working-class families and communities, they had never visited this neighborhood and were nervous about visiting and conducting ethnographic research there. Walking and meeting people from the community assuaged their fears almost immediately and helped them to appreciate and learn from the people in the community.

Denisse and Juan learned much from talking with different members of the community, and they labeled this section in their ethnographic report, "Voices from the community." By talking to Ms. Ana (pseudonym), who sells bread next to the park to support her family (Figure 9.1), they were able to capture her view about the economic inequality visible in her neighborhood: "There is a bit of everything [SES]. There are people who have a high level, and others who need support. There are people who sometimes do not have money to eat" (Denisse's interview).

Besides Ms. Ana, Denisse and Juan spoke to "Don Felipe," a man who had migrated to the USA; "Sr. Mario," the gardener at the mayor's office; "Sr. Gabriel," an older man who knew a lot about the history of the neighborhood; César, a

Figure 9.1 Ms. Ana selling bread to get by.

teenager; and Naomi, a young elementary schoolgirl. Not only did Denisse and Juan learn about economics, religion, politics, history, social issues, and languages in the community from all these *people*, but they also came to respect these individuals as real individuals who know a lot about their community and who strive to get by on a daily basis. They had met and spoken with the relatives and friends of their future students, which gave Denisse and Juan confidence and the basis for their decolonizing teaching praxicum, where they would continue learning—from their students, as we discuss next.

Learning About, and From, the Children

Denisse and Juan focused on two children for their case study, learning not only about them, but from them, as developing language teachers. "Antonio" and "Jacobo" (pseudonyms) had been born and raised in the community. Antonio was ten while Jacobo was eleven years old. Denisse and Juan chose these two students because they were both extroverts and willing to participate in class. In their ethnographic portrait, Denisse and Juan included an episode from Denisse's journal where Denisse brought candy to the class as a reward for the children who answered correctly. Antonio was the focus of this episode. According to Denisse:

> The activity was planned in such a way that all students had the opportunity to get the candy as a prize. Antonio was one of the first students to participate and when he answered correctly, he got his candy. He did not sit down and stayed close to the board to see if the others answered correctly. If someone failed, Antonio's reaction was as follows: "Teacher, teacher, I'll tell you," to which I replied, "Antonio, please, let your classmates participate." His insistence was so great that he would not let his classmates participate.

In the same way that Antonio wanted to compete to get the candy, Jacobo was also eager to participate and be the first in class, even in coloring tasks. Denisse and Juan included the following journal excerpt, written by Juan, in their ethnographic portrait:

> Since the Day of the Dead was coming, I took the opportunity for my students to practice the colors in English using a drawing of an altar for the Day of the Dead (Figure 9.2). A very short time had passed when Jacobo came up to me and said, "Teacher, can you check my work?" I realized that, in fact, Jacobo had finished and was anxious to check on his other classmates to see if he had finished first.

In their ethnographic portrait, Denisse and Juan included multiple episodes that highlighted both Antonio's and Jacobo's active participation and competitiveness. They also wrote about the two boys' behavior in class, which was challenging, and their relationships with their classmates and the different feelings that go with being competitive.

Reflecting on their teaching praxicum, which included competitive games, Denisse and Juan realized that such games are connected to coloniality. In their ethnographic portrait, they wrote:

> Competitiveness is something that happens every day in a classroom. By analyzing this more deeply in the case of Antonio and Jacobo, we can infer that their competitiveness comes from a need to prove to their teachers that they *do* know and that they know more than the other students. As we had previously talked about in our debriefings, this may have its root in our colonial past, as argued by Germana. "The know-how of the European 'whites' prevailed as superior to that of the 'Indians', 'blacks' and 'mestizos'" (2010: 216). So when we are teaching the English language to children, we awaken that feeling in them of wanting to prove that they do know and that their knowledge is better than that of their peers.

Developing Decolonizing Language Teachers in Colonial Sociopolitical Contexts 161

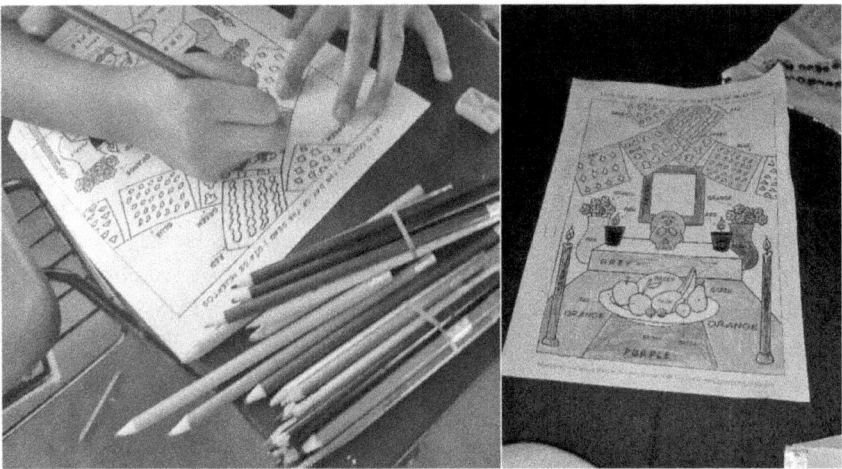

Figure 9.2 Jacobo coloring his Day of the Dead altar.

Clearly, Denisse and Juan were being critical as to how their teaching praxicum was unintentionally reproducing coloniality and "colonialist regimes of knowledge" (Calderón 2016: 5), something they also noticed in other aspects of their teaching praxicum, as discussed in the next section.

Gaining Critical Praxicum Insights Related to Decoloniality

Denisse and Juan realized that decolonizing pedagogies requires constant reflection about our teaching and how we relate to students. In their critical analysis of their teaching praxicum, Denisse and Juan included the following excerpt from Denisse's journal:

> Vielka [one of Denisse's students] was copying from the board and did not understand a letter, so she stopped and addressed me: "Denisse, what letter is that?" Her question was too informal for me, so I said, "Vielka, one says Professor Denisse." Vielka just smiled and returned to her place to continue copying. Later she asked me something again and this time when she said it, she addressed me in the following way: "Maestraaaa Denisse" ["Teeeeacher Denisse"], which I found a bit funny as Vielka wanted me to know that she had not forgotten to address me as a teacher.

In their critical analysis about this episode, Denisse and Juan added the following:

It was a bit strange for Denisse to hear that she was called by her name when she was teaching the class. When she was a student, she never heard a student calling the teacher by their name, since it was considered rude and disrespectful. Coloniality shows up in schools day by day. In this episode, we can see a clear example of the reproduction of coloniality, since Denisse instinctively corrected her student and asked her to address her as a "teacher," when calling her by her name was not necessarily wrong or disrespectful. Schooling has taught us that within a classroom there are hierarchies and that the teacher is considered the most knowledgeable person who should be respected at all times. For this reason, there is a gap between students and teachers, in which "respect" is confused with "hierarchies."

Denisse and Juan discovered that coloniality is disguised by "good" manners or behaviors. They identified the thin line between "respect" and "hierarchies," where teachers have been positioned as the colonizers who must "help" and "educate" the "colonial other" (the students). Throughout their praxicum, they became close to their students, allowing them to call them by their first name should they choose to do so. In their critical analysis, they included episodes when they talked to their students about their feelings, problems at home, and discrimination experienced both in the community and in their classroom.

Not only did Denisse and Juan challenge colonial hierarchies in terms of personal relationships, they also did it in terms of world language hierarchies, as laid out in Denisse's and Juan's critical analysis, which included a diary kept by Juan:

> Being language teachers, we have realized that there are certain preferences between one language and another and that these preferences are very marked in a class. Most children are more inclined toward a foreign language than an Indigenous language. For example, in one class, Juan encountered the following situation, as described in his diary:
>
> I asked my students, "Do you think English is important?" They all said, "Yes!" To which I responded, "Why do you think it is important?" Some children quickly raised their hands. I called on a boy named Diego. Diego said, "I think it is important because when we go to look for a job, they will give it to us because we speak English." I said, "Sure, very good, Diego." I immediately called on another boy, named Samuel. He commented: "Also when we study medicine and we want to study in another country, they will let us go because we speak English." I commented that his was a good idea. Later I asked them, "And what about the indigenous languages of Oaxaca?" The whole room became silent.

Reflecting on this episode, Denisse and Juan wrote the following in their critical analysis:

As we can see, children have been taught that learning a foreign language (English) will give them more opportunities and that they will become better people, but apparently this is not the case with Indigenous languages.

Throughout their teaching praxicum, Denisse and Juan challenged the colonial perceptions regarding the English language, as the language that would open doors (Sayer 2015) and make us "better" people (López-Gopar 2016). In their teaching praxicum, multiple languages (Spanish and English, including words in other languages the students, Denisse and Juan, know) were embraced, appreciated, and used to talk about health as well as other important aspects of the children's lives that arose during their classes.

Conclusion

In this chapter, we have described the curricular journey of Denisse and Juan leading to their reflexive teaching praxis with a decolonizing agenda. With this agenda, Denisse and Juan are representative of decolonial-minded pre-service teachers of English not only in Mexico but also in other formerly colonized nation-states in the Americas and elsewhere. For this reason, the present study has implications for BA ELT programs in Mexico as well as other post-colonial countries. One implication, for instance, is that teacher educators working in these programs should directly incorporate decolonial theories and readings on ELT in particular and language education in general into their pre-, in-, and post-praxicum class activities and discussion sessions. In addition to learning about decolonial theories, space should be built into the courses of the ELT program through which future teachers have the opportunity to discover the presence of modernity/coloniality and/or decoloniality in their own university classrooms as they acknowledge and reflect about the diversity present in their program. It is essential for future teachers to approach this diversity with a positive mindset, which does not equate difference with inferiority. This can be accomplished through cooperative learning methodologies whereby the pre-service teachers learn from one another. Finally, it is important to look beyond the classroom walls by having pre-service teachers visit and learn from the community, or by inviting community members (elementary school teachers and their children, the children's parents, small business owners, Indigenous speakers, etc.) into the university classroom and have them participate in the class activities and discussions with the pre-service teachers. Learning from one another and community members may help future teachers to develop a social vision and to work for the common benefit. These teachers, who will find themselves working in communities that face economic, social, and political issues, need to develop a critical awareness in order to better equip themselves for teaching in such contexts and join the decolonizing efforts that may be occurring in those communities.

In this tenor, we conclude with Denisse's and Juan's words about decolonizing pedagogies included in their critical analysis:

> When we analyze all this, we realize that decolonizing is not an easy task in these times, since we have certain deeply ingrained thoughts. From the moment we are born, we are told how we should be or look, or even what we should know to be able to fit into our society. All these parameters are governed by modernity. In our teaching praxicum, we realized that we colonized a lot. Sometimes we did not realize it until we wrote about it, but doing this reflection and realizing our actions is the first step to decolonize. If we want to decolonize classrooms, we must begin by decolonizing ourselves, as teachers, in order to start making a small difference and influencing children in this way.

As Denisse and Juan indicate, the teaching of English in Mexico requires teachers to be reflexive decolonial agents, should they escape "[becoming] the proletariat tool of the new economical world situation, which benefits very few people while negatively affecting most" (López-Gopar and Sughrua 2014: 109).

Note

1 Denisse and Juan wrote their journal entries, diaries, and reflections in Spanish. They also conducted their interviews in Spanish. In directly quoting from Denisse and Juan, here and throughout this and the next section of the chapter, we as co-authors (Mario, Vilma, and Bill) have translated the text from Spanish to English.

References

Asher, N. (2009), "Writing Home/Decolonizing Text(s)," *Discourse: Studies in the Cultural Politics of Education*, 30 (1): 1–13.

Banegas, D., L. Jacovkis, and A. Romiti (2020), "A Gender Perspective in Initial English Language Teacher Education: An Argentinian Experience," *Sexuality & Culture*, 24: 1–22.

Calderón, D. (2016), "Moving from Damage-Center Research through Unsettling Reflexivity," *Anthropology & Education Quarterly*, 47 (1): 5–24.

Carbajal, B. (2021), "Ganan 1% de Millonarios 141 Veces Más que la Mitad de los Mexicanos," *La Jornada*, December 8. https://www.jornada.com.mx/2021/12/08/economia/024n1eco.

Cummins, J., and M. Early (2011), "Introduction," in J. Cummins and M. Early (eds.), *Identity Texts: The Collaborative Creation of Power in Multilingual Schools*, 3–19, London: Trentham Books.

Diversi, M., and S. Finley (2010), "Poverty Pimps in the Academy: A Dialogue about Subjectivity, Reflexivity, and Power in Decolonizing Production of Knowledge," *Cultural Studies-Critical Methodologies*, 10 (1): 14–17.

Enciso, A. (2013), "En México, 56% de los niños menores de cinco años viven en la pobreza," *La Jornada*, April 4. http://www.jornada.unam.mx/2013/04/04/sociedad/040n1soc.

Enciso, A., and F. Camacho (2013), "Enfrentan indígenas más carencias que el resto de mexicanos pobres," *La Jornada*, August 9. http://www.jornada.unam.mx/2013/08/09/sociedad/033n1soc.

Freire, P. (2005), *Pedagogy of the Oppressed*, New York: Continuum (original work, 1970).

Galeano, E. (1992), *Ser como Ellos y Otros Artículos*, México: Siglo Veintiuno Editores.

Germana, C. (2010), "Una Epistemología Otra: El Proyecto de Anibal Quijano," *Nómadas*, 32: 211–221.

Goodwin Seadler, D., O. Narváez Trejo, C. Macola Rojo, and P. Nuñez Mercado (2015), "Introduction," in D. Goodwin Seadler, O. Narváez Trejo, C. Macola Rojo, and P. Nuñez Mercado (eds.), *Percepciones Interinstitucionales sobre la Formación de Profesores de Inglés*, 13–22, Jalapa, Veracruz: Universidad Veracruzana.

Granados Beltrán, C. (2016), "Critical Interculturality: A Path for Pre-Service ELT Teachers," *Ikala*, 21 (2): 171–187.

Grosfoguel, R. (2013), "The Structure of Knowledge in Westernized Universities: Epistemic Racism/Sexism and the Four Genocides/Epistemicides of the Long 16th Century," *Human Architecture: Journal of the Sociology of Self-Knowledge*, XI (1): 73–90.

Hawkins, M. (2011), "Introduction," in M. Hawkins (ed.), *Social Justice Language Teacher Education*, 1–6, Bristol: Multilingual Matters.

Kemmis, S. (2002), "La Teoría de la Práctica Educativa," in W. Carr (ed.), *Una Teoría para la Educación: Hacia una Investigación Educativa Crítica (P. Manzano, trad)*, 17–38, Madrid: Ediciones Morata, SL.

Kitsiou, R., M. Papadopoulou, G. Androulakis, R. Tsokalidou, and E. Skourtou (2019), "Beyond Conventional Borders of Second Language Teachers' Education: A Digital, Interdisciplinary, and Critical Postgraduate Curriculum," in A. Kostoulas (ed.), *Challenging Boundaries in Language Education*, 229–245, Cham: Springer.

Kumaravadivelu, B. (2016), "The Decolonial Option in English Teaching: Can the Subaltern Act?," *TESOL Quarterly*, 50 (1): 66–85.

López-Gopar, M. E. (2016), *Decolonizing Primary English Language Teaching*, Bristol: Multilingual Matters.

López-Gopar, M. E., and W. Sughrua (2014), "Social Class in English Language Education in Oaxaca, Mexico," *Journal of Language, Identity and Education*, 13: 104–110.

López-Gopar, M. E., O. Núñez Méndez, L. Montes Medina, and M. Cantera Martínez (2009), "Inglés Enciclomedia: A Ground-Breaking Program for Young Mexican Children?," *Mextesol Journal*, 33 (1): 67–86.

Madison, D. S. (2012), *Critical Ethnography: Method, Ethics, and Performance*, Los Angeles, CA: Sage.

Mignolo, W. (2000), *Local Histories/Global Designs: Coloniality, Subaltern Knowledges, and Border Thinking*, Princeton, NJ: Princeton University Press.

Mignolo, W. (2007), "Delinking: The Rhetoric of Modernity, the Logic of Coloniality and the Grammar of De-coloniality," *Cultural Studies*, 21 (2–3): 449–514.

Mignolo, W. (2009), "La Colonialidad: La Cara Oculta de la Modernidad," in S. Breitwieser (ed.), *Modernologias: Artistas Contemporáneos Investigan la Modernidad y el Modernismo*, 39–49, Barcelona: Museo de Arte Contemporáneo de Barcelona.

Morgan, B. (2016), "Language Teacher Identity and the Domestication of Dissent: An Exploratory Account," *TESOL Quarterly*, 50 (3): 708–734.

Motha, S., and A. Lin (2014), "'Non-Coercive Rearrangements': Theorizing Desire in TESOL," *TESOL Quarterly*, 48 (2): 331–359.

Ng, R. (2018), "Decolonizing Teaching and Learning through Embodied Learning," in S. Batacharya and Y-L. R. Wong (eds.), *Sharing Breath: Embodied Learning and Decolonization*, 33–54, Edmonton, AB: Athabasca University Press.

Quijano, A. (2007), "Coloniality and Modernity/Rationality," *Cultural Studies*, 21 (2–3): 168–178.

Quijano, A. (2014), "Colonialidad del Poder y Clasificación Social," in B. de Sousa Santos and M. P. Meneses (eds.), *Epistemologías del Sur (Perspectivas)*, 67–107, Madrid: Akal Cuestiones de Antagonismo.

Ramírez Romero, J. L., P. Sayer, and E. N. Pamplón Irigoyen (2014), "English Language Teaching in Public Primary Schools in Mexico: The Practices and Challenges of Implementing a National Language Education Program," *International Journal of Qualitative Studies in Education*, 27 (8): 1020–1043.

Rawls, J. (2003), *A Theory of Justice*, Cambridge, MA: Harvard University Press (original work, 1971).

Sayer, P. (2015), "'More & Earlier': Neoliberalism and Primary English Education in Mexican Public Schools," *L2 Journal*, 7 (3): 40–56.

Sharma, B. K., and P. Phyak (2017), "Criticality as Ideological Becoming: Developing English Teachers for Critical Pedagogy in Nepal," *Critical Inquiry in Language Studies*, 14 (2–3): 210–238.
Smith, L. T. (2012), *Decolonizing Methodologies: Research and Indigenous Peoples*, 2nd edition, London: Zed Books.
Toohey, K., and S. Smythe (2022), "A Different Difference in Teacher Education: Posthuman and Decolonizing Perspectives," *Language Education*, 36 (2): 122–136.
Walsh, C. (2007), "Interculturalidad, Colonialidad y Educación," *Revista de Educación y Pedagogía XIX*, 48: 25–35.
Walsh, C. (2020), "Decolonial Learnings, Asking and Musings," *Postcolonial Studies*, 23 (4): 604–611.
Warren, A. N. (2021), "Toward an Inclination to Advocate: A Discursive Study of Teachers' Stance Toward Linguistically-Responsive Pedagogy in Online Teacher Education," *Language and Education*, 35 (1): 60–77.
Yazan, B. (2019), "Identities and Ideologies in a Language Teacher Candidate's Autoethnography: Making Meaning of Storied Experience," *TESOL Journal*, 10: e500. https://doi.org/10.1002/tesj.500.

Afterword: Interrogating and Destabilizing the Canon of TESOL Teacher Education

Peter Sayer

As an educator, and an optimist, I want to read the arc of history as moving us towards a more just and equitable world. In the past two centuries, we have done away with state-sanctioned slavery, expanded representative democracies, and formed the United Nations out of the ashes of world wars. And as a TESOL educator, I also want to believe that English language teachers have a positive contribution to make in increasing individuals' access to social, political, and economic opportunities. I'm inspired when I see TESOL teacher education become a space for dialoguing across historical wounds in a divided Cyprus,[1] part of the peace and reconciliation efforts in post-FARC conflict Colombia,[2] or part of HIV/AIDS prevention efforts in Uganda (Norton, Jones, and Ahimbisibwe 2013). However, as Reynolds (Chapter 2) reminds us, broader sociopolitical changes are not unidirectional; change can also be regressive, and more often than not, lately, progress has felt like one step forward, two steps back. If history does arc towards greater justice and equity, it is not because it is necessarily inclined to do so, but rather because of the individuals who acted on their beliefs grounded in ethical and moral principles.

All of us in TESOL who are committed to social justice have a professional and ethical obligation to be leaders in both words and deeds to call out inequities in our field and advocate for making TESOL policies, pedagogies, and practices more critically accountable. As this volume has illustrated, this often entails developing teachers and teacher candidates with the disposition to interrogate how their practices will either challenge or reinforce existing educational conditions. As the editors De Costa and Uştuk argue (Chapter 1), this critical consciousness is not an accidental by-product of training teachers with a set of technical skills. Instead, it must be inculcated through an orientation to teacher education that places a sociopolitical agenda at the center of our endeavor to prepare effective language teachers. In my concluding remarks, I would like to highlight three main contributions that this volume makes: destabilizing the canon of TESOL teacher education, a critique of Global English, and the foregrounding of teacher education as identity work. I conclude by underscoring that the authors of this volume do not merely present a critique of the shortcomings of current frameworks and practices of TESOL teacher education, they provide a constructive vision for implementing a sociopolitical agenda, and I summarize what I consider to be the key elements of this agenda.

Destabilizing Categories in Teacher Education

Much of the work in English language teacher education (ELTE) emphasizes the essential role of reflection in developing teachers' ability to connect the knowledge base of the field to the everyday practice of teaching (Mann and Walsh 2017). Teacher reflection is a retrospective deliberation on past actions that aim to increase understanding of the teaching-learning process (Schön 1983). The movement to make reflection integral to teacher education was part of the reform efforts to "transform teachers from technicians rigidly and obediently following a prescribed curriculum into teachers able to analyze and adapt their teaching to particular students in particular social, cultural, and political contexts" (Liu 2015: 136–137). However, as Mann and Walsh (2017) point out, even as reflection has become integral to professional development in many language teacher education programs, at the same time reflective practice has often become reduced to an evaluative tool for assessing competence. What good is reflection, if it becomes a normative process that serves only to reinforce the canon of the field? As the chapters in this volume have illustrated, the canon in TESOL has been built on highly problematic notions such as native speakerism, normative monolingualism, and assessment of achievement defined by curricular standards.

Liu (2015) therefore argues that we must adopt a framework of *critical reflection*, which centers the wider social, historical, political, and cultural contexts of education, and examines the relationships between educational practice and the construction of a more equitable, just, and democratic society (Dinkelman 2000). This is echoed in Johnson's sociocultural approach to language teacher education in emphasizing the microgenetic elements of teacher learning: "if the goal of L2 teacher education is to prepare the individual teacher to function in the professional world of L2 teaching, then it is critical to account for how an individual's activities shape and are shaped by the social, cultural, and historical macro-structures which constitute that professional world" (2009: 77). This also aligns with Foucault's (1972) genealogical approach: "Genealogical analysis traces how contemporary practices and institutions emerged out of specific struggles, conflicts, alliances, and exercises of power, many of which are nowadays forgotten [and suggests] that institutions and practice we value and take for granted today are actually more problematic or more 'dangerous' than they otherwise appear" (Garland 2014: 372). This type of critical reflection goes beyond examining and acknowledging the origins of concepts and relationships of power, it actively seeks to interrogate and destabilize them. The seminal early example in TESOL is Pennycook's (1989) genealogical critique of the concept of the Teaching Method. Like Pennycook did 30 years ago with the notion of *method*, a sociopolitical approach to educating language teachers must challenge and destabilize the canon.

An innovative approach to critical reflection, and one that brings the concept up to the present in the 2020s, is Kayi-Aydar's (Chapter 7) implementation of an *intersectional approach* with MA-TESOL students in a graduate teacher education program in the United States, drawing on the concept of intersectionality from Crenshaw (1991). Kayi-Aydar argues that an intersectional pedagogy explicitly challenges the knowledge base of TESOL, by openly questioning who produced it. She notes books on TESOL methods have been overwhelmingly written by White, Western, native-English speaking scholars. She argues that an intersectional approach helps English language teachers (1) challenge the US centric knowledge and perspectives in TESOL methodology, (2) question naming and labeling in TESOL praxis, and (3) make invisible identities visible in TESOL teacher education.

One way to look at this volume, then, is a collective effort at destabilizing some of the most taken-for-granted and entrenched categories of TESOL. Schissel and Hornberger (Chapter 5) give us an illuminating example of how canonical concepts become baked into an educational system, despite the fact that they often marginalize the very students they contend to be supporting. In their chapter, they demonstrate that in the United States the push toward "accountability" for schools and teachers has resulted in the creation of an assessment apparatus built on standardized testing. Within this system, the terminology around English language learners (ELs), the achievement gap, and the procedures for providing accommodations to ELs, all contribute to normalizing a regime that is, quite frankly, an insane form of educating system. Ultimately, their point is that part of critical reflection for TESOL professionals should include the capacity to question test use, in particular standardized test use, with their students; this is to say, the disposition to interrogate the knowledge base of TESOL. As Freeman (2020: 11) has argued:

> Following the financial approach known as "zero-based" budgeting in which no expenditure is assumed to carry over from previous budgets, we need to re-examine – and not necessarily carry forward de facto—usual ideas to formulate these new proposals. This is the only way, to my mind, that we can challenge the conceptual expenditures which represent the practices of the center.

The need for destabilizing categories stems from the broader concern for pushing back against the neoliberal discourses that have become deeply ingrained in English teacher education. Selvi's (Chapter 4) formulation of *non-native speakerism* is one prominent example from this volume of how the canon can be destabilized and reframed. In my own work on the expansion of early English programs in public education in many countries (Sayer 2015, 2019), I've examined how the increase of English at the primary level curriculum in places like Latin America or Southeast Asia is discursively linked to modernizing the country's education system. While this is a boon for us as language teacher educators, since the demand is high, the sociopolitical agenda demands that we ask how our work then contributes to the corporate interests of teaching English in order to develop human capital, and how we can push back against that (Murray 2020).

Critique of Global English

The debate about the role, or perhaps collusion, of TESOL and the rise of English as the dominant global language goes back 30 years, to Phillipson's (1992) seminal work on *Linguistic Imperialism*. Phillipson's argument was that English language teaching is a value-laden enterprise that profits from the linguistic domination of English in peripheral ("Third World" or nonnative English-speaking) countries. The work that extended and critiqued Phillipson's thesis, especially ethnographic work that documents the ways that TESOL educators and students from the "periphery" exercise agency (cf. Canagarajah 1999), was central in pushing TESOL and applied linguistics to examine its own ideological foundations rooted in native speakerism, linguistic definitions of language, and Western pedagogical approaches to teaching and learning.

López Gopar and colleagues (Chapter 9) bring this debate into the present. First, they show how the history and neocolonial reality of Mexico have shaped the language identities of Indigenous peoples. Next, they describe how the English teacher education undergraduate program at a public university in Southern Mexico has an explicit goal to: "provide the Oaxacan and larger Mexican community with critical language teachers who are aware of the hegemony of English and other so-called modern languages (e.g., French and Italian) over Indigenous languages and Spanish." It may seem paradoxical to model a program to train English teachers around a counter-hegemonic approach to English, but as the ethnographic descriptions of the journey's two teacher candidates reveals, the insights gained support a decolonizing agenda. I would add, it also paints a portrait of a deeply humanizing pedagogy, both for the teacher candidates and their students. For example, the reflections that the teachers have on the kindness shown by the people in the community where they are doing their practicum, and even on the assumptions that we have for using names and showing respect between students and teachers, speak to the power of small insights about everyday practice in bringing about broader sociopolitical changes. This moves the sociopolitical agenda from the abstract sense of "teaching toward social justice," to the specific sense of the local concerns and struggles of the teacher's students.

Within the canon of international TESOL, the native/nonnative teacher (NEST/NNEST) dichotomy is perhaps the most contentious and pernicious, and the most in need of destabilizing. Selvi's (Chapter 4) chapter is clearly an attempt to destabilize the ingrained NEST-NNEST categories and the privileging of *native speakerism* (Seidlhofer 1999). He begins by pointing out that the NNEST movement, even as it advocates for policy, initiatives, teaching activities, and research efforts, to some extent legitimizes its very object of scrutiny. Interestingly, rather than trying to break down this dichotomy as a fallacy, Selvi takes a very different tact by rewriting the distinction in terms of *nonnative speakerism*. Instead of destabilizing by deconstruction, Selvi's move is an ideational push-back which essentially flips the script:

> The term *nonnative speakerism* refers to the idealization and promotion of teachers who are positioned or self-described as *nonnative speakers* as *more* viable models of learning and teaching. Similar to *native speakerism*, this ideology (and related discourses and practices) builds upon and extends (and even expands) the mutually exclusive binary categorization of teacher identity.

He goes on to argue that from a position of privileging nonnative speakerism, diverse multilingual English teachers (and especially those whose putative native language is not English) are the ones with the greatest potential to serve as agents of change, since their positionality affords them a perspective from which they know, inherently and viscerally, the ways that dominant ideologies and identity categories can marginalize.

Language Teacher Education as Identity Work

One of the clearest strands that runs through the chapters in this volume is that educating English teachers must entail creating spaces for participants to explore and build their identities, both in the sense of developing their professional and personal relationship to the work they have chosen to do (Varghese et al. 2016). Part of the sociopolitical agenda for TESOL teacher education, therefore, must be a vision for how the forms of critical reflection that programs and teacher educators strive to engage their teacher candidates in can positively support the development of their identities. Three of the chapters (Chapters 3, 6, and 8) present approaches that align with this vision with novice language teachers in different contexts.

Both Peercy, Sodani, and Hall (Chapter 6) and Yazan (Chapter 8) start with the premise that language teacher education with novice teachers is identity work. Peercy, Sodani, and Hall's approach in an undergraduate teacher licensure program in the US connects strongly to the one implemented by López Gopar and colleagues in Mexico, in that they are centered around collective structures. They call this approach *humanizing induction*. Identity work and humanizing education through collaboration and collective experiences, support the development of teachers' agency, which in turn is fundamental to novice teachers' capacity to advocate for language minoritized students. They explain that their intention was to re-center the process of teacher induction from supervisory and hierarchical activities to ones that were fundamentally collaborative and dialogic. This shift allowed candidates to "leverage their own experiences, questions, dilemmas, doubts, and ideas to collaboratively examine problems of practice as equals."

There is a strong parallel here with Yazan's (Chapter 8) approach to organizing language teacher education around identity work through a sociopolitical agenda called *critical autoethnographic narrative* (CAN). Yazan characterizes CAN as an identity-oriented teacher learning activity that allows participants to examine "the sociopolitical situatedness of (a) languages, (b) language learning and teaching, and (c) themselves as teachers and users of languages." He illustrates this process through a deep dive into the autographic project by Kateryna, a novice teacher in an MA-TESOL program who is herself an immigrant from

Ukraine, who provides several telling critical incidents. I was struck in particular by the dilemma that Kateryna faced as a student teacher, in her disagreement with her mentor teachers over whether students would be allowed to use L1 sources and Google Translate to support their academic writing in English. In her journal entry, she concludes that: "In the end we did compromise but I still felt as though my classroom authority was dominated by both the co-teacher but largely and more importantly by English Language Ideologies."

Kateryna's insight here underscores the importance of language teacher education to support the development of participants' voices and agency. As the chapters acknowledge, a sociopolitical approach to working with teachers does not occur in a vacuum; quite the opposite, teachers with a critically conscious approach to working with students are very likely going to encounter ideological and institutional structures that push back strongly against their attempts to destabilize mainstream and normative practices. During a recent reflection session with my students in the undergraduate TESOL licensure program, one of the critically engaged students was discussing an issue she was facing as she tried to get the school to provide appropriate accommodations for one of her English learner students, and after her classmates shared similar stories of struggling, she exclaimed in frustration: "I was really excited with all the critical stuff we were talking about last semester because, I mean, I know that's just what our kiddos deserve, but then you get into the classroom and in the school, it's like you realize that all that theory you have to figure out how to make it work in practice with your colleagues who just aren't down with that at all."

The chapter by Çomoğlu and Dikilitaş (Chapter 3) provides a telling example of how discursive spaces for critical sociopolitical reflection can be created even within the teacher preparation system in Turkey, which emphasizes decontextualized knowledge and is rigidly standardized. Like Peercy et. al. and Yazan, Çomoğlu and Dikilitaş argue that a sociopolitical approach to educating English teachers in Turkey should be organized around developing teachers' identities and agency. However, they explain that in the Turkish context the broader framework for training teachers is based almost entirely on the commodification of generic pedagogical knowledge with little consideration of teachers' voices and critical interpretation. In order to get a job, prospective teachers must take a professional standards exam on six main competencies, 31 sub-competencies, and 233 performance signs. The aim is the homogenization of English language teacher education programs across the country. Another result, they explain, is the systematic marginalization of the minoritized areas by sending teachers with the lowest test scores to the east/southeast parts of the country. Nevertheless, they present four cases within ELTE programs which show that small openings for dialogue and reflection, even the chatbox function in an online class, can be significant places to project and develop teachers' voices within rigid institutional spaces.

I reference Freeman and Johnson's (Freeman and Johnson 1998; Freeman 2020; Johnson 2009) seminal work on the knowledge base of TESOL teacher education. However, what comes through from the contributions in this book is that at the heart of teacher education as identity work is not the acquisition of the general TESOL knowledge base, but engagement and meaning-making with local knowledge (Canagarajah 2005). After all, teachers do not work generically in "TESOL," they work as these teachers do in a specific school with particular students in Turkey, Oaxaca, Florida, and Arizona. The ways that the teacher understands her own practice and the meaning the teacher attaches to her teaching is a meaning that she ascribes to the specific activity in her classroom with her students, not in some theoretical or generalized sense. This moves the sociopolitical agenda from the abstract sense of social justice, to the specific sense of the local concerns and struggles of the teacher's students, what we could call *social justice as pedagogical practice*.

The Sociopolitical Agenda: From Critique to Constructive Proposals

The sociopolitical agenda laid out in this book contributes to the debate in critical applied linguistics about the role of global English, and the agency that teachers have a say in how the role of global English might be a more positive one in the lives of their students. This debate is almost 30 years old now, going back to the work of Robert Phillipson, Tove Skutnab-Kangas, Alastair Pennycook, Suresh Canagarajah, Jim Tollefson, Braj Kachru, and others. However, what the authors in this volume offer is not just a re-hash and update of these critiques of the problem of teaching global English, but a set of examples that can be taken, collectively, as a proposal for a sociopolitical agenda for TESOL teacher education. What this agenda offers is a constructive approach(es) to educating ELT professionals that is at once cognizant of the realities and constraints of working in English language teaching at this moment in history, but is purposeful and even optimistic about the possibilities for TESOL educators to be agents of change by implementing critical language pedagogies.

Çomoğlu and Dikilitaş (Chapter 3) reference López Gopar's (2019) conceptualization of the development of critical pedagogy within ELTE programs as a transformative process of conscious resistance to discrimination and injustices both broad (e.g., the imposition of non-local and fixed expert knowledge) and mundane (e.g., teachers' work schedule and lack of planning time, or feedback and non-judgmental pedagogical support). This resistance is the *critique* part of critical pedagogy. But López Gopar (2019) also emphasizes the *constructive* aspects of critical pedagogy that we see detailed in this volume: the development of teachers' voice and agency to implement teaching practices based on their critical consciousness that are responsive to the local and specific needs and identities of students. Kubanyiova eloquently formulates: "the task of language teacher education in the age of paradox involves educating 'responsive meaning makers in the world': teachers who do not shy away from the politics of the social worlds in which their practices are located, but who are, at the same time, committed to growing their capacity of 'knowing what to do' in the particular moment of an educational encounter" (2020: 50).

In looking across the chapters, we should ask: what are the core elements that define the sociopolitical agenda for TESOL teacher education? First off, what we do *not* find are recipes or prescriptions for "this is what it means to be a sociopolitically aware English teacher." Multilingualism and multiculturalism in teacher education, divorced from critical reflection and reduced to standardized and measurable professional competencies, become their own shallow forms of dogma. Therefore, what we see in these chapters are accounts of teacher education that are the opposite of reductionist; they are extended dialogic spaces, projects, and collaborations. Methodologically, they are documented through ethnography and narratives. The cases presented in Part II of the volume, whether it is the intersectional approach (Kayi-Aydar, Chapter 7), humanizing teacher induction program (Peercy et al., Chapter 6), critical autoethnographic narrative project (Yazan, Chapter 8), or decolonizing language teaching praxicum (López Gopar et al., Chapter 9), exemplify and underscore the main tenants of a sociopolitical agenda that I have identified: *critical reflection, critical pedagogy, dialogue, advocacy, collaboration, ethnography, narratives.* As the chapters demonstrate, these tenets are both orienting concepts and the methodological tools that we can use as teacher educators as we embrace a sociopolitical agenda of TESOL teacher education that is rooted in the material concerns of the local context: social justice struggles that are immediately relevant to the lives of teachers and their students.

Notes

1 In the 1990s/early 2000s, there were ELTE programs to bring Greek Cypriot and Turkish Cypriot English teachers together as part of broader UN-endorsed reconciliation efforts following the 1974 partition of Cyprus.
2 The FARC is the Fuerzas Armadas Revolucionarias de Colombia, an insurgent group that was active from the 1960s until 2017, when a ceasefire accord went into effect.

References

Canagarajah, A. S. (1999), *Resisting Linguistic Imperialism in English Teaching*, Oxford: Oxford University Press.
Canagarajah, A. S., ed. (2005), *Reclaiming the Local in Language Policy and Practice*, Mahwah, NJ: Lawrence Erlbaum.
Crenshaw, K. (1991), "Mapping the Margins: Intersectionality, Identity Politics, and Violence against Women of Color," *Stanford Law Review*, 43 (6): 1241–1299.
Dinkelman, T. (2000), "An Inquiry into the Development of Critical Reflection in Secondary Student Teachers," *Teaching and Teacher Education*, 16 (2): 195–222.
Foucault, M. (1972), *The Archaeology of Knowledge and the Discourse on Language*, trans. S. Smith, New York: Dorset Press/Pantheon Books.
Freeman, D. (2020), "Arguing for a Knowledge-Base in Language Teacher Education, Then (1998) and Now (2018)," *Language Teaching Research*, 24 (1): 5–16.
Freeman, D., and K. Johnson (1998), "Reconceptualizing the Knowledge-Base of Language Teacher Education," *TESOL Quarterly*, 32 (3): 397–417.
Garland, D. (2014), "What is a 'History of the Present'? On Foucault's Genealogies and Their Critical Preconditions," *Punishment & Society*, 16 (4): 365–384.
Johnson, K. E. (2009), *Second Language Teacher Education: A Sociocultural Perspective*, New York: Routledge.
Kubanyiova, M. (2020), "Language Teacher Education in the Age of Ambiguity: Educating Responsive Meaning Makers in the World," *Language Teaching Research*, 42 (1): 49–59.
Liu, K. (2015), "Critical Reflection as a Framework for Transformative Learning in Teacher Education," *Educational Review*, 67 (2): 135–157.
López Gopar, M. (2019), "Introducing International Critical Pedagogies in ELT," in M. López Gopar (ed.), *International Perspectives on Critical Pedagogies in ELT*, 1–15, Cham: Palgrave Macmillan.
Mann, S., and S. Walsh (2017), *Reflective Practice in English Language Teaching*, New York: Routledge.

Murray, D. E. (2020), "The World of English Language Teaching: Creating Equity or Inequity?," *Language Teaching Research*, 24 (1): 60–70.

Norton, B., S. Jones, and D. Ahimbisibwe (2013), "Digital Literacy, HIV/AIDS Information and English Language Learners in Uganda," in E. J. Erling and P. Seargeant (eds.), *English and Development: Policy, Pedagogy and Globalization*, 182–203, Bristol: Multilingual Matters.

Pennycook, A. (1989), "The Concept of Method, Interested Knowledge, and the Politics of Language Teaching," *TESOL Quarterly*, 23 (4): 589–618.

Phillipson, R. (1992), *Linguistic Imperialism*, Cambridge: Cambridge University Press.

Sayer, P. (2015), "'More & Earlier': Neoliberalism and Primary English Education in Mexican Public Schools," *L2 Journal*, 7 (3): 40–56.

Sayer, P. (2019), "The Hidden Curriculum of Work in English Language Education: Neoliberalism and Early English Programs in Public Schooling," *AILA Review*, 32 (1): 36–63.

Schön, D. A. (1983), *The Reflective Practitioner: How Professionals Think in Action*, New York: Basic Books.

Seidlhofer, B. (1999), "Double Standards: Teacher Education in the Expanding Circle," *World Englishes*, 18 (2): 233–245.

Varghese, M., S. Motha, J. Trent, G. Park, and J. Reeves (2016), "Language Teacher Identity in Multilingual Settings," *TESOL Quarterly*, 50 (3): 545–571.

Contributors

Irem Çomoğlu is a Professor at Dokuz Eylul University, Faculty of Education, English Language Teaching Department, Izmir, Turkey. In her research, she focuses on pre-service/in-service teacher learning and development, teacher research, and research skills for pre-service teachers, mainly from a qualitative research paradigm. ORCID: 0000-0003-0186-9122.

Vilma Huerta Cordova has a PhD in Critical Studies of Language. Vilma is a member of the National System of Researchers in México and Professor and Researcher at the Language Department (FI) at the University "Benito Juárez" of Oaxaca, Mexico. She is part of the teaching staff of the following educational programs: Bachelor's Degree in Language Teaching, Master's Degree in Critical Language Teaching, and PhD in Critical Language Studies. Her areas of interest are collaborative learning, peer tutoring, and interpersonal relationships in the classroom. ORCID: 0000-0002-2914-7132.

Peter I. De Costa is an Associate Professor in the Department of Linguistics, Languages & Cultures and the Department of Teacher Education at Michigan State University, where he directs the Master's in TESOL program. As a critical applied linguist, his research areas include emotions, identity, ideology and ethics in language learning, language teaching, and language policy. In addition, his ecologically- and social justice-oriented work looks at the intersection between second language acquisition (SLA), second language teacher education (SLTE), and language policy. He is the co-editor of *TESOL Quarterly* and the First Vice-President of the American Association for Applied Linguistics. ORCID: 0000-0003-0389-1163.

Kenan Dikilitaş is a Professor of University Pedagogy at the University of Stavanger in Norway. He previously worked in Turkey on graduate and undergraduate programs. His recent research interests include teacher education and professional development with an emphasis on mentoring action research and bilingual teaching, and he has published related articles and books. ORCID: 0000-0001-9387-8696.

Wyatt Hall is an Assistant Professor of Curriculum and Instruction at Georgia Gwinnett College, USA. Wyatt is a former elementary ESOL teacher and has served as a university field supervisor. His research in ESOL teacher education includes pre-service language teachers' relationships with their mentors during their internships and pre-service teachers' integration of their multilingual learners' funds of knowledge into instruction. He is also interested in professional learning and teacher communities of practice in schools. ORCID: 0000-0003-0537-5859.

Nancy H. Hornberger, Professor Emerita at the University of Pennsylvania, USA, is an internationally recognized educational linguist and anthropologist researching multilingual education policy and practice in immigrant, refugee, and Indigenous communities. A prolific author and editor, her books include *Indigenous Literacies in the Americas: Language Planning from the Bottom Up* (1997), *Continua of Biliteracy* (2003), *Can Schools Save Indigenous Languages?* (2008), and *Honoring Richard Ruiz and his Work on Language Planning and Bilingual Education* (2017). Recent awards include an honorary doctorate from Umeå University, Sweden and elected membership in the National Academy of Education, USA. ORCID: 0000-0003-4357-6424.

Hayriye Kayi-Aydar is an Associate Professor of TESOL in the Department of English, University of Arizona, USA. Her research focuses on identity, agency, intersectionality, and positioning theory.

Maggie Kubanyiova is a Professor and Chair of Language Education at the University of Leeds, UK, where she is Director of the Centre for Language Education Research. Her ethnographic, discourse analytic, conceptual, and arts-based research spans a range of topics investigating human encounters with difference. She has primarily drawn on educational sociolinguistics, philosophy, and the arts to examine the role of formal and informal (teacher) education in facilitating such encounters in diverse multilingual contexts and in settings of social stigma. Her current research is concerned with creating spaces for transdisciplinary working and engagement across sectors to tackle issues of societal polarization. ORCID: 0000-0002-8848-0293.

Mario López-Gopar (PhD, OISE/University of Toronto) is a Professor at Universidad Autónoma "Benito Juárez" de Oaxaca, Mexico. His main research interest is intercultural and multilingual education of Indigenous peoples in Mexico. His articles have appeared in the *Journal of Language Education and*

Identity, Applied Linguistics, ELT Journal, and the *International Journal of Multilingualism,* among others. He has published numerous book chapters in Mexico, USA, Canada, Argentina, Brazil, and Europe. His latest books are *Decolonizing Primary English Language Teaching* (2016) and *International Perspectives on Critical Pedagogies in ELT* (2019). ORCID: 0000-0001-5121-3901.

Juan Ignacio Martínez Martínez was born in Salina Cruz, Oaxaca and was raised in Juchitán de Zaragoza, Oaxaca. He has a BA in Language Teaching from Universidad Autónoma "Benito Juárez" de Oaxaca, Mexico. He is currently on a trainee program for Hospitality in Williamsburg, Virginia, USA. He wants to return to Mexican classrooms after his program.

Megan Madigan Peercy is a Professor and Associate Dean for Undergraduate and Graduate studies in the College of Education at the University of Maryland. Her research examines pedagogies of teacher education and the preparation and development of teachers throughout their careers, as they work with linguistically and culturally diverse learners. She is deeply invested in understanding the ways in which practice and theory can be in dialogue. Her research has been funded by the Spencer Foundation and the Institute of Education Sciences. Examples of her recent work appear in *Teaching and Teacher Education, Action in Teacher Education, TESOL Quarterly,* and *TESOL Journal.* ORCID: 0000-0002-4322-5520.

Dudley Reynolds is the Senior Associate Dean for Education and Teaching Professor of English at Carnegie Mellon University, Qatar. He served as President of TESOL International Association 2016–17 and has been a teacher and researcher of multilingual language learners for over 30 years, working primarily with learners of English. His research addresses language education policy, developmental patterns in additional language learning, curricular and pedagogical approaches to literacy development, teacher education and learning. ORCID: 0000-0002-4706-2474.

Denisse Concepción Zárate Ríos was born and raised in Oaxaca de Juárez, Oaxaca. She has a BA in Language Teaching from Universidad Autónoma "Benito Juárez" de Oaxaca, Mexico, and is currently studying her for master's degree in Education. She has been teaching English for the last three years in a private school. She dreams about becoming a good teacher.

Peter Sayer is Professor of Multilingual Language Education in the College of Education & Human Ecology at the Ohio State University, USA. His work focuses on educational sociolinguistics, and he has published on topics including language ideologies in education, translanguaging, the linguistic landscape and social class, and additional language teaching. ORCID: 0000-0002-1468-6256.

Jamie L. Schissel is an Associate Professor of TESOL at the University of North Carolina at Greensboro, USA. Her research using historical analyses and participatory action research collaborations focuses on inequities surrounding educational assessments and policies for linguistically and culturally diverse communities. In 2021, she was the recipient of the Bilingual Education Research SIG in AERA Early Career Research Award. Her book, *The Social Consequences of Testing for Language-Minoritized Bilinguals in the United States* (Multilingual Matters), was published in 2019. Since 2018, she has co-facilitated Asociación Mexicana de Evaluación de Lenguas Indígenas with Drs. Mario López-Gopar and Constant Leung. ORCID: 0000-0002-6298-8443.

Ali Fuad Selvi is an Assistant Professor of TESOL and Applied Linguistics at the University of Alabama, USA. His research interests include Global Englishes and its implications for language learning, teaching, teacher education, and language policy/planning; issues related to (in)equity, professionalism, marginalization, and discrimination in TESOL; and second language teacher education. In addition to his scholarship in these areas, he was recognized as one of TESOL International Association's 30 Up and Coming Leaders in recognition of his potential to "shape the future of both the association and the profession for years to come." ORCiD: 0000-0002-1122-9770.

Danielle Gervais Sodani is currently pursuing her PhD in Teacher Education/ Professional Development in the Teaching and Learning, Policy and Leadership program in the College of Education at the University of Maryland, College Park, USA. Her research interests focus on how educators in research-practice partnerships encourage the use of research by school leaders and teachers to support equitable educational outcomes for students. She also serves as the Director of the Institute for Innovation and Education in the School of Education at American University, Washington, DC where she cultivates partnerships with educational organizations to jointly implement research-informed professional development initiatives. ORCID: 0000-0003-2734-667X.

William M. Sughrua (PhD, Applied Linguistics) is a Postgraduate Lecturer and thesis advisor at the Language Faculty of Universidad Autónoma "Benito Juárez" de Oaxaca, Mexico. His research interests and publications are in the areas of English language teaching, critical pedagogy, epistemology, qualitative inquiry, and autoethnography. ORCID:0000-0001-6567-7483.

Özgehan Uştuk is a teacher educator and a Postdoctoral Fellow in the Department of English and Communication at the Hong Kong Polytechnic University. His research areas include practitioner inquiry, language teacher education and professional development, teacher learning, identity, tensions, and emotions. He also researches drama-in-education pedagogies in language and language teacher education. His research has appeared in academic journals including *Language Teaching Research*, *TESOL Quarterly*, *Research in Drama Education*, *TESOL Journal*, and *International Journal of Lesson and Learning Studies*. He is the chair (2023) of TESOL International Association's Research Professional Council. ORCID: 0000-0002-7486-1386.

Bedrettin Yazan is an Associate Professor in the Department of Bicultural-Bilingual Studies at the University of Texas at San Antonio, USA. His research focuses on language teacher learning and identity, collaboration between ESL and content teachers, language policy and planning, and World Englishes. Methodologically he is interested in critical autoethnography, narrative inquiry, and qualitative case study. His work has appeared in *TESOL Quarterly*, *Language Teaching Research*, *RECALL*, *Linguistics and Education*, *Language and Intercultural Communication*, *Pedagogy, Culture, and Society*, *Critical Inquiry in Language Studies*, and *World Englishes*, among other journals. He is currently serving as Co-Editor of *TESOL Journal* with Kristen Lindahl. ORCID: https://orcid.org/0000-0002-1888-1120.

Subject Index

Ableism, xiv
achievement gap, xix, 5, 65, 66, 67, 68, 69, 70, 72, 73, 75, 76, 77, 80, 81, 171
activism, xx
advocacy, 50, 53, 54, 56, 57, 80, 90, 91, 92, 94, 95, 96, 97, 101, 136, 177
African(-American), 91, 146
agency, 5, 6, 20, 21, 23, 24, 27, 28, 36, 38, 39, 87, 90, 94, 98, 101, 115, 125, 127, 135, 137, 172, 174, 175, 176, 177
American Association for Applied Linguistics (AAAL), 138
American Educational Research Association (AERA), 2
anti-racist, 7
assessment, 5, 46, 49, 67, 72, 73, 74, 75, 77, 79, 81, 113, 148, 155, 170, 171
autoethnography, 127, 128, 133, 138, 142
autonomy, 28, 29

bilingual education/school, 33, 34, 38, 69, 72, 76, 78, 133, 145
bilingualism, 34, 51, 71, 150
Black(ness), 110, 114, 115, 147, 160
Border, 3, 14, 46, 49, 56, 132
Burnout, xxi, 2

case study, 36, 156, 157, 159
capital, 22, 172
capitalism, 153
citizenship, 110, 114
climate change, 1, 3, 22, 70
colonialism, 14, 22, 146, 150, 152, 153
    coloniality, 147, 150, 152, 153, 156, 157, 158, 160, 161, 162, 163
    colonization, xviii, xiix, 107
communication, xx, 45
community of practice (CoP), 34, 124
Complexity Theory, 18
counter-ideology, xix
Covid-19, 2, 19, 100, 107
Creole, 132, 133, 134, 146

critical
    critical applied linguistics, 1, 45, 149, 176
    critical approach, xiii, xiiv, xvi, 124, 149, 154
    critical autoethnographic narrative (CAN), 6, 123, 126, 127, 128, 129, 130, 131, 132, 133, 134, 136, 137, 138, 142, 174, 177
    critical inquiry, 28, 110, 111
    critical pedagogy, 39, 177
    critical scholarship, xiv, xvi, 52
    critical translingual awareness, 4
Cultural Historical Activity Theory (CHAT), 36
Culturally responsive pedagogy, 45
Curriculum, xix, 6, 22, 23, 31, 49, 89, 107, 116, 117, 120, 123, 135, 136, 145, 148, 153, 170, 172

Decolonization/decolonizing, 107, 145, 146, 148, 149, 150, 151, 152, 153, 155, 159, 163, 164173, 177
    Decoloniality, 146, 153, 157, 161, 163
    Decolonizing/decolonial pedagogy, 149, 150, 151, 156, 161, 164
dehumanization/dehumanizing, xix, 29, 98
democracy, 169
destabilization/destabilizing, xvi, 4, 48, 59, 169, 170, 171, 172, 173
dialogic, 27, 99, 174, 177
disability, 65, 71, 114
discrimination, 3, 27, 49, 50, 51, 53, 54, 56, 58, 110, 162, 177
discriminatory practices, xix, 49, 53
Douglas Fir Group, 136
Dynamic Systems Theory, 18

Ecological perspective, 20
educational linguistics, 127
educational policy, 2, 65
election, 13, 65

emotion, 127
English as a Foreign Language (EFL), 33, 34, 36, 38
English as a Lingua Franca (ELF), 46, 48
English as an International Language (EIL), 48
English learner (EL) classification, 66, 67, 68, 70, 71, 75, 76, 79, 80
English medium instruction (EMI), 36
Equity, 46, 47, 52, 53, 54, 56, 57, 58, 87, 88, 90, 100, 102, 148, 149, 160
ethnicity, xiv, 46, 50, 53, 65, 66, 69, 91, 102, 110, 114, 115, 116, 146
ethnographic portrait, 146, 157, 159, 160
ethnography, 154, 177
Every Student Succeeds Act, 67

gender, xiv, 46, 50, 53, 65, 110, 114, 115, 125, 150, 153
Genealogical Analysis, 171
Global North, 3, 5, 54, 113
Global South, 3, 6, 7
Global warming, 19
globalization, xiv, 18, 19, 22, 107
glocalization, 46

hegemony, 5, 7, 48, 151, 173
heterogeneity, xix, 69, 71, 80
high-stakes, xiv, 2, 66, 68, 69, 70
home language, 68, 69, 95, 96, 131, 133
humaning, xviii, xx
    humanizing (teacher) induction, 89, 92, 174, 177
    humanizing pedagogy, 88, 89, 95, 99, 173

identity
    identity-oriented pedagogy (language) teacher learning, 125, 136, 137, 174
    identity politics, 3
    identity position, xiv, 130
    identity work, 27, 117, 123, 127, 137, 170, 174, 176
ideology, xiii, xiv, xv, xvi, 3, 4, 6, 46, 49, 51, 52, 54, 56, 113, 115, 125, 126, 128, 132, 134, 135, 136, 137, 173, 174, 175
immigrant, 14, 108, 114, 131, 133, 174
immigration, 97, 100, 107, 150

indigenous, 6, 7, 145, 146, 147, 148, 150, 151, 153, 154, 162, 163, 173
inequality, 6, 14, 22, 49, 51, 89, 107, 110, 111, 113, 117, 118, 120, 145, 147, 158
inequity, xvi, 1, 2, 5, 46, 47, 49, 50, 66, 67, 70, 79, 101, 110, 111, 118, 169
injustice, 3, 5, 14, 27, 111, 120, 148, 149, 150, 177
initial (language) teacher education, 4, 28, 29, 37
innovation, xiii, 125
in-service (teacher), 4, 28, 29, 30, 31, 37, 39, 57, 75, 80, 100, 101
International Association of Teachers of English as a Foreign Language (IATEFL), 19
Intersectionality, 50, 108, 110, 111, 113, 115, 116, 117, 118, 119, 120, 171
intersectional pedagogy, 6, 107, 108, 110, 113, 117, 118, 119, 171
investment 125, 127, 142

justice, 87, 88, 89, 102, 169

language ideology, xiii, xiv, xv, 46, 126, 135, 175
language portrait, 126
Latinx, 115
leadership, 5, 14, 17, 18, 19, 21, 24, 27, 70
lesson study, 100
linguistic bias, 5, 75
linguistic identity, 50, 89, 114, 117
linguistic imperialism, 52, 115, 172
linguistic minority, 6
linguistically diverse (students/learners), 3, 58

marginalization, xiii, xv, 46, 47, 49, 50, 51, 52, 53, 54, 56, 58, 110, 125, 145, 175
    marginalized student/learner, 66, 98, 99
mentoring, 88, 100, 101
middle class, 48, 54, 108, 110, 151
Ministry, 20, 29, 148
minoritized (language) learner, 66, 73, 74, 87, 101, 137, 174
monolingual fallacy, xiv

Subject Index

monolingualism, 72, 170
multiculturalism, 177
multilingualism, 6, 74, 75, 77, 81, 145, 177
Muslim, 14, 108, 114, 116

Narrative inquiry, 108, 109
National Assessment of Educational Progress (NAEP), 67, 69, 73, 75, 76, 77
National Center for Education Statistics (NCES), 69, 70, 71, 77
nationality, xiv
nationalistic ideology, 19
nationalism, 19, 22
native speaker (NS), 4, 36, 37, 46, 47, 48, 49, 51, 52, 53, 54, 55
native English-speaking teacher (NEST), 39, 46, 47, 48, 49, 50, 52, 54, 55, 56, 57, 58, 173
native speakerism, xix, 5, 45, 47, 48, 50, 51, 52, 53, 55, 57, 58, 59, 170, 172, 173
native speaker fallacy, xiv, 52, 56
neoliberal, 1, 2, 6, 19, 22, 34, 45, 50, 126, 145, 172
No Child Left Behind Act (2001), 67
nonnative speaker (NNS), 46, 47, 49, 52, 54, 55, 173
nonnative speakerism, xix, 45, 47, 48, 53, 54, 55, 56, 58, 59, 173
nonnative English speaking teachers (NNEST), 39, 46, 47, 49, 50, 51, 54, 55, 56, 57, 58, 173
normativity, 3

Office of English Language Acquisition (OELA), 75
Office of Refugee Resettlement (ORR), 70, 71
oppression, xviii, 67, 110, 111, 115, 116, 117, 118, 119

pandemic, 19, 100, 107
participatory action research, 35, 36
passport, 19, 50, 53
peer interaction, 87, 89, 98, 101
plurilingualism, 51
power, 14, 16, 35, 48, 52, 87, 95, 113, 119, 151, 171, 173

power dynamics, xiiv
power relation, xv, xvi, 36, 39, 125, 137
practicum, 23, 30, 32, 89, 127, 155, 173
practitioner research, 31
praxicum 6, 146, 147, 149, 150, 151, 152, 154, 155, 156, 157, 159, 160, 161, 162, 163, 164, 177
praxis, xx, 6, 27, 108, 110, 118, 146, 150, 155, 163, 171
precarity, 2
pre-service (teacher), 28, 29, 30, 31, 32, 33, 37, 75, 80, 89, 90, 91, 97, 100, 101, 109, 146, 163
privilege xiii, xv, 46, 47, 48, 49, 50, 52, 53, 54, 56, 58, 99, 108, 110, 114, 115, 116, 120, 125
professionalism, 4, 13, 14
professional development, 4, 14, 18, 27, 28, 29, 30, 31, 32, 35, 37, 39, 49, 58, 88, 119, 170
professional learning, 4, 5, 27, 32, 39, 40, 100

queer, 7

race, xiv, 46, 50, 53, 65, 66, 69, 91, 100, 102, 110, 114, 115, 116, 125, 126, 146, 147, 153
racialized identity, 14, 126
racism, 99, 101, 113
recession, 3
reflective practice, 32, 170
reflective practitioner, 155
reflexive teacher, 3, 6
reflexivity, xvi, 4, 6, 156
reform, 2, 15, 29, 57, 145, 148, 170
refugee, 3, 14, 19, 114
   Refugee learner of English, 3
Religion, 19, 50, 53, 66, 100, 102, 125, 154, 159
research-practitioner gap, 7
resurgent nationalism, 3

sexuality, xiv, 46, 110, 115
social class, 116, 146, 147, 153
social justice, xiii, 1, 6, 29, 120, 127, 146, 147, 149, 150, 155, 169, 173, 176, 177
social media, 57, 91, 100, 153

social positioning, 124, 130, 135, 136
socioeconomic status (SES), 33, 65, 69, 100, 101, 102, 110, 145, 146, 148, 149, 155, 157, 158
socioeducational context, xvi, 137
sociopolitical agenda, xvi, xviii, xix, xx, 1, 4, 7, 48, 56, 57, 59, 127, 136, 169, 172, 173, 174, 176, 177
sociopolitical awareness, 37
sociopolitics, 1, 4
speakerhood, xix, 55, 58
standardized test/assessment, 20, 29, 65, 66, 68, 69, 70, 72, 79, 80, 81, 171, 172
subtractive fallacy, xiv
superdiversity, 46

teacher
   teacher agency, 3, 5, 15, 20, 88, 89
   teacher candidate, 58, 112, 118, 123, 126, 127, 128, 129, 130, 136, 137, 138, 169, 173, 174
   teacher cognition, 18
   teacher emotion, 125
   teacher identity, xiv, 3, 6, 34, 35, 46, 48, 55, 58, 88, 92, 108, 115, 123, 124, 125, 126, 127, 130, 132, 134, 135, 136, 137, 173

teacher induction, 87, 90, 98, 101, 174, 177
teacher leadership, 4, 13, 14, 15, 16, 17, 18, 19, 20, 21, 23, 24
teacher learning, 4, 31, 123, 125, 126, 128, 136, 137, 138, 170, 174
teacher mentoring, 4
teacher reflexivity, 4
teacher research, 31
tension, 3, 46, 98, 125, 133, 134, 135
TESOL International Association (TESOL), 13, 16, 17, 18, 20, 21
TESOL methodology, 6, 107, 108, 109, 111, 113, 117, 118, 119, 171
Translanguaging, 38, 132
translingual identity, 126
translingualism, 126
transnational identity, 126
transnationalism, 126

vulnerability, 2, 128

wellbeing, 148
White(ness), 3, 5, 48, 54, 74, 79, 91, 99, 101, 108, 109, 110, 112, 112, 114, 115, 116, 118, 120, 147, 160, 171
working class, 151

www.ingramcontent.com/pod-product-compliance
Lightning Source LLC
Chambersburg PA
CBHW052116300426
44116CB00010B/1680